Virginia Colleges 101

The Ultimate Guide for Students of All Ages

by Christina Couch

Palari Publishing
1113 W. Main St.
Richmond, VA 23220

www.palaribooks.com

Printed in the United State of America

Library of Congress Cataloging-in-Publication Data

Couch, Christina.
Virginia colleges 101 : the ultimate guide for students of all ages /
by Christina Couch.
p. cm.
Includes index.
ISBN-13: 978-1-928662-11-2 (pbk.)
ISBN-10: 1-928662-11-0 (pbk.)
1. Universities and colleges--Virginia--Entrance requirements. I. Title.
LB2351.3.V8C68 2007
378.1'61609755--dc22

2007033475

Cover Design: David Perry and Brian Bear

Interior: David Perry and Brian Bear

Disclaimer: While all efforts were made to ensure that the facts and figures in this book are accurate, information is subject to change. Use this guide as a resource and then make sure to verify the information on your own.

For My Mother, Who Made College an Expectation.
Thank you.

A Word of Thanks: To all of the college admissions counselors and advisors who made this book possible as well as to Dave Smitherman and Ted Randler of Palari Publishing. A special thanks also extends to Celena Church, Maura Pond, and Mark Kantrowitz for their help and contribution to this work. Finally a thank you to Linda and Billy Call, Stephanie Brown, and Richard Couch for their lifelong support.

Table of Contents

Introduction

Why Choose Virginia?

Planning Your Future (Cue the Scary Music)

Welcome to the college application process, a time that's chock full of questions, confusion, and more paperwork than you can shake a stick at. If you're feeling lost, overwhelmed, or just plain frustrated, never fear. This book is here to help you figure out what your next educational step should be, how to get there, and how to pay for it. This book is designed to give you a guide to the educational and financial opportunities in your own backyard and hopefully provide you with a few options you hadn't considered before. So let's jump straight to the important questions:

Is College Really Worth the Cash?

If you've splurged on this superb book, you're probably tremendously good looking...no really, like WAY above average...AND you already know that getting a college education is one of the most lucrative things you can do for your future. In fact, it's a million-dollar decision. Over the course of a lifetime, those who graduate with a bachelor's degree earn an average of $1 million more than those with high school diplomas. Beyond bigger salaries, college grads also have more employment opportunities, better benefits, and more freedom to choose where they live and what they do for a living than graduates with a high school degree alone. Aside from the post-graduate advantages, college gives students the ability to explore subjects they've never even heard of before, learn from some of the finest minds in the country, travel to exotic destinations, take part in groundbreaking research, meet people from across the globe, create projects bigger than themselves, make invaluable professional connections, gain on-the-job experience, and put their brains, bodies, and creative juices to the test in a community of motivated people determined to better their future. Convinced yet?

Why Choose Virginia?

Here are three good reasons:

1 **Virginia has fantastic schools.** Got your doubts? Just ask Katie Couric, Jon Stewart, Glenn Close, Pearl S. Buck, John Warner, Jim Gilmore, Robert F. Kennedy, Tom Wolfe, Tina Fey, Fred Willard, Frank Beemer, Perry Ellis, Samuel J. Goldwyn, Jr., and John McAfee (of McAfee Anti-Virus fame) if their Virginia education paid off. What's even better is that Virginia has A LOT of fantastic schools, something to fit any and every serious student who comes here to study. From huge state-funded research universities to small, private colleges to historically black schools, military academies, arts conservatories, distance learning institutions, single sex schools, community colleges, and trade schools, this state offers an enormous spectrum of programs that will help you get anywhere you want to go.

2 **It's cheap!** On top of having fantastic schools (see #1), Virginia residents who attend in-state colleges and universities also avoid paying out-of-state tuition, a financial burden that costs the average out of state student $9,947 more per year than their in-state peers. That's nearly $40,000 saved over a four-year period in tuition alone! The truth is unless you land the scholarship package of your dreams or decide to spend the decade after you graduate paying back student loans, in-state tuition will almost always be your best fiscal bet. In addition to spending less, Virginia college savings programs will help you save more before you ever step foot on campus. This state offers some of the best long-term savings plans in the nation as well as some pretty generous grants packages for students attending VA-based schools, making it that much easier to fund your education.

3 **Location, Location, Location!** Whether you're looking for a gritty, urban campus in the middle of a thriving city, a quiet study sanctuary in the mountains, or a school smack dab in the middle of suburbia, Virginia is one of the few states that can accommodate all of these requests and more. No matter what you want to learn or where you want to learn it, Virginia offers an affordable way to do it.

How do I Use this Book?

Simple kid, check out the table of contents, flip to the chapter you need, and go to town. Unlike your chemistry textbook, the mini-masterpiece you're holding isn't meant to be read straight through. This book is divided into three sections. The first will address what you need to get into and pay for colleges and universities in Virginia, the second will be a comprehensive guide to programs, costs, and other vital statistics about regionally-accredited four-year Virginia schools, and finally, you'll find a few indexes in the back that will provide practical information on things like scholarships available only to Virginia residents and summer programs that can help you sweeten up that college application a bit. If you get lost or need a quick reference, there's a short cheat sheet in the back of each chapter that can help catch you up on major points covered.

Higher ED Basics

Like people, schools have personalities too. Some you might fall in love with at first glance; others you might loathe with every cell in your body, so it's crucial that you choose a school that fits your specific needs and wants. The toughest question you'll need to answer is "What Do I Really Want?" Well, what DO you really want? Even if you're throwing your hands up in dismay right this very second, it's ok. Chances are that you do have some idea of how you'd like to continue your education. To help you make your decision, here's a short breakdown of your options:

Four-Year Schools

Get ready to invest a big chunk of your time, energy, and money if you attend a four-year school. Four-year college and university freshmen typically live on-campus, spending about half of their academic career fulfilling general education requirements and the other half completing coursework in their major. Four-year schools focus on giving you a well-rounded education so expect to be introduced to new subjects and to take a wide range of classes, some of which you'll love and some of which you'll hate with the fire of 1,000 suns. Other four-year school perks include study abroad programs, internship opportunities, the ability to participate on college sports teams, the once-in-a-lifetime chance to live in a tiny, tiny room with someone you've never met, and access to on-campus resources including libraries, student organizations, and school-funded programs and presentations. Though four-year schools are undeniably the biggest financial investment, consider your cash just that...an investment. According to the College Board, graduates with a four-year degree earn approximately 73% more over their lifetime than those only holding a high school diploma. Just don't spend it all in one place.

Two-Year Schools

While four-year schools tend to receive all the hype, the College Board reports that many high school grads (22% nationwide to be exact) choose two-year schools. As opposed to a broad, liberal arts education, community colleges and technical schools typically focus on preparing students to enter the workforce. Two-year schools require a fraction of the time and cash that it takes to earn a four-year degree; however, graduates do not live on-campus or have access to many of the programs and resources their four-year counterparts enjoy every day. The good news is, for those who want to save money or for students with a less-than-perfect high school record, community colleges are an excellent way to transition into a top-notch four-year school.

Specialty Schools

These are schools that don't fit into a single category simply because their programs are unlike anything else. Schools like Virginia Military Institute and Shenandoah Arts Conservatory put their own spin on education and play by a different set of rules than everyone else. What these schools have in common is that all of them offer programs and curricula that are radically different than anything else the state offers and each school draws a different type of student than you'll see strolling across the trimmed lawns of typical colleges and universities. Do your homework, plan on making at least one campus visit, and ask to interview a current student before sending your specialty school application off. You'll need to know exactly what you're jumping into.

Distance Learning Programs

Earn your degree without ever putting on pants? What is this, heaven? Thanks to the wonders of modern technology (the internet), you can earn your associate, bachelor's, masters, or even Ph.D. without ever being exposed to pencils, books, or teachers' dirty looks. The catch is that students who opt for distance learning courses MUST be twice as disciplined as their brick-and-mortar counterparts AND have to be willing to forego the nice-ities of in-person contact with both professors and other students. Good luck getting a study group to come over when you're not wearing pants.

Trade Schools

You'll find beauty school, tractor-trailer training, and everything in between here. Trade schools are the fast, cheap way to move directly into a chosen profession. Although program lengths, costs, and time required vary tremendously from school to school, all trade institutions are focused on giving you one skill that you can use to move into a specific job upon completion of the program. These programs are NOT for the curious, unsure, experimental, or exploratory student, nor are they for those who seek a multifaceted education. Students who fare well in trade school know exactly who they want to be and won't settle for anything else.

What it Takes to Get In

Students eyeing trade and two-year institutions, you're in luck. These schools (with very few exceptions) tend to accept anyone with a high school diploma or G.E.D. who walks through the door, so you won't have to worry about stiff competition. All you'll need to do is pick up your application, send it in by the deadline, pay for your classes, and you're in. The only thing you've got to worry about from here on out is passing. For everyone else, brace yourselves. Four-year, specialty, and distance learning schools usually require an entire application packet (don't worry, we'll walk you through that process in the next chapter) and, depending on what school you've got your eye on, range in admissions competition from Easy-As-Pie to Straight-A's-Only.

Choosing What Type of School Fits You Best

A Greek philosopher once wrote, "Know Thyself." Had the Greeks been college admissions counselors today, they'd have tacked on "And Visit Lots and Lots of Schools Too." Nobody can make the higher education decision for you, so before you even start organizing your application paperwork, securing your recommendations, perfecting that essay, scrounging up the cash for those application fees, getting in some extra community service hours, brushing up on your S.A.T. vocab, and trying to recall all of those extracurricular activities you did since freshman year, take a moment to evaluate yourself and think about your educational goals, your favorite (and not-so-favorite) classes, your dream job, and what you choose to read and learn about when given total academic freedom. While you're exploring who you are, explore what's out there as well. Make use of the guidance counselors, admissions reps, financial aid officers, and college tour guides that come to work every single day to help students like you figure out which schools fit you like a glove. While you're at it, also make use of those excused absences you get for college visits. Visiting a college campus and sitting in on a couple of classes will give you more information about what life is really like at that school than any web site or brochure will ever be able to provide. The secret to finding the school that fits you is knowing what you want (that's all you) and finding the program that can help you achieve it. Hopefully this book will be able to help with that last part.

Top FIVE Reasons to Attend Virginia Schools

5 **The eats.** With the cash you'll save on in-state tuition in one year alone, you'll be able to feed yourself, your roommate, and the rest of your dorm for all of freshman year. With an extra $9,947 floating around, you could buy 621 large Papa John's pizzas and still have enough leftover for breadsticks. Bon appetite

4 **Because success is sexy.** Virginia's four-year public colleges and universities boast significantly higher six year graduation rates than the national average. By staying here, you statistically have a better shot of earning that flat hat than the average non-Virginia student.

3 **Jon Stewart graduated from a Virginia school.** Read that out loud to yourself to get the full effect. J-O-N S-T-E-W-A-R-T graduated from a VA school. Do you really need a better reason?

2 **Virginia is for lovers...of knowledge.** With VA's Early College Scholars program, motivated students can earn up to an entire semester's worth of credits before they ever step foot on a college campus. Helloooooooo savings.

1 **Virginia makes it easier for parents.** This state is one of just 17 in the nation where parents, grandparents, relatives, and guardians can choose to invest their cash in either a state-supported pre-paid tuition plan or a 529 college savings plan. Drawing a blank? We'll go over what these plans are and why they're important in later chapters.

Chapter One

The Painless Way to Plan for College

The early bird catches the worm. In this case, the proverbial early bird catches the highest test scores, the well-written recommendations, the enviable scholarship packages, and the acceptance letters from top-tier schools. Like college academics, acing the application process boils down to one thing—Planning. Capital P. No matter where you choose to go, those who prove that they've got ninja-level planning skillz find themselves with more college options and more cash to pay for it all than slackers who wait until the last minute. To help you become a Planning black belt, here's a year-by-year breakdown of what you should be doing, broken down by the big three things colleges will be looking for - your grades and curriculum, your extra activities, and how mentally prepared you are for the road ahead.

What Everyone Should Know

In order to graduate from a Virginia high school, you're going to have to take the following classes:

- 4 English classes
- 3 Math, Science, and History classes
- 2 P.E. classes
- 1 Fine Arts class
- 6 Electives

In addition to passing SOL tests in English, Math, History, Science, and one course of your choice. But that's just the bare minimum and colleges are going to encourage—no, scratch that—expect you to go above and beyond the minimum if you want to get in. The harder the classes you take and do well in, the more likely you are to WOW the pants off an admissions rep (not literally of course, that would just be awkward). Doing well is the important part. Your goal is to take courses that will both challenge you intellectually and encourage you to perform at your peak. That means a B+ in a lower-level course looks better than a D in an AP class and chances are you won't sacrifice other grades (or your sanity) for the lower-level class. Try to be as academically competitive as possible without breezing through your classes and without drowning in coursework that's over your head. Aim for an Advanced Studies diploma (4 English, Math, Science, and History credits, 3 Foreign Language, 2 P.E., 1 Fine Arts course, and 2 Electives) and take the hardest courses you can handle while still pulling those A's and B's we all love to see. **Got it? Good.**

A Word on Magnet Schools

Congratulations! You're gifted! Now what, smarty pants?
For an increasing number of Virginia students, that means making a tough decision before you set foot in a 9th grade classroom. With gifted programs and magnet schools in nearly every part of the state, bright, motivated students have more choices when it comes to their education than previous generations ever dreamed of having. The bonus of attending a magnet school is that you'll have different (in some cases better) learning experiences than other students, you'll most likely be surrounded by like-minded peers, and you'll be receiving a name-brand high school education, much in the same way that those who attend a notable university receive a name-brand college education

The flip side to attending a magnet school is that you'll have to stay academically competitive even though the competition is more fierce. Name means little if it's not backed up by high grades, solid test scores, and positive recommendations. Whether you attend a public, private, or magnet high school, grades and the level of your curriculum come first —AP or IB-level C's look just as bad coming from magnet schools as they do from public ones. When deciding if a magnet program is right for you, forget about the name and your college app for a second and consider whether or not the school's mission and learning opportunities match your interests and educational goals.

Freshmen: Getting Adjusted

Thought you were off the hook? Yeah right. When it comes to colleges, it's never too early to start looking. Students who begin planning early, long before they ever even think of taking the SATs, are far more prepared for the application process, and ultimately the college experience, than their procrastinating peers. Your mission, should you choose to accept it, is to lay the groundwork for a successful high school career and begin investigating what colleges and universities appeal to you.

The Academics

Welcome to the next four years of your life. This year your goal is to learn your way around high school and set yourself up for academic success. The first step is to make sure you're in classes that fit your interests and ability level. Spend the first quarter working with your teachers and guidance counselor to make sure you're in classes that challenge but don't overwhelm you. Once your schedule is set, all you've got to do is maintain those grades baby. If you find your grades dropping at any point, don't be afraid to ask a friend or teacher for help.

The Extras

This is your time to try out any and everything that catches your eye. Check out what clubs are available, try out for a team, find a volunteer job, or audition for the school play. If you can't find anything you like, think outside of your school's short list of activities. Start a club, long-term project, small business, volunteer project, community activity, or nonprofit agency (yep, it's been done by kids your age before). Whatever you do, be involved, keep a record of your hours put in, and absolutely, positively DON'T do it because it will look good on your college app. Colleges are looking for students that are passionate, creative individuals, not suck-ups out to brown nose an admissions committee.

The Future

Graduation probably seems eons away but it will be here faster than you can say "Accepted." Begin thinking about what colleges interest you and what you'd like to study. If you haven't a clue, don't freak out. You've got four whole years to figure this stuff out. Visit your guidance counselor to talk about the college process, what you need to do, and what colleges and universities are nearby. Also find out where your parents, older siblings, teachers, church leaders, coaches, bosses, all of their adult friends, and all of their friends' friends went to school—they might be able to recommend something you've never even heard of before. If possible, go and visit at least one college or university nearby just to get a feel for collegiate life and don't even think about making the argument that all of the information is listed on the web. According to some very scientific calculations, visiting schools and seeing for yourself how the classes and on-campus life there works will provide you with approximately 10 kabillion times the information you'd be able to gather from a web site.

While you're in college mode, keep in mind that you've got to get a feel for paying for college as well. Translation? Begin the scholarship hunt right this very minute, even if you're only six years old and using this book to learn to read. Start today. Scholarships available to first and second-year high school students typically get overlooked by both students and guidance counselors. The best place to start is by visiting your guidance counselor for info on local scholarships, then scouring area businesses and community associations for scholarship info. You can create your own scholarship profile at Fastweb.com or Collegeboard.com; however, these sites will provide you (as well as thousands of other kids across the country) with information on national, rather than local, awards. For your best shot at college cash, check out the list of scholarships only available to Virginia students in the back of this ridiculously useful book. Free college bucks are given out to students of all ages every single month of the year, so do your research and start filling out forms as soon as possible. You could have college paid for before you become a sophomore.

Sophomores: Getting Active

Crunch time is coming up, but don't start sweating yet. Your second year in school should focus on finding out who you are, what you love to do, and how you can be a leader in your chosen activities. Spend the year exploring the academic, extracurricular, and human resources offered in your high school and figuring out what places and programs appeal to you for life after high school.

The Academics

Year two—you should have the routine down by now. Keep the grades sky high (or at least try to), stay in touch with your favorite teachers (hey, you'll need recommendations one day), and schedule routine check-ups with your guidance counselor. What you may not be prepared for is the PSATs. Wipe the sweat off your forehead, the PSATs have nothing to do with the real SATs, are optional for sophomores, and only count when taken during the junior year. The PSATs simply determine whether you're eligible to win a National Merit or National Achievement Scholarship. Score high and you could bank big before you've even chosen a school. Score lower than you'd like and you'll have some idea of where you can improve before you take the real SATs. Hooray! Everybody wins! But wait! If it doesn't count until next year, why bother with another stupid test? The simple, anti-climactic answer is this: Because practice makes perfect, or at least closer to perfect. Taking the PSATs will help prepare you for bigger, tougher tests, will show you where your strengths and weaknesses lie, and may qualify you for a fatter scholarship check. Take your scores with a grain (or quarry) of salt and work on your soft spots.

If you're feeling really confident and have room in your schedule, consider taking an Advanced Placement or Dual Enrollment course this year. Showing colleges that you have the ambition and the ability to do university-level work while still in high school is a good indicator that you'll be an academic asset to their campus. If you can't take one this year, think about squeezing one in next year, taking a class on the side at a local community college, or preparing for an AP exam on your own. AP exams are open to any student willing to take them regardless of whether the student has actually taken the AP class or not. If you can't get into an official AP class, consider asking a teacher to help you get ready for an AP exam or start preparing online at VirginiaMentor.org. Another way to get ahead is by taking - prepare to cringe - summer school. Think of it this way - the more credits you can get out of the way now, the fewer college credits you'll have to pony up for down the road.

The Extras

Spend this year trying something old and something new. Hopefully you've already found your passion and at least one club or organization that shares it. If so, keep up the good work sport and try branching out into at least one different area. If you haven't found anything that catches your eye, forget about last year and start anew. Find at least one in-school activity (think clubs, sports, school plays, music groups, or speaking teams) and one out-of-school activity (like a part-time job, internship, externship, volunteer position, small business, punk rock band, study abroad trip, or independent project) that tickles your intellectual fancy. When picking your activities, think big, think bold, and think beyond the box. Every year college admissions counselors encounter thousands of applications from students who were treasurer of the drama club or volunteered two hours a month with a local homeless shelter, but kids who began their own catering business at the age of 15, became champion jugglers, or spent their summer walking across Italy truly stand out as young pioneers.

In between organizing your school's blood drive or putting the finishing touches on your first screenplay, plan on working on more than your tan this summer. Schools like the University of Virginia, James Madison University, and George Mason University offer summer programs for high school students that will not only introduce you to new people and ideas (as well as sweeten your college app a little), but will also give you a chance to scope out a real college campus. If you're having trouble getting started, check out the list of summer programs in the back of this chapter. Whatever activities you decide to try, keep a record of the hours you spend doing it. Admissions reps will want to know just how much of your blood, sweat, and tears went into those clubs.

The Future

Now's the time to seriously start thinking about colleges. Talk to your guidance counselor (who should be your BFF by now), read every college brochure you can get your grubby little hands on, and check out the web site of any and every school that sounds interesting. If you have no clue what exactly you'd like to study, that's ok. You can start narrowing down schools by thinking about what kind of campus you'd like, what size school you'd like to attend, what majors interest you, and where in the country you'd like to end up. If you have any friends that have graduated, make it a point to go visit them. If you don't have any friends that have graduated, make some, then go visit them, even if they attend a school you wouldn't apply to if your life depended on it. Go visit anyway. Visiting schools and observing classes is the single best way to find out how college life works and what you should expect.

Now that you've taken the PSATs, you'll be eligible for bigger, better scholarships, so stay on top of the hunt for college funding. Start a scholarship filing system of awards you're eligible for this year, those you've applied for already, and awards you'll be eligible for in later years. Think local, stay persistent, and keep sending in those applications. Your bank account will thank you later.

Juniors: Getting Organized

Ready to get down to business? If you've been preparing all along, you should be. Since you've already got the grades and the activities down pat, this year you've got to focus on which colleges you'll be applying to and where you'll get the green to pay for it all. Make the college and financial aid hunt a priority and you'll earn the right to have a mild (that's Mild, not Wild) case of Senioritis next year.

The Academics

Maintain your grades, make nice with your teachers, blah, blah. You know how it works by now. This year, it's time to take the PSATs for real. This round you'll know what to expect and hopefully you've been tweaking your weak spots. Go into the test calm, cool, and collected and remember that the scores have no bearing on where you get into school. Once you've conquered the PSATs, set your sights on the big tests...that's right...plural. Before this year's over, you'll need to take the SATs at least once (don't sweat it, we'll help you ace the SATs and ACTs in a later chapter), any SAT II subject tests your colleges require, the ACTs (if you can), and the IB or AP exams for any courses you're taking this year. Register early, bring sharpened #2 pencils, and prepare for hand cramps and nervous sweating. Academically, this will be your toughest year.

Speaking of academic challenges, students who are serious about getting a jump on college and who wouldn't mind saving up to $5,000 on tuition should check out Virginia's Early College Scholars Program. Designed to save motivated students credit hours and tuition dollars, the Early College Scholars Program allows academically advanced high school students to complete up to 15 hours, or one full semester's worth, of transferable college credits before they graduate high school. Students must have a solid B (3.0) average, be pursuing an Advanced Studies Diploma, and sign a participation agreement in conjunction with both their parents and their high school. In exchange, students will be able to take any AP, IB, or dual enrollment course their high school offers as well as any college-level courses offered online through the Virginia Virtual Advanced Placement School without paying a dime. While having a boat load of college courses under your belt may turn some admissions counselors heads, earning AP-level C's can actually make you look less prepared for college than a student armed with fewer college credits. Should you opt for Early College Scholars, visit your guidance counselor during the first week of school to sign up and make sure to plan carefully, budget in enough time for studying, and stay in close contact with teachers and guidance counselors just in case you get in over your head.

The Extras

You've found your creative, athletic, and employment outlets, now all you've got to do is look for ways to excel. Try taking on at least one leadership position this year or heading up a school or community project on your own. Spend this year searching for schools that will not only accommodate your academic needs, but your social and extracurricular ones as well. Also, check out whether your outside-of-school interests can pay off. National organizations such as DECA, the National Forensic League, Girl/Boy Scouts of America, and the National Foundation for the Advancement in the Arts all offer huge scholarships for students who have put in their time and companies including Wal-Mart, McDonald's, and Chick-Fil-A provide monetary rewards for student employees. The catch is that you'll be competing against the crème de la crème from across the country. To narrow down the competition, take a look around. Area businesses such as Ukrop's Super Markets and Erikson Retirement Communities offer generous educational rewards for student employees and local chapters of national associations including the American Legion, Rotary International, and the Lion's Club provide funding to area college-bound kids. Your high school could be another scholarship source and your college of interest could offer departmental or memorial scholarships. A little digging and a few phone calls could result in a serious chunk of change being thrown your way.

The Future

Hear that? It's the sound of your future sneaking up on you. Scary, isn't it? By the end of this year, you should have a list of six to ten schools you wouldn't mind attending, including at least two schools that are practically begging you to apply, two you may or may not get into, and two you've got a better shot of sprouting wings than attending. When deciding where you'll apply, keep a couple of out-of-state schools in mind too. In-state competition for Virginia schools is tough and in some cases you'll have a better shot of getting accepted to a more academically prestigious school as well as landing a more generous scholarship package if you aim for an institution that's not in your home state. Once you've got your list, find out everything you can, schedule some visits, and gather applications. By the time you're a senior, you should be able to rattle off those schools' vital stats in your sleep. Just knowing about colleges isn't enough. You've got to keep costs in mind too. Keep adding to that scholarship folder and aim for local cash. Staying well-organized and on top of it all will save you significant stress next year

ACEing High School:

1. Academics come first, plain and simple. Admissions counselors both in-state and nationally cite high grades and a challenging curriculum as the number one thing they look for in applicants. Take the hardest and most diverse curriculum you can handle, but remember that a B in a lower-level class looks better than a C- in a higher one. If you find yourself slipping, study harder, ask a teacher for help, get a tutor, organize a study group, do some extra credit, or if all else fails, slip down to a lower level class. A couple of C's won't kill you, but more than a few will damage your application packet.

2. College planning. Start early, be thorough, get organized, and don't forget to use those human (ahem, your BFF guidance counselor) and physical resources to make the planning process easier. Visit as many schools as you can (who doesn't love a good road trip?), tap local organizations for scholarships, and apply for any financial aid you're even remotely qualified for. Ace planning for college and you'll be well-prepared for your upcoming freshman year.

3. Extracurriculars. Remember that they're just that—extras. If your schedule gets too hectic, sacrificing a club isn't nearly as bad as getting a poor grade. Do what you love, try something unique, record how much time you spent doing it, and take advantage of your summers off. Above all, keep in mind that extracurricular activities are supposed to be fun, not more work.

Seniors: Getting In

It all comes down to this. Time for your hard work to pay off. Expect six, jam-packed, paperwork-riddled months and then a little time to breathe and finish out the school year. Remember, all you have to do is survive until those applications are in the mail, then you can return to being a normal high school student...you know...until you graduate forever. Dun Dun Duuuuuuuuuuuun!!!!!!!!!!

The Academics

The biggest misconception about the college admissions process is that nobody cares about your senior year grades...oh contraire. Although sleeping through your morning classes and spending the rest of the day drawing nasty renditions of your teachers would be nothing shy of glorious, colleges reserve the right to take back your acceptance letter should your grades plummet. The first semester will be critical in determining whether or not you can take on college courses, so keep your nose begrudgingly in those books. Instead of thinking of your senior year as punishment, think of it like a blue-light sale on education. This is your last year to cram in as many college-level courses as you can handle before having to pay full price for them on-campus. Focus your attention on the APs, IBs, CLEPs, and Dual Enrollments you're currently taking. Do well on those and the scholarship search will become that much easier.

The Extras

The main thing you should do with your extracurricular activities this year is enjoy them. If you're working on a huge project you've spent the past three years building up to, put in the extra hours and finish it before you send in your apps. Colleges will be interested in seeing the fruits of your high school labors. To take full advantage of the time you've put in, don't forget that coaches, directors, club organizers, and employers see a different side of you than your teachers and have known you for a longer period of time. When compiling your recommendations, think about including one from someone who knows the non-academic you.

The Future

You've got your list of schools. You've got the paperwork to go with them. You've got a scholarship filing system that would make Dewey envious. Now all you've got to do is fill those suckers out (we'll help you in the next chapter) and send them in ON TIME. Remember that planning is the name of the game here. Start working on your personal statements and figuring out which lucky teachers you'll ask to fill out your recommendations this summer, you know, before you've got two club meetings, enough homework to kill a man, and a test tomorrow you haven't even begun studying for. The next chapter will walk you through creating an air-tight application packet.

FOR HOME SCHOOLERS:

You guys are like the outlaws of the education world—playing by your own rogue set of rules, that is, all the way up until you apply for colleges. The good news is that Virginia is a very homeschool-friendly state. Even the most selective VA schools including the University of Virginia, George Mason University, Virginia Military Institute, Virginia Tech, Washington and Lee University, Emory and Henry College, Hollins University, and the University of Richmond have all accepted homeschooled students before....but that doesn't mean getting in is easy. Because you're outside of a formal school system, you're going to have to go out of your way to prove to admissions reps that you're hard-working, ambitious, and capable of doing college-level work. It will be essential that you find people other than your parents and relatives who can attest to your academic and leadership abilities. On the academic side, homeschool students should heavily consider taking a few community college courses, CLEP exams, SAT II tests, or courses offered through the Virtual Advanced Placement School at www.virtualvirginia.org. You've also got to focus on nailing the SATs. Since homeschool transcripts vary tremendously from student to student, many schools place added emphasis on standardized tests like the SATs and ACTs. Think about taking an SAT prep course or at least taking a few practice tests so you're ready. You'll also need to get involved in at least one (preferably two or three) community activity such as a sports team, club, volunteer group, internship, summer camp, or part-time job to make that college app shine. For more info on how to apply for college as a homeschool student, check out the Homeschool Supplement at the end of this chapter.

Chapter *Recap*

Let's review, shall we?

FRESHMEN:

- Set the precedent for good grades early on.
- Establish open communication with your teachers, they're here to help.
- Meet and greet your guidance counselor.
- Get involved in something you're interested in, not something that you think will look good to admissions reps.
- Start investigating colleges, visit at least one.
- Spend your summer doing something productive. If you need help coming up with the ideas, take a peek at the list of possibilities in the back of this chapter.

SOPHOMORES:

- Maintain the grades and contacts with your teachers and guidance counselor.
- Take the practice PSATs.
- Consider taking an AP or Dual Enrollment class. If you can't do it this year, aim for next or take a community college class this summer.
- Find a passion (preferably a unique one) and run with it. Establish your in and out-of-school extracurricular activities.
- Apply for scholarships. The list of scholarship opportunities in the back of the book will help you get started.
- Use your summer wisely.

JUNIORS:

- Keep the grades, keep contacts with your teachers, keep visiting your guidance counselor.
- Sign up for the Early College Scholars Program now if interested.
- Take some AP classes, the PSATs (for real this time), and the SATs at least once.
- Take on a leadership position in your extracurricular activities.
- Investigate what scholarships and grants are offered through your extracurriculars.
- Make a list of 6 – 10 schools where you'd like to apply, including 2 safety schools, 2 target schools, and 2 reach schools.
- Research, visit, and contact those schools' admissions and financial aid departments.
- Apply for local and national scholarships available near you.

SENIORS:

- Sign up for a challenging year and keep the grades up.
- Enjoy your extracurricular activities and keep your extracurricular leaders in mind for recommendations.
- Start filling out your college applications this summer, you'll need the extra time.
- Send those suckers in ON TIME.
- Wait anxiously to hear back and try not to bite your nails to the quick.

Top FIVE Web Sites for College-bound Students

5 **Collegeboard.com**—Your one-stop shop for information about SAT registration, testing locations, preparation tips, and practice tests. Students with a serious case of test anxiety can test their skills on College Board's online SAT training course.

4 **Collegiatechoice.com**—View student guided tours of over 350 colleges and universities across the U.S., Canada, England, Ireland and Scotland, including 11 Virginia schools.

3 **Getthatgig.com / Idealist.org**—Fine, fine, this is actually two sites, but both will help you find internships and volunteer opportunities around the corner or around the world. These will come in handy when you're planning out your summer.

2 **VirginiaMentor.org**—Plug in your requirements and this site's Undergraduate Matching Assistant will find Virginia schools that fit your needs. Other bonuses include online applications to 8 VA schools, a scholarship search, information on how to find AP courses near you, and the ability to get your guidance counselor in on the red-hot, electronic action.

1 **FinAid.org**—Hands down the most comprehensive financial aid resource on the web. What sets this site apart from the dozens of other sites that offer scholarship searches and loan information is the financial aid calculators that allow you to compute everything from your loan payments to projected aid packages to life insurance needs.

ADMISSIONS Q+A

What's the #1 thing you look for in an applicant?

"The first thing is curriculum, both how far you've gone and the level of rigor. The second thing we look at is grades, mostly in core subjects. We don't look at GPA because everyone calculates that differently."

-*Michael Walsh,* Admissions Director for James Madison University (Harrisonburg, VA)

"We are looking for students who challenge themselves with tough courses and have thrived in their academic program in high school...For an in-state student to be admitted, that student needs to look at what's offered in their high school and to take a rich offering of AP, IB, or other advanced courses offered by their school."

-*John Blackburn,* Dean of Admissions for the University of Virginia (Charlottesville, VA)

"I think first and foremost we look for applicants that have taken the most demanding curriculum in their school."

-*Josh Henry,* Assistant Dean of Admissions for the College of William and Mary (Williamsburg, VA)

"It's a combination of your grades, the courses you took, the trends in your grades, the opportunities you had in high school, all of that packaged as an academic profile...What a student can do in order to maximize their chance of getting in is to pick the right courses and do the best they can. It's really terribly simple."

-*Andrew Flagel,* Dean of Admissions for George Mason University (Fairfax, VA)

What's the number one mistake students make when planning for college?

"A lot of students pick courses in their areas of strength and it's really important for them to take courses in all subject areas and really work on their weaknesses."

-*Josh Henry,* Assistant Dean Admissions for the College of William and Mary

"Believing that it's important to have a super long resume of involvements and forgetting or not realizing that particularly selective schools often value quality of involvement of quantity... Having the look of a joiner when applying for school versus having the look of someone who's committed."

-*Jonathan Webster,* Associate Dean of Admissions for Washington and Lee University

"Students assume that there's an individual school that's perfect and that they should tailor their lives to getting admitted to that school...Instead of picking what matches their interests, students are trying to guess what admissions counselors want."

-*Andrew Flagel,* Dean of Admissions for George Mason University

"Students don't visit the college that they're interested in early on. Sometimes students will visit during their senior year and then find out it's not what they thought it would be. Students need to visit during their junior year if at all possible."

-*Rebecca Eckstein,* Admissions Director for Hollins University

"The choice of courses. That's one thing that I see time and again where if a student had only taken a tougher program, they would be more competitive. A lot of times in the senior year, students drop off and say 'Well, I'll take a lighter load until I get to college.' You're about to go to college, it's not good to be taking a lighter load."

-*John Blackburn,* Director of Admissions for the University of Virginia

Chapter Two

Admissions, Schmadmissions: The Application Process Made Easier

Hopefully by this point you have some idea of what kinds of schools you'd like to attend. Bonus points if you've visited a few schools and/or have already started collecting the necessary paperwork. No matter what institution you attend after high school, you're going to have to brave the application process in order to get there. Know this—the application process is **OF THE UTMOST IMPORTANCE** if you're planning on attending a college or university next year. So important in fact, that it is totally worthy of being written in bold and underlined. Your application materials are the only tools colleges will have to figure out who you are and if you're ready to handle their curriculum. This is your one chance to shine so get ready to invest some serious time and thought into creating the most well-written, professional-looking, head-turning, eye-popping, acceptance letter-winning application packet the known universe has ever seen. Ready? Let's do this.

Step One: Know Thy Enemy

In order to conquer the college admissions process, you've got to know what you're up against. Your application packet will contain the following:

- *A completed paper or online application*—Don't get worked up, this section is a breeze. Here you'll fill out basic information about your educational background, test scores, and college programs of interest, yada, yada, yada as well as info about your high school jobs, ongoing projects, and extracurricular activities. The first step in acing this section is simply gathering the paperwork. To obtain your paper application, request one directly from the schools where you're applying or check out commonapp.org to see if your schools of choice accept the Common Application.

- *An official high school transcript*—That means it's sealed and signed by a school administrator. Since your entire graduating class will all be requesting transcripts at the same time, be a dear and let your registrar or guidance counselor know exactly how many transcripts you'll need and where they'll need to be sent by October of your senior year.

- *Your test scores*—Colleges are going to want to see your SAT, ACT, and SAT II scores as well as results from any CLEP, AP, or IB exams you've scored well on ("well" in this case meaning a 3 or above for AP tests, a 5 or above for IB credit, and for most institutions a 50 or above for CLEP exams). If English is not your native language, you're highly encouraged to take a Test of English as a Foreign Language (TOEFL) as well. Information on when and where to take the TOEFL is available at www.ets.org. After you've studied up and taken the tests, don't forget to have your scores sent to directly to your schools. AP scores can be sent by contacting the College Board at (888)-225-5427. For IB scores, contact your local Diplome Coordinator or the International Baccalaureate Organization at (212) 696-4464. You can send your SAT, CLEP, and SAT II scores by contacting the College Board online at www.collegeboard.org and your ACT scores can be sent by telephone at (319) 337-1313 or online at www.actstudent.org.

- *At least one essay or personal statement*—Chill out, it doesn't have to be Pulitzer-worthy, it just has to give the admissions committee a glimpse into what makes you, you. Essays and personal statements usually range from 150 words (that's under a page you lucky duck) to 500 words (about 2 pages). While some colleges will give you specific questions to answer, others will simply ask you to submit a personal statement of your own choice. Think **HONEST**. Think **CREATIVE**. Think **UNIQUE**. If you need help kicking those brain juices into gear, read a few of the rockstar admissions essays in the back of this chapter.

- *At least three glowing recommendations*—These can come from your teachers, coaches, guidance counselors, advisors, bosses, community service coordinators, or any other professional outside of your family who can attest to your academic and leadership abilities. Most colleges will require at least one recommendation come from a teacher (preferably a teacher in a non-elective course you've had in the past two years) and prefer that another recommendation come from a guidance or career counselor.

- *An application fee*—Get ready to fork over anywhere from zilch to $60 per application for schools in Virginia. If you need a little financial assistance on the application fees, ask the school about how to apply for a fee waiver.

- *An interview*—For most schools the admissions interview is optional, but this is an option you'll want to take. An interview is an in-person chance to show an admissions rep that you're a dynamic student who can bring academic integrity as well as creativity to campus. When preparing your application packets, call the admissions department of each of your schools to request an interview. If you're lucky enough to score one, prepare by answering the sample interview questions on the next page, take a hard look at your transcript, and get ready to account for any low points. For instance, if you got low grades one year due to illness or a family crisis, this is your time to let an admissions counselor know why there's a dip in your transcript. Also have a couple samples of your best high school work on hand to whip out at a moment's notice. Though you might feel like you're the only one in the hot seat, this is your chance to grill the school as well. In addition to bringing materials that highlight your interests and academic strong points, bring a list of researched questions (i.e. questions whose answers you won't find on the school's web site). If you can't come up with any, check out the sample list in this chapter. Dress professionally, be on time, stay cool, and remember that a successful interview can turn a hardened admissions reviewer into your personal cheerleader.

If you're applying for a certain major or if you're applying to a specialty school, you may also have to fulfill additional requirements such as an audition or portfolio review along with the application packet. Read your application carefully and make sure you fulfill ALL of the requirements before dropping that bad boy in the mail.

Timing is Everything

What you put in your application isn't the only admissions decision you'll make. You'll also have to choose when to apply. Most schools nationwide offer incoming freshmen not one, but two chances to apply for fall semester admissions. Students may submit their applications by the regular admissions deadline (usually in December or January) or may choose to apply early, typically in November. The benefit of applying earlier than the rest of the pack is that some (but definitely not all) schools admit a higher percentage of the early applicant pool than the regular applicant pool, potentially giving you a better shot of getting in. Additionally, students who apply earlier also hear back earlier (usually in November or December), allowing time to regroup and apply for other schools during the regular admissions season if necessary. The catch is that your senior year grades and projects won't be considered in your application pack AND your application may be binding. Early application programs come in one of two flavors - early decision and early action. Schools such as Virginia Tech, Sweet Briar College, and Virginia Military Institute offer early decision programs that require students to sign a legally-binding promise to attend that particular school if admitted. That means early decision students won't have the opportunity to apply to any other schools and won't have the chance to compare financial aid offers. On the flip side, schools that offer early action programs—like Hampton University, UVA-Wise, and Radford University—do not require students to commit to attending the school if accepted.

What both early application programs have in common is that they each offer students the opportunity to get the dreaded college application process out of the way early. Those who crave choice, expect their senior year grades to substantially improve their academic record, or who have a senior project they'd like to highlight in their college application will probably want to hold off until the regular application deadline so their first semester stats will be considered.

Top 10 Questions...

Questions an Admissions Interviewer May Ask You:

1. What can you bring to the school's campus?
2. What was the greatest lesson you learned in high school? How did it impact your life?
3. What obstacles have you overcome in your high school career?
4. How does this school fit into your future goals?
5. How do you spend your free time?
6. What were your favorite and least favorite high school courses? What did you learn from them?
7. What's your favorite book, quote, and song and why?
8. What do you see yourself doing ten years from now?
9. What are you most passionate about?
10. If you were a billionaire, how would you spend your time?

Questions to Ask an Admissions Interviewer:

1. What do you think draws students to your campus?
2. What does your interviewer consider to be the school's greatest asset?
3. What's the most popular major and extracurricular activity on campus?
4. What percentage of freshmen return for their sophomore year?
5. Does the school offer independent study or independent research courses?
6. Can you create your own major?
7. Can you intern off campus for credit?
8. What percentage of graduates find jobs within six months of finishing their degrees?
9. How big is the school's Greek system?
10. What percentage of grad students teach first-year courses?

Q+A ADMISSIONS

Four Interview Faux-Pas:

4 **Not taking one**: "If an interview is offered and you don't take it, that's a mistake. At schools that receive too many applications from qualified kids, an interview can really help you out."

– *Jonathan Webster*, Associate Dean of Admissions for Washington and Lee University (Lexington, VA)

3 **Letting mom and dad do the talking**: "If a student has their parents speak for them, that's a big mistake. We like to meet the parents, but we also want the student to articulate for herself in the interview."

– *Rebecca Eckstein*, Admissions Director for Hollins University (Roanoke, VA)

2 **Forgetting Your Homework**: "Do the basic research on the school before you get to the interview. Do not ask an interviewer how many students go to this college or do they have a certain major. The interview ought to be more substantive discussion. Go in there with some questions that you want to know, but also be ready to answer when you're asked about what you're most proud of in your academic or extracurricular background."

– *Jonathan Webster*

1 **Sweating Bullets**: "Try to be as comfortable as possible...When students have no direct eye contact, look at the floor a lot, or are visibly uncomfortable, we can tell that they don't want to be there or they haven't put a lot of thought into it."

– *Rebecca Eckstein*

Timeline of the Most Important Events in History

35,000 BC
Paleolithic Era

2,000 BC
The Bronze Age

1492
Discovery of the New World

1865
Assassination of Lincoln

1989
Fall of the Berlin Wall

August (before your senior year), Get Prepared—Finish researching your potential schools. Once you've got your list of schools in hand, gather those applications, and get to work. Before summer is over, you should have the paper application portion of each filled out, a draft of your essays ready to be critiqued, and a list of who you'll ask to fill out your recommendations.

September, Get Paperwork—Here's where the mountain of papers come in. As soon as the school year kicks in, request copies of your transcripts and start passing out your recommendation forms to the lucky, lucky teachers and counselors who will help you land those acceptance letters. Also, get a teacher or two to proofread your essays just to make sure that your i's are crossed and your t's are dotted. Feel free to take a moment to groan aloud at that absurdly corny joke. If you need to take the SATs, ACTs, or SAT IIs again, now is the time to get registered. This is your last chance to raise your scores before admissions officials take a look. If you need a little monetary help, SAT and ACT testing fees can be waived for qualified students.

October, Get the Scores—SAT/ACT time. Take the SAT's and/or ACT's one last time, arrange to have your scores sent to your schools of choice, and don't forget to collect your recommendations and transcripts. If you're applying early decision or early action, pay attention to those deadlines and get your application in ON TIME.

November, Get Moving—It's crunch time now. November 1st and 15th are when most early decision and early action apps are due. It's your job to put the finishing touches on your application packet and get em in the mail.

ON A ROLL

Deadlines got you down? There is an alternative. A few VA schools ditch the deadlines and instead have a rolling admissions policy in which applications are accepted year-round or until there are no more openings available. Because applications tend to flood in during the regular admissions season (December and January), getting your packet in early, preferably by the end of September, can greatly increase your chances of getting in.

CALLING REALLY EARLY BIRDS

If you can't wait to get to college, you might not have to. Virginia Intermont College, Mary Baldwin College, and Liberty University all offer admission to select students of "unusual academic ability" who haven't graduated from high school. All you need is a lot of A's behind you, a challenging roster of classes, solid SAT or ACT scores, and a few good recommendations.

December, Get the Grades—Exam cram. Try to finish the semester off with a bang, the bigger, the better. Colleges can, and definitely do, consider your mid-term semester grades, so study hard, do some extra credit, and try to kiss up as much as you can. While you're at it, stay on top of those application deadlines and begin gathering your financial aid paperwork. If you know nothing about the mind-blowingly tedious process that is applying for financial aid, get ready to break a mental sweat in chapters three and four.

January, Get the Cash—New year, new semester, new cha-ching in your bank account. This month, you should focus first and foremost on getting your FAFSA finished (with the help of the rents) and filed as close to January 1st as humanly possible. If you have no clue as to what your parents will earn in the upcoming year, don't stress, slip in some estimated income figures and send your FAFSA off the minute it's been completed and proofread. Once you've filed FAFSA, contact your schools and ask for information and paperwork for private scholarships for which you may be eligible. Just in case Uncle Sam doesn't send you a fat check, you may be able to score a quick tuition reduction through school-sponsored scholarships and grants. But what good is college cash if you have no college to attend, right? Be aware of your looming admissions deadlines and finish up those pesky application packets.

February, Get 'R Done—Close your eyes, breathe deeply, and let out a gigantic sigh of relief. February is the month when everything begins to wrap up and you can start to look forward to hearing back from your schools (Huzzah!). If you've got any applications left to send, do it and turn your attention to applying for private scholarships and grants.

March, Get the Credits—Applications: Done, FAFSA: Done, Scholarship apps: Done, all that's left is your AP exams. APs are your chance to get college credit at a ludicrously discounted rate, so don't miss this sale. Forget about college for a second and bury your nose in the books. By the end of the month, you should receive your Student Aid Report from the government, letting you know exactly how much dough they're willing to fork over for your education. If you don't get exactly what you're looking for, check out Chapter Four for a few tips on getting the most bang for your buck.

April, Get the Answers—Your hard work is about to pay off! Acceptance letters and financial aid awards should both find their way to your door before the month is over. All you've got to do is compare options and make the final call. If you don't make it into the school of your dreams and you're absolutely, positively, without a doubt committed to going there anyway AND you feel that there was crucial (as in life-altering) information missing from your first application, you can try to file an appeal to the admissions committee before the end of the month. You can read up on how to file an appeal on page 27.

May, Get Registered—The bad news is that college deposits are due. The good news is that you'll get your AP scores back and you'll finally be able to go back to being a normal student. The things you will need to do before you graduate include thanking those teachers that provided you with an excellent education (especially the ones that wrote you those radiant recommendations), requesting that a final transcript of your grades get sent to the school you'll be attending next year, and finishing up any straggling financial aid forms your school needs in order to send you your check.

June, Get Graduated—Kiss high school goodbye and say hello to a new life on campus.

What are admissions representatives really looking for?

Glad you asked. Although admission formulas vary from school to school, most admissions departments are looking for consistently high grades in challenging classes first and foremost, decent test scores and strong extracurricular activities secondly, solid recommendations third, and a killer application packet fourth. That means if you have the choice between stressing over your admissions essay or your AP bio test, your best bet is to spend some extra time in the lab rather than on the personal statement. Above all, colleges are looking for students that will not only fit the school's academic profile, but will also contribute to the school's name, both academically and creatively. Now is a good time to play the "What If?" game. When putting together your application packet, imagine what your life would be like if you went to that school. What academic programs interest you? What extracurriculars would you get involved in? Where would you make your mark on campus? Present a clear, compelling argument that you can and will live up to the school's academic expectations, that you would fit right in on campus, and that you know both of these facts because you have already accomplished great things academically and found your extracurricular niche in your high school, and your chances of getting a big, fat YES from that school will get a little better.

"If we get an application and there's some unusual pattern, if we don't have an explanation for it, we assume that the student didn't work very hard...if we know what's happening, that's when admissions committees can take that into account."

– *JohnBlackburn*, Admissions Director for the University of Virginia.

My transcript isn't perfect, help!

A couple of blemishes on that transcript? Don't fret. While you can't remove them from your transcript, you can address weak spots in your application packet and hopefully put a positive spin on your academic record. The key is to accentuate your strong points, directly address your weaknesses, and show admissions counselors how and why you're striving for improvement. If you have a justifiable reason for low grades during one year or semester (for example, a close family member passed away, personal health problems, a family divorce, etc.), let admissions reps know that either in your personal statement or in your admissions interview. While all of your grades will still be taken into consideration, admissions reps will understand that your semester in the dumps probably isn't indicative of your study habits and work ethic in general. If you're consistently lacking in a particular subject, you could also have teachers from that subject attest to your work ethic, your willingness to attend study sessions and work harder than the rest of the class to keep up. If you had a slow time adjusting to the high school work load, ask your guidance counselor to write a recommendation that addresses how you've improved over your four years and why you're prepared to handle college-level material. The secret to minimizing the impact of academic weaknesses is to address them head-on and provide evidence to show that despite a low grade here and there, you're still a motivated and conscientious student.

What are SAT's and ACT's and do I really need to take them both?

The SATs and ACTs are both standardized tests designed to measure your ability to reason and comprehend problems. Do you have to take both of them? Nope. Is it a good idea? Absolutely. The SATs and ACTs each emphasize a different set of skills, so taking both only increases your chances of doing well and earning an acceptance letter to the school of your choice. Though there's a large amount of cross-over material between the two tests, the ACTs tend to focus more on content questions, questions on the core curricula taught in high school, whereas the SATs focus more on critical thinking and problem-solving questions. The chart on the next page will give you a full breakdown of how each test works and what you can expect.

Taking the Easy Road

"Every year we have straight-A students who apply and they haven't taken the top courses and those students rarely get in. The levels of the grades and of the performance are the most important things we consider."

– *John Blackburn*, Director of Admissions for the University of Virginia.

SATs VS. ACTs

The Structure

SATs

Students will be tested on three basic areas:

- Writing—One short multiple-choice section (35 minutes) designed to test your grammar, word choice, and ability to improve both sentences and larger paragraphs. There's also an essay section (25 minutes) designed to showcase your ability to thoroughly develop and support a thesis statement.
- Critical Reading—All multiple-choice (70 minutes). Critical reading questions will test your reading comprehension, sentence completion, vocabulary, and ability to recognize context clues.
- Math—Ten pencil and paper problems, the rest multiple-choice (70 minutes). This section will cover a wide array of geometry, algebra, data analysis, quantitative comparison, and number operations questions.

ACTs

Students will be tested on five basic areas:

- English—75 questions, 45 minutes to do them. The English section tests how well you've mastered the semantics of the English language including punctuation, sentence structure, and grammar as well as your grasp of how to organize paragraphs, use word choice to communicate ideas, and develop an idea in writing.
- Math—60 questions, 60 minutes, calculators are welcome, but leave your laptops or personal organizers at home. Expect questions covering algebra, geometry, and trigonometry. Unlike the SAT's, you won't be required to solve any problems on paper or show your work.
- Reading—40 questions, 35 minutes. Basically this section tests your ability to analyze. Covering four basic types of texts (social studies, natural sciences, prose fiction, and humanities), this section will present a passage and require you to interpret the main and implied points as well as analyze content-dependent statements.
- Science—40 questions, 35 minutes, no calculators allowed. Covering introductory biology, chemistry, physics, and Earth science, the ACT science test requires students to draw inferences from graphs, tables, and diagrams, design experiments and interpret their results, and compare scientific data and hypotheses.
- Writing—30 minutes, 2 points of view, 1 essay. In this section, you'll be presented with one issue as well as with arguments supporting two conflicting views on the issue. Your job is to take a stance and develop a concise essay that reflects why you've taken that position and why your side could kick the daylights out of the other side.

Scoring

SATs: For every correct answer, you get a point. For every question you miss, you lose one-quarter of a point and those you don't answer count as zero. Students are scored on a 200 – 800-point scale for each section. That means you'll get a composite score of somewhere between 600 and 2400. You'll also get a subscore between 20 and 80 for the essay portion. The average SAT score nationally is 1,511.

ACTs: One point for every question you get right, nothing for those you miss. Once scores for each section have been tallied, raw scores are converted to a 36-point scale and writing scores are converted to a 12-point scale. Students receive a composite score between 1 and 36 as well as a writing score between 2 and 12. The average ACT score nationally is 21.1.

Sending Scores

SATs: Students can send their SAT scores to up to four colleges or universities for free every time they take the test. For every additional school, there's a minimal surcharge of $9.00. Scores can be sent online at www.collegeboard.com.

ACTs: Students can send their ACT scores to up to four colleges or universities for free every time they take the test. For every additional school, there's a minimal surcharge of $7.00. Students can send scores by calling (319) 337-1313 ($10 extra surcharge for ordering by phone) or can download a copy of the scores request form at www.actstudent.org/pdf/asrform.pdf.

Getting Registered

SATs: Students can register online at www.collegeboard.com or by mail. A list of testing locations and dates will be available online or through your guidance counselor.

ACTs: Students can register online at www.actstudent.org or by mail. 2007-2008 testing dates and locations will be available online or through your guidance counselor.

Getting Prepared

SATs: The College Board publishes a few sample SAT questions from each section of the test as well as a free practice test at www.collegeboard.com/student/testing/sat/prep_one/practice.html. Students who want to beef up their scores even more can check out The Official SAT Study Guide (available for $19.95) or can register for the online SAT prep program for $69.95. Yahoo! Education also publishes free practice questions broken down by type of question and subject covered at http://education.yahoo.com/college/essentials/practice_tests/sat/.

ACTs: Step one is to check out the ACT student test prep center at www.actstudent.org/testprep/index.html. There you'll find sample tests, a scoring key, and more practice questions than you can handle all for the low, low cost of absolutely nothing. If you want to take your test prep one step further, students can gain access to the ACT Online Test Prep program for $19.95 or can order the official prep book for $25. 4tests.com also contains a free online practice test and Testpreppreview.com contains free self-assessment quizzes broken down by type of question and subject covered.

The Differences

- Scoring: The SATs count off for wrong answers, so limit your guessing! Guess away on the ACTs. Wrong answers and those you skip are counted equally.
- Presentation: While you can take both tests as many times as you like, schools will receive all of your SAT scores and be able to track your progress (or lack thereof) whereas the ACTs let students decide which scores schools will view.
- Format: The SATs incorporate a multiple-choice section as well as write-in response and essay sections. The ACTs do not include a write-in response section.
- Material: The SATs cover writing, critical thinking, and math. The ACTs include all of the above plus questions on English grammar and science.
- Requirements: The SATs require students to complete a writing section, whereas essays are optional (but typically preferred by most colleges) on the ACTs.
- Costs: Expect to pony up $41.50 to take the SATs and $29.00 to take the ACTs without the writing test ($43.00 with the writing test). Students who need fee waivers on either tests should visit their guidance counselor.

No Scores Attached!

If you're scores are stressing you out, think about applying to George Mason University. The only school in the state that has a scores optional admissions review policy, GMU applicants with an unweighted GPA of 3.5 and who rank in the top twenty percent of their class can choose whether or not they'd like to include their SAT and ACT scores in their application packet. In lieu of showing their scores, applicants must submit two extra teacher recommendations as well as an additional essay. Certain restrictions apply. For more information, check out: http://admissions.gmu.edu/scoreoptional/.

What are SAT IIs and do I need to take them?

The SAT Is measure your ability to problem-solve across a wide variety of disciplines. The SAT IIs are hour-long, multiple-choice subject tests that measure your knowledge in one particular area. Although the SAT IIs are optional for many schools in the state, most institutions prefer to see scores from at least two tests (usually in Writing and Math) and some of the most selective schools (including UVA, Hollins University, and the University of Richmond) require them. Students who are applying for a specific program of study such as physics or a foreign language, should also take the SAT II test in that area.

The essay/personal statement really freaks me out!

I Have No Idea What to Write About. A Little Help Please!

The good news is that the essay usually counts for relatively little in the application packet. Grades, curriculum, test scores, extracurricular activities - these things carry much more weight than the personal statement. The bad news is that there's no formula for the perfect admissions essay. A good admissions essay is concise, honest, directly addresses the essay question, and reveals something about the student's style, background, and character. The best way to give you essay pointers is simply to show you an excellent example...or three. Conveniently you can find three admissions-winning essays in the back of this chapter.

I attend a specialized or magnet high school. Will colleges understand that my curriculum is different than other schools?

Not if you don't tell them. Students who attend specialized schools need to include information about how their school's curriculum works in the application packet. While some schools include information about how the school works in every student's transcript, it's wise to make sure that the colleges you're applying to understand how and why your high school is more competitive than the rest. Your guidance or career counselor will have information about whether informing colleges about your specialty school will be taken care of within your high school or if it's up to you.

Making the Most of the Magnet

"Most magnet or specialized schools give us a school profile that tells us all about how the school works. When we read an application, we look at that profile to understand how the school works. What's important for the student is to show us how the school's specialization has made a difference. The essay can be an opportunity to do that."

– *Michael Walsh,*
Director of Admissions for James Madison University

I need special accommodations, where do I go?

Students who can document hearing or vision impairment, an ongoing psychiatric or medical condition, or a physical or learning disability can apply for special testing accommodations for both the SATs and ACTs. The first step is to see your guidance counselor to obtain school-signed documentation forms then to apply for the accommodation you'll need by contacting Act.org or by calling (319) 337-1270. For the SATs, contact Collegeboard.com or call (212) 713-8000.

I'm a homeschooled student, is there anything extra I need to do for the application process?

Boy howdy, have we got a supplement for you. Rules, regulations, and general tips for homeschool applicants can be found in the back of this face-meltingly awesome chapter.

I didn't get into my dream school, what now?

Relax, you've got options. If you've applied to a few safety schools (you know, like this book told you to), you'll have a place to kick off your freshman year, even if it's not your first choice. Who knows? You may wind up falling in love with your safety school after you've spent a semester there. Another route is to knock out a few credits in a community college before making the leap to a four-year institution. Many four-year schools have established transfer agreements with area community colleges. Do well in a cheaper two-year institution and you could have a better shot of getting into your dream school than you did fresh out of high school. A third option is to check out schools with rolling admissions policies. Accepting applications all year long, institutions like Virginia Intermont College and Virginia Union University admit students long passed the admissions deadlines at most schools. If you've got an extensive research project, internship, volunteer job, or trip on your mind, you could also spend a gap year accomplishing personal goals, saving up for college, and preparing to re-apply the next year. The key to having a successful gap year, one that will add something new to your college application for the next time around, is to spend your time wisely doing something that will turn heads whether it be working in the rainforest for six months, writing that book you've always wanted to pen, or turning your business idea into a small LLC. Whatever you do, go big or don't bother. Students who spend their year out of college working the same ho-hum job and not pushing themselves to do, see, and think in different ways usually end up having a gap year count against them for the next college application season. A good place to start the hunt for What Next? is with your guidance counselor then check out the index of student summer programs in the back of this book for ideas.

I didn't include something crucial on my college application and I wasn't accepted, is there anything I can do?

The technical answer is yes. If you've been rejected and you feel that your application packet was lacking pertinent information about your academic or family situation, you may be able to appeal. In reality, you have the same probability of appealing an admissions decision as you do of winning an Olympic medal, a Nobel Prize, and the lottery all on the same day. Admissions appeals are incredibly difficult to obtain; however, if you're brave enough to try, talk with your guidance counselor about what new information you'll use to convince admissions reps that they should have sent you an acceptance letter in the first place then ask your dream school about how to start the appeals process.

Chapter *Recap*

Review time

- Remember the Grades – Your grades will stand out far more than anything else you write on your application, so stay on top of your work during the application process.
- Start Early – Organizing your test scores, asking for recommendations, laying out all of your extracurricular activities, and composing the best essay you've ever written will take time...lots of time. Start early, preferably in August, to give yourself (and your teachers, guidance counselors, and testing agencies) enough time to put together a commendable application packet.
- Go Above and Beyond – If your school allows it, submit a resume, creative work, or extra essay to accompany your application packet. Request an admissions interview as well. Proving that you're dedicated to impressing an admissions committee will reflect how dedicated you are to your education.
- Accentuate the Positive – When preparing your application packet, keep in mind that nobody's perfect. Your goal is to highlight your strong points, address your low points, and bring attention to what you're doing to improve upon them. Your guidance counselor can help.
- Give 'Em a Crash Course in You 101 – The point of the application packet is to give admissions committees a glimpse at what makes you a cut above every other applicant out there. Feel free to get creative, get personal, and get honest while remaining professional and organized.
- Watch Your Timing – When you apply to college can affect your chances of getting in. Decide in advance if you're applying Early Action, Early Decision, or Regular Admission and no matter when your application deadline rolls around, make sure your application is completed and in on time.
- Remember Your Options – Even if you don't get into your top choice school, keep in mind that you've got a sea of options, not to mention time, on your side.

Think of it as organization on a platter. This Deadlines Chart will help you stay on top of the looming dates ahead.

Your Schools	Early Application Deadline	Regular Admissions Deadline	Financial Aid Deadline	Acceptance Deadline	Contact Info
#1					
#2					
#3					
#4					
#5					
#6					
#7					
#8					
#9					
#10					

Tales from the crypt: Admissions horror stories that landed smart students in the dead pile:

"The Gallagher Essay, we see three of four of those every year. If you Google 'Hugh Gallagher,' you'll come up with his essay. It's a student who's describing how he's cured cancer and it goes on for a page and a half about his or her accomplishments and then at the end, it says that 'but I haven't been to college yet.' We see 3 or 4 of those every year, they paraphrase it and put in their own things, but it's plagiarism as far as we're concerned."
- *John Blackburn,* Director of Admissions for the University of Virginia (Charlottesville, VA)

"One time I got an app that was written in crayon. I'm not sure what the student was trying to prove to us."
- *Michael Walsh,* Director of Admissions for James Madison University (Harrisonburg, VA)

"We've had applications with stickers on it, children's sticker book stickers on an application. That's not really something we like."
- *Rebecca Eckstein,* Director of Admissions for Hollins University (Roanoke, VA)

with admissions directors . . .

What should every college bound student know before applying to college?

"Don't believe the hype that you have to get into a top-ranked school or allow stress and external expectations to interfere in your consideration."
- *Jonathan Webster,* Associate Dean of Admissions for Washington and Lee University (Lexington, VA)

"Doing their homework is the most important thing and by that I mean figuring out what we have, to have visited our campus, and to investigate us. We have people who come here and enroll and say, 'gee, I thought you had this program here.' I think it's very important that students know what they're getting into."
- *John Blackburn,* Dean of Admissions for the University of Virginia (Charlottesville, VA)

"Students should get out of the mentality that a school fits them best. They should be looking at multiple schools that fit them best...I've yet to work with a student in the past twenty years for whom there weren't multiple institutions that were great fits."
- *Andrew Flagel,* Dean of Admissions for George Mason University (Fairfax, VA)

ESSAY 911

Need a little help on writing your application essay? Look no further. These three essays each helped earn the students that wrote them admittance into the school of their choice. What these essays have in common is that they're honest, easy to read, spell checked, and each highlights a meaningful experience or philosophy that reveals a bit about the students' character. Check out what turned the heads of some of the most selective schools in the state.

#1: *Personal statement from student admitted to Hampden-Sydney College* (reprinted with permission)

So what is a "personal statement" anyway? Honestly, my current personal statement would be: "I am hungry." But I don't think you are looking for that. Shall I entertain you with an anecdote featuring one of the many activities that "looks good on applications" and frames me as a god among men? Sorry to disappoint, but I am a man. I am confident, however, that I am a unique, multifaceted, dynamic man. On paper, I am a two-time state championship athlete, thespian, and student government participant. I am proud of these accomplishments, but the phrase "on paper" makes me queasy - mostly because "paper" routinely loses to its nemesis, "scissors," in Rochambeaux. It is my character, not my statistics, that I have been most interested in forging.

I have grown up significantly in my educational career. Being voted a member of the homecoming court was a stark contradiction to my kindergarten days, when I was told that I had "lily-pad ears" and was harassed for my speech impediment and lack of coordination. I was lucky to make it through the day without tripping or crying (though I usually did both).

Once I learned how to roll with the proverbial punches, I learned how to "dish it out" (but in a way that prevented crying AND tripping). Being voted class clown, loudest, and most likely to embarrass you in public earned me a triple crown of which even my hero Jon Stewart would be proud. My other hero, my mother, was voted "nicest" and was asked to play the part of the Virgin Mary in our Christmas pageant her senior year. Although my apple fell far from the tree, I think she is still proud. Plus, striving to be the next Virgin Mary would be unrealistic; my ability to grow sideburns makes me a better Conrad Birdie anyway.

I am also the only boy in my family. And while the application merely inquired about my age and schooling of my sisters, I must tell you that they are two incredibly influential forces. Kathleen is the big brother I never had but always needed. She dragged me outside to throw a baseball, football, lacrosse ball, or what-have-you on a regular basis. If I didn't comply, there was a physical penalty of some sort. She played football her sophomore year of high school and is now a soccer player at William and Mary. She showed me that love of competition triumphed over genetic makeup. Lauren, my oldest sister, sparked my interest in theatre, which I intend to pursue in college. Pursuing theatre revealed to me elements of my character of which I was otherwise oblivious. I am forever grateful that she opened that door.

While "paper" does succumb to "scissors," I have managed to find the Rocks of character I have needed in all my endeavors. Life has been a series of full plates and nauseous moments (usually on stage). But I guess my proposed personal statement is true: I am hungry for more.

#2: *Personal statement by Chase Hathaway, a student admitted to the University of Richmond* (reprinted with permission)

The anticipation had been building. It was like Christmas morning, only...more exciting, more artistic, more diverse, and more beautiful. Every day over the summer, as I drove to my senior mentorship project, or to volunteering at church, I glimpsed with hope that it would be ready. Then it finally happened. The first burrito bar opened in Virginia Beach, Virginia.

As a connoisseur of burritos, I have eaten everywhere from Taco Bell, to Guadalajara, to Poncho Villa of New York. Taco Bell was child's play to me, mere meat on a plain tortilla, while Guadalajara and Poncho Villa were too slow to produce the food. I needed something more, something that would quench the burrito-sized hole in my stomach. I found that something at a burrito bar in Richmond: Chipotle. It was simple: walk in, give the burrito-artists my order, and walk out with a creation as intricate as M.C. Escher's tessellations and as perfect as Da Vinci's "Mona Lisa." Chipotle was my first outlet, my first burrito love, my first burrito passion, but I knew there was more out there.

While the Virginia Beach burrito bar is not Chipotle, it is Machismo's, meaning macho. And these burritos are macho. Upon entering, I find the kinds of burrito-crafting offer one of five tortilla flavors, followed by selection of meats, rice, and beans. There is a choice of twelve condiments with everything from guacamole to jalapeno peppers followed by the salsa choices, the true personality detector. My brazen, outgoing personality calls for the spiciest sauce available. By the time my masterpiece is complete, my diverse burrito – filled with steak, corn, jalapenos, green peppers, and so many other items – forms a stomach-sized cylinder. I exit Machismo's with my breathtaking burrito wrapped in aluminum foil, ready to be consumed.

I've told all of my friends of the ingenious invention that is the burrito bar. We stop in at the restaurant after we meet to discuss community service and school improvement ideas. We've adopted it as our new favorite food, assimilated it into our school work, and added it to our extracurricular eating places. Machismo's has become a part of our friendships. My Machismo's peers and I have decided how important these next four years will be to our future. My closest friends and I have discussed everything from communication degrees, to leadership degrees, to even business degrees. Our degrees aren't settled, but there is a dream among my group of friends: bring our passion of burritos to teenagers across Virginia. My future holds great successes, regardless of whether I become a burrito bar builder or not. I will follow my passions to my future.

Faith, school, leadership, friends, art, and volleyball are among my large list of passions. But the passion stirred by the burrito bar shows my bold, gregarious side. Creating burritos gives me a way to express exactly who I am in a way besides prayer, song, quadratic equations, or pastels. But the best part of the burrito passion is whenever my chef-d'oeuvre of food is finished, I know I won't have problems creating another masterpiece.

#3: *Personal statement from student admitted to Sweet Briar College* (reprinted with permission)

One hundred fifty milligrams of Zantac, 25 milligrams of Prednisone and make sure to take it with food, or was that for the 200 milligrams of...of, well I know it starts with an M. Dispose of the needle in the sharps container after each Methotrexate injection and don't forget the daily calcium plus D and multivitamins. I can't leave out the Remicaide infusions every six to eight weeks, making sure to take Benedryl prior to reduce allergic reactions and...oh, yes the folic acid, how could I forget? After reciting my lengthy regimen, I was finally able to lean back in my seat, when I heard one of the doctors say, "Never let the disease get hold of you." Right, I thought to myself and is there a drug for that you could prescribe for me?

Barely a freshman in high school and so suddenly the plethora of my responsibilities vastly increased. Not to mention the medication side effects, physical therapy appointments, and school of course. It's not exactly the simplest task to explain to your fourteen year old best friend that you...well, have rheumatoid arthritis. Isn't that an old person's disease? Carting a heavy backpack to and from school, secretly hoping to not be passed the ball in gym class or hurrying to finish a test before the bell rings, when your hand has been throbbing since five minutes into the exam, are the constant reminders of the disease.

One day, sitting in my anatomy and physiology class during my junior year, I nervously bit my lip and sensed my foot shaking under the desk. Looking around the room I wondered if anyone knew. Could anybody tell, as my heart began to race, that I suffer from an autoimmune disease similar to the disorder which our teacher was lecturing on for the past forty-nine minutes? Scanning the room, I guessed not, considering half the class wasn't paying attention anyway. I smiled to myself as the bell rang, thinking I would have nothing to worry about. I will be the only one to know the truth. It is not anyone else's business to know about my health problems, I reassured myself. They will never know if I never tell. However, as I grabbed my backpack and headed for the door, my teacher stopped me to inform me of my topic for a presentation on Rheumatoid Arthritis. Well, at least I can easily complete the project considering I basically know all the specifics of the illness.

As I was shuffling my notes cards back in order, immediately, after my presentation, I felt relieved. Suddenly, my teacher asked the class if anyone knew of anyone with the disease. I looked up, and once again felt the extreme rush of adrenaline throughout my entire body. No one in the class raised their hand, the room was silent. I felt my face get hot and my palms became sticky and sweaty. I fumbled to grab hold of the desk. I stared blankly at the motionless sea of faces glaring back at me. Questions began flooding my head: What should I do? Why is this happening to me? Do I tell them? After what seemed like an eternity I smiled and blurted out, "Yes, I do know someone with the disease. In fact, I was diagnosed with Rheumatoid Arthritis myself." Just as quickly as I was overburdened with the onset of the disease, I was revived and felt reconnected with the part of me that had remained absent for three long years.

The wall I built around me, block by block for three years, came crumbling down that afternoon. For the first time in several years, I was free, free from the burden of hiding the illness as well as the symptoms themselves. The real me, for the first time, in a long while, stood naked and exposed. I started to realize that feeling ashamed and embarrassed about my condition is not the outlook I want to have in life. I should not let this disease define me as a person. I too, have goals and aspirations about the future and my health should never prevent me from success. At that pivotal moment, I shed my cocoon and was able to fly freely into my new world— a world where my motto of 'living with the disease' transformed into something so much greater.

Bit by bit, as I continue to uncover my true self, I recognize that person I wish to become. I anxiously await that day in the near future when Rheumatoid Arthritis will become a lesser focus in my life. Reflecting back on my experiences throughout high school, I recognize the battles I have fought and cherish the lessons I have learned. Today, looking forward to the future, as I will soon begin the next chapter of my life, I am left with a sense of hope for what my new experiences may bring.

Homeschool Supplement

If formal schooling isn't really your cup of tea, you've got a lot more work ahead of you when it comes to applying for college. The good news is that Virginia is an excellent place to attend college if you're coming from a nontraditional high school background. Even the most prestigious and selective schools in the state including the College of William and Mary, the University of Virginia, the University of Richmond, Virginia Military Institute, Emory and Henry College, Virginia Polytechnic and State Institute, and Hollins University all have homeschool-friendly admissions policies, giving you just as good a shot of gaining admittance as your formally educated peers. The first question you're probably asking is ***Where Do I Begin***? That's easy – as soon as you start covering high school-level material (i.e. your "freshman" year in a high school curriculum), you should start documenting every standardized test and community or technical college class you've taken. You should also keep a close record of all major independent projects you've completed, exemplary essays you've written, awards you've won, jobs you've worked, and leadership positions you've held in your community. The major hurdle homeschool students have to get over is providing documentation of their accomplishments and community impact. Documenting your extracurricular activities now will make the application process A LOT smoother down the road. With that in mind, here's a quick breakdown of how to plan for and apply to college without a formal high school background.

Mapping Out the High School Years

In order to be competitive, homeschooled students have to start thinking about and planning for college much earlier than students enrolled in formal schools where on-site guidance counselors, career counselors, librarians, and college recruiters are there to help with the college admissions process. Homeschooled students are on their own when it comes to planning a curriculum that will turn admissions reviewers' heads, so it's essential to start planning early, to plan carefully, and to make community connections that will strengthen you as a student. When planning your high school curriculum, there are two basic things to keep in mind. The most important by far is documenting your academic progress. As you move through your high school curriculum, consider taking some SAT II subject tests, CLEP exams, and/or AP tests just to prove your intellectual skillz on paper. One of the best resources for homeschool students the state offers is the Virtual Advanced Placement School located at www.pen.k12.va.us/VDOE/Technology/VAPS.html. Offering online AP and foreign language courses, the Virginia Virtual Advanced Placement School allows students to prepare for AP exams on their own time under the instruction of a professor trained to teach distance learning courses. Taking some community college courses is also strongly recommended. Not only will a few courses provide you with some grades that didn't come from your parents, they'll also provide you with teachers you can turn to for outside recommendations. Even better than taking community college courses is enrolling in a few non-degree classes at a local four-year college or university. In addition to the grades and the recommendations, non-degree classes will give you a foot in the door at that school. With a few classes under your belt (and a few college professors eating out of the palm of your hand), there's a chance that you'll be able to bypass typical admissions requirements (including submitting SAT scores and a high school transcript) and simply apply to that school as a degree-seeking student.

Testing isn't the only way to prove you're well equipped for college. Entering county-wide science fairs, writing a grant for a local organization, building a friend's web page, and organizing a local fundraiser are all great ways to prove that you're a bright, motivated kid whose just as capable (if not more capable) than formally schooled applicants. If you need some help coming up with things to do that will make your application shine, check out the list on page 34. The second thing to remember is that you'll need connections with the outside world to make your college application stand out. By becoming a part of your community, applying for local, state, and national awards, and taking at least a few classes at a local university or community college, you'll have no problem finding adults besides your parents to help you with those application recommendations.

Minding the Paperwork

With a folder full of impressive accomplishments occupying a VIP spot in your home, it's time to start compiling the college paperwork. For a homeschool student, the paperwork should begin the year before the student is ready to apply for school. Since many colleges require homeschooled students to complete extra paperwork in addition to everything that goes with a standard paper application, it's essential to first figure out what exactly you need to do and secondly, who you can go to with questions. Watch out, many institutions only publish application requirements for formally schooled students, so it could be up to you to figure out exactly what they expect you to send. The best way to do that is simply to call the admissions office and ask to speak with the admissions counselor who handles homeschool applications. While some schools won't require any extra materials, others may ask for additional essays, SAT II tests, an interview, a portfolio of writing samples, reading lists, course descriptions, and/or outside recommendations.

Once you have a checklist of the materials you'll need, you and your parents will need to put together a transcript of your high school curriculum. The advantage that you have over the average high school student is that you hold the power to create an honest transcript that accentuates your strong spots and downplays your weak points. How your transcript looks will depend entirely on the format and timing of your curriculum. Since many homeschool students do not abide by a standard semester curriculum, required courses, or grading system, you'll have to tailor your transcript to accurately reflect your learning environment.

Before you sit down to write anything, take a look at the sample transcripts included on the next few pages just to get some ideas about how you could format your transcript and what information you might consider including. Please note that the first student (Jane Doe) has an outstanding academic record as well as test scores and that these are prominently featured on her transcript whereas student number two (John Doe) has chosen to accentuate his extracurricular activities, travel, and independent projects. Keep in mind that these sample transcripts are by no means the only ways to present your high school work, they're simply a few ideas to help get the ball rolling.

As a rule, your transcript should include the following:

- Identification information like your name, address, date of birth, sex, social security number, phone, e-mail, the name of your primary instructor, etc.
- A list of what courses you took as well as the grade. Some students also include the number of credits each course was worth in order to give admissions counselors an idea of how much of your education focused on that subject.
- A list of courses outside of the home you took including those taken through community colleges, professional agencies, online institutions, religious organizations, technical schools, etc. Grades, when possible, should be included as well.
- A list of any extra certifications, professional licenses, or credentials you've earned.
- Scores from standardized, AP, SAT II, and CLEP tests you've taken.
- A list of local, regional, or national academic awards you've won.
- A list of internships, volunteer positions, co-op classes, and/or apprenticeship programs you've completed.

Q+A . . .

with admission: How can homeschool applicants be competitive with traditional students?

"It's difficult for us to evaluate homeschool students because we don't have an external evaluation. The grades are mostly given by the parents and it's mostly A's that we see. We recommend that they take as many Collegeboard subject tests as they can."

— *John Blackburn*, Director of Admissions for the University of Virginia (Charlottesville, VA)

"If I have 30 apps from homeschooled students, there's probably 25 different curriculums I'm looking at. I think the key thing for the homeschooled student is to speak directly with an admissions person and say 'Look, I'm homeschooled. What do I need to provide you with?'... We may ask them for a syllabus, we may ask them for a narrative evaluation. It would be very good for a homeschool student to have a conversation with the university to make sure that they make a fair decision."

— *Michael Walsh*, Admissions Director for James Madison University (Harrisonburg, VA)

"Try to restrain mom and dad when it comes to the letters of recommendation. We want some impartial letters that can comment on a student's academic potential. It's fine for mom and dad to fill out the counselor form, but that shouldn't be the primary voice of recommendation on file."

— *Jonathan Webster*, Associate Dean of Admissions for Washington and Lee University (Lexington, VA)

Four Resources for Homeschool Students:

1 **Virginia Standards of Learning**
www.pen.k12.va.us/VDOE/Superintendent/Sols/home.shtml - Although homeschooled students (thankfully) aren't required to take the SOL's, this site will help you track your own progress and find out which areas you need to brush up on.

2 **Virginia HomeSchoolers - www.vahomeschoolers.org**
This is where homeschooling families from across the state come to find educational resources, exchange tips, and network with other homeschooling families. The support group page will help you find homeschool groups in your area.

3 **National Center for Home Education - http://nche.hslda.org**
What's happening in homeschooling on the national level? Find out here. This site contains a wealth of information on everything from taking the PSATs to tips on applying for educational tax credits (a topic which is also outlined in Chapter Four).

4 **Home School Foundation - www.homeschoolfoundation.org**
Scholarships are hard to come by for homeschooled students. The Home School Foundation gives away thousands each year to kids from homeschool backgrounds.

Consider asking your parents to write a short, one-page mission statement that describes their teaching philosophy and homeschooling methods. This gives admissions counselors a better idea of what your homeschool experience was truly like. Some families also include a list of textbooks and primary source material covered in the homeschool curriculum as well as a transcript of extracurricular activities.

When discussing the requirements with your college's homeschool rep, it's wise to ask if the school is willing to accept additional documentation from homeschool applicants. Beefing your application up with a stellar portfolio of creative work or tacking on an in-person interview could mean the difference between an acceptance and rejection letter.

HOMESCHOOL FUN FACT

Patrick Henry College in Purcellville, VA is the only college in the nation where the majority of the student body (80-90%) comes from a homeschool background. Dubbed "The Harvard for Homeschoolers," Patrick Henry has a strong reputation for helping fresh-faced teens score enviable internships in the White House and high-profile government think tanks. The downside is that Patrick Henry College is not a regionally accredited institution, meaning that credits and degrees earned from the school could, but won't necessarily, be universally accepted by employers or other colleges and universities. Because of this fact, the school is not included in the college guide section of this book. For more information on Patrick Henry College, go to www.phc.edu or call (540) 338-1776.

30 Ways to Shine as a Homeschool Student

1. Ace a few community college courses. The grades and recommendations will help your application immensely.
2. Pass some CLEP, AP, or SAT II tests!
3. Land a National Merit Scholarship thanks to your SAT scores.
4. Enter a local science fair, speech contest, film festival, or art competition.
5. Attend an academic summer camp (there's a list in the back for your reference).
6. Publish an article, poem, or even your own book.
7. Start your own business. It could be anything from building backyard sheds to selling used clothes on eBay.
8. Write a software program or video game to show an admissions counselor.
9. Start a band. Let the rock begin.
10. Take it to the stage. Getting involved in community theatre or radio station will let you showcase your creative side.
11. Volunteer. Just remember to keep a record of your hours. Check out idealist.org for a list of excellent volunteer opportunities in your area.
12. Intern for an organization that sparks your interest. Do well and it could land you an acceptance letter AND a job after college. Double bonus.
13. Enter a cooperative education program. Offered through many community colleges, co-op programs give students technical skills and a paycheck.
14. Become an apprentice. If technical areas catch your eye, consider apprenticing in the industry of your choice.
15. Start a fundraiser. It will benefit your college admissions packet and your community.
16. Take lessons somewhere. No matter if it's swimming lessons at your local YMCA or Spanish lessons at a nearby coffee shop, getting a tutor will broaden your education.
17. Get physical. Joining a local sports team will improve your body and get you involved in your community.
18. Set a goal and stick to it. Whether you've got your mind set on visiting all 50 states or reading Jane Austen's entire catalogue, setting a goal and accomplishing it will show colleges you've got drive and follow-through.
19. Travel. Seeing the world is one of the best educational experiences out there.

20. Create an independent project. The luxury of being a homeschooled student is getting to create your own projects, so do it! Writing a thesis on invertebrates, building a visual representation of a math equation, or researching your family's genealogy will make your application stand out and give you something concrete to show an interview committee.
21. Build something big. Put those mental skills to the test by constructing your own homemade radio, miniature rocket, or legobot.
22. Get political. Joining a local political campaign is a great way to see government first-hand and rub shoulders with area big wigs.
23. Attend conferences. Something catch your eye? Make an effort to meet and greet the people in that community.
24. Be a leader. If the club or organization you desire isn't in your area, take the initiative and start one.
25. Attend on-campus activities. Many local colleges have very liberal policies regarding who can take part in their extracurricular activities. Getting involved with a college, whether it's through joining a club or attending a guest lecture series, will give you one more thing to put on a resume and a good understanding of how the college works.
26. Join national organizations. Organizations such as the National Home School Honor Society, Key Club, and 4-H all are open to interested homeschool students.
27. Exchange yourself with a student from another country. Participating in an international exchange, study abroad program, or international volunteer project are fantastic ways to see the world and gain admissions cred.
28. Learn a foreign language. Being bilingual is both practical and in-demand in today's society. To sweeten your admissions packet, get a private tutor, join a community language club, or attend a language immersion program.
29. Find a mentor. Many colleges and universities offer independent study programs that allow you to design your own coursework under the supervision of a college professor. Besides simply earning a good grade, you'll also have something concrete to show admissions counselors by the time your course is over.
30. Launch a nonprofit. It may be easier than you think. Starting your own nonprofit organization will help you meet and greet those who are passionate about making the world a better place and teach you business, communication, finance, management, and public relations skills.

Sample Transcript I

Transcript of Home Education Program

Student: Jane Doe
Address: 231 Any Street
Anytown, Anyplace USA
Date of Birth: 00/00/00
Date of Attendance: January 2002 – January 2006

Phone: (555) 555-5555
E-mail Address: anyone@anyone.com
Social Security Number: 000-000-0000
Sex: Female

Home Education Supervisor: Mrs. Paulette Doe

Phone: (555) 555-5556
E-mail Address: paulette@anyone.com

Academic Record

FRESHMAN YEAR (2002 – 2003)
Credits Earned: 19
Quality Points Earned: 68.5
Grade Point Average: 3.61

Course Title	Grade	Credits	Quality Points
English 9	A	3	12.0
World History	B+	3	10.5
Algebra	B	3	9.0
Earth Science	B	3	9.0
Physical Ed	A	1	4.0
Music Appreciation	A	1	4.0
Bible Study	A	1	4.0
Spanish II	A	3	12.0
Computer Literacy	A	1	4.0

SOPHOMORE YEAR (2003 – 2004)
Credits Earned: 20
Quality Points Earned: 72.0
Grade Point Average: 3.60

Course Title	Grade	Credits	Quality Points
English 10	B+	3	10.5
World History II	B	3	9.0
Geometry	B+	3	10.5
Biology	A	3	12.0
Physical Ed	A	1	4
Violin Performance	A	1	4
Bible Study	A	1	4
Spanish Study	A	3	12.0
HTML Programming	A	2	6.0

JUNIOR YEAR (2004 – 2005)
Credits Earned: 19
Quality Points Earned: 67.5
Grade Point Average: 3.55

Course Title	Grade	Credits	Quality Points
English 11	B+	3	10.5
AP U.S. History	B	3	9.0
Calculus I	A	3	12.0
AP Chemistry	A	3	12.0
Driver's Ed	B	1	3.0
Violin Performance II	A	1	4.0
Bible Study	A	1	4.0
Spanish III	B	3	9.0
C++ Programming	A	1	4.0

SENIOR YEAR (2005 – 2006)
Credits Earned: 21
Quality Points Earned: 70.5
Grade Point Average: 3.36

Course Title	Grade	Credits	Quality Points
English 12	B+	3	10.5
AP Psychology	B	3	9.0
Calculus II	B	3	9.0
Physics	B+	3	10.5
Economics	C+	3	7.5
Violin Performance III	A	1	4.0
Bible Study	A	1	4.0
AP Spanish	A	3	12.0
Advanced Computer Programming	A	1	4.0

Total Credits Earned: 81 Total Quality Points Earned: 286.5 Cumulative GPA: 3.53

Test Scores

PSAT: 2003
Verbal: 70
Math: 70
Critical Reasoning: 70

SAT: 2005
Verbal: 720
Math: 700
Total: 1420

AP U.S. History: 2005 / Score: 5
AP Chemistry: 2005 / Score: 3
AP Psychology: 2006 / Score: 4

SAT II English: 2006 / Score: 750
SAT II Math: 2006 / Score: 700
SAT II Biology: 2004 / Score: 710

Outside Classes Awards

Course Title	School	Grade	College Credits
Intro to Bioethics	Robert Frye Community College	A	3
Intro to Psychology	Robert Frye Community College	A	3
United States Government	Robert Frye Community College	A	3

Member of National Honor Society since 2005.

Sample Transcript 2

Offical Home School Transcript

January 2002 – June 2006
231 Any Street, Anytown, Anyplace, USA
(555) 555-5555

Student: John Doe — Instructor: Paulette Doe
Date of Birth: 00/00/00 Phone: (555) 555-5556
SSN: 000-00-0000 — E-mail address: paulette@anyone.com

Cumulative GPA: 3.45 — Class Rank: 1 out of 2

Grading Scale:	A = 100 – 91	B = 86 – 81	C = 76 – 71	D = 66 – 61	F = 60 and Below
		B+ = 90 – 87	C+ = 80 – 77	D+ = 70 – 67	

Community College Credits Earned: 15 / *Technical College Credits Earned:* 9 / *CLEP Exams Taken:* 2 / *GED Earned:* Yes

Standardized Test Scores:
SATs:—Verbal: 620, Math: 600, Cumulative: 1220
ACTs:—English:33, Math: 28, Composite: 30, Science 31, Reading 30

Coursework

Course Title	Letter Grade	Numeric Grade	GPA
English			
American Lit.	B+	89	3.5
British Lit	B	81	3.0
World Lit	B+	88	3.0
Composition	A	94	4.0

- 40-page Senior Thesis completed on the role of men in the works of Jane Austen
- 2002 – Won Honorable Mention in the Anytown Weekly's annual poetry contest

Course Title	Letter Grade	Numeric Grade	GPA
Science			
Ecology	B	83	3.0
Chemistry	B	82	3.0
Physics*	B+	87	3.5
Botany*	B+	87	3.5

- 2004 – Won 2nd place in the Anytown Community Science Fair for creation of steam-powered toy car.
- 2005 – Won Honorable Mention in the Anytown Community Science Fair for comparing the pH levels in various Anytown bodies of water.
- Completed 3-month

Course Title	Letter Grade	Numeric Grade	GPA
History/Social Studies			
World History	B+	87	3.5
U.S. History	B	82	3.0
European History Travel Program	A	93	4.0
Civil War Travel Program	A	97	4.0
History of Architecture*	A	93	4.0

- 2003 – Completed 3-month travel/study program to Germany, Austria, and Hungary. Completed coursework in European History.
- 2002 – Completed 2-month travel/study program to Virginia, Maryland, and West Virginia. Completed coursework in Civil War History.
- May – August 2004 - 4 month internship completed with the Anytown Preservation Society
- 2004 – Attended the Virginia Governor's School regional summer residential program. Took courses in film, archaeology, and music.

* Coursework completed for dual enrollment credit through Robert Frye Community College ** Coursework completed for dual enrollment credit through Anytown Technical College
*** Coursework completed for dual enrollment credit through University of St. Petersburg

Course Title	Letter Grade	Numeric Grade	GPA
Math			
Algebra	B+	87	3.5
Algebra II	B+	89	3.5
Geometry/Trig	A	94	4.0

Course Title	Letter Grade	Numeric Grade	GPA
Foreign Language			
Russian I*	A	96	4.0
Russian II*	A	98	4.0
Russian III***	A	93	4.0

- 2005 – Completed 6-month travel/study program to St. Petersburg, Russia. Completed coursework in Russian language at the University of St. Petersburg.

Course Title	Letter Grade	Numeric Grade	GPA
Electives			
Basic Woodwork**	A	95	4.0
Carpentry I**	A	95	4.0
Carpentry II**	A	98	4.0
Swimming (Phys Ed)	A	97	4.0
Weight Lifting (Phys Ed)	A	96	4.0
Cardio Training (Phys Ed)	A	98	4.0

Independent Projects

- 2004 – 2006 – Launched Inthedirt.com, a web site devoted exclusively to promoting dirt bike racing and culture. The site currently brings in more than 2,000 visitors each month and through advertising, raises approximately $250 each month to benefit the Anytown Boys and Girls Society.
- 2003 – Hiked approximately 200 miles of the Appalachain Trail. Hike began in Harper's Ferry, Maryland to Damascus, Virginia.
- Began Sheds 4 U, LLC with partner John Doe, Sr. Currently operating part-time, the company specializes in building high quality backyard sheds for clients. In 2005, the firm built 15 sheds and in 2006, we plan to build at least 20.

Awards and Honors

Winner of the 2005 Community Leadership Award given by the Anytown Boys and Girls Society for raising $3,000 through the web site Inthedirt.com.

GED and CLEP Exams Taken

GED Exam / Score: 470 CLEP American History / Score: 70
CLEP Freshman Composition / Score: 73

Chapter Three

Paying For It All – The Long-Term Plan

The battle isn't over yet, you've still got to pay for higher ed. Those of you who have an unsightly amount of cold, hard cash just lying around are too smart (or rich or both) to need this chapter. Those of you who need to scrounge up some fast cash, pay attention. Put simply, college is mind-blowingly expensive. So expensive in fact that it will undoubtedly be one of the priciest things you'll ever pay for in your life, alongside buying a home, supporting a family, and saving for retirement. The upside is that like buying a home or supporting a family, higher education is an investment, arguably the ultimate investment, one that will pay off ten-fold in the years to come both in terms of how much money you'll earn as well as how many opportunities a college education brings. Luckily you've got some help on the financial end. From federally-funded grants and scholarships to tuition reimbursement programs, educational tax credits, and loan forgiveness programs, Virginia offers a tremendous number of options to bright young minds seeking to better themselves. Before we get down to what's available in the state, let's break down how financial aid works and how to fiscally plan for college.

How it Works

Financial aid is the amount of monetary help you'll need when it comes time to pay for higher education. While some financial aid is merit-based, meaning that you earn it because of your skills in a particular area whether it be academics, sports, the arts, whatever, most financial aid is based on how much money your family needs in order to send you to a particular school. Both colleges themselves and the federal government calculate the amount of aid you'll need by estimating how much money your family can put towards education (based on a number of factors including your parent's income, savings, financial assets, your income, the number of siblings you currently have in college, etc.) and subtracting that from how much your school will cost to attend, taking into account the cost of tuition, room, board, books, and other school-related expenses. The difference between the Cost of Attendance (COA) and your Expected Family Contribution (EFC) is, in theory at least, the amount of help you'll need to attend the school of your dreams without starving in the process. **Write this down: COA – EFC = Cash4U**

Contrary to what many parents believe, financial aid, even need-based financial aid, isn't always just a free check families are handed to subsidize college. While colleges as well as the federal government do offer grants and scholarships, most financial aid comes in the form of low-interest student loans you'll have to pay back once you've graduated and work-study programs that will require you to earn your aid.

Paying for College the Easy Way

The most important thing to remember about financial aid is that it's a fall-back measure, not a reliable way to financially plan for college. The fastest and simplest way to pay for college is to have your parents and grandparents plan for your education early, preferably as soon as you're born. Putting a little away on a regular basis over a number of years will significantly diminish both the amount of aid you'll need when you apply to college and the stress of scraping together funds at the last minute to pay for your education. Since tuition rises an average of six to eight percent every year, it's crucial that your savings increase as well. The College Board reports that currently tuition and fees for one year at a public, in-state school costs $5,836 on average and for a private college or university, you can expect to pay $22,218 on average per year. But that's just where the tuition headache starts. Factoring in tuition inflation, ten years from now, a public, in-state school will cost an estimated $12,599 each year to attend, more than twice today's price. By 2026, the tuition price will have risen to over $27,000 per year. For students who attend private schools, the situation is much worse. In ten years, one year at a private school will cost an estimated $47,967 and in twenty years, it'll be over $100,000 to buy one year's worth of education! Tuition is also just the beginning of your college price tag. You're also going to have to pay for room and board, books, school supplies, phone, a computer, laundry, transportation, student and lab fees, internet access, printing costs, club dues, and don't forget to budget in a night out on the town every now and then. Tack on another $6,000 to $11,000 per year to cover non-tuition expenses and you're looking at a staggering education bill. With such intimidating numbers ahead, planning early and taking advantage of the miracle of compounded interest is essential.

If a family starts saving just $20 a week in a mutual fund or high-yield savings account with a 4% interest rate, beginning the day their child is born, they'll have more than $27,000 stored away by the time their child graduates high school. If they up their ante to $50 per week, they'll have over $68,000 in tuition money ready to go by the time Junior is moving into his or her dorm.

The obvious question here is, *If I don't save anything, won't my need be higher and my financial aid check be fatter?* Sounds like a brilliant plan, Einstein. The only problem is that financial aid is designed for people who can't afford college, not for poor planners or those who live beyond their means. All government, state, and privately funded need-based aid takes your family's income into account as well as your savings, meaning those writing the check are going to know if your family needs aid due to a lack of funding coming in or if it's because you haven't been saving for school. Because a significant amount of financial aid is made up of student loans, it makes sense to knock out all or a large part of your education expenses on your own rather than borrowing and paying them all back with interest later. Let's say you start saving now (you smart cookie you), stashing away $200 a month ($50 per week) for the next ten years. Factoring in a 4% interest rate, you'll have nearly $30,000 by the time you're ready to use your cash. Well played smart saver. Well played indeed. If you choose to borrow your $30,000 instead of saving it yourself, you'll pay a lot more than $200 a month. Assuming your loan charges a 6.8% interest rate, you'll have to cough up more than $340 a month over the next decade. The alternative to paying for it yourself is scoring a sweet scholarship package. While possible (Chapter Four will give you the low down on that), scholarships and grants aren't a surefire way to pay for college either, even if you're a straight-A, sports team captain, yearbook editor, student council president, overachieving type. According to FinAid.org, only 7% of all students receive private sector scholarships and the average undergraduate scholarship package is just $2,000. Saving for college is the only way to ensure that you'll be as financially prepared as you are academically prepared.

> Parental Alert! Mom, Dad, Gran, Gramps, as you read up on the specifics of each investment option, keep in mind that college is just one of several long-term investments you should be writing checks for. Paying off your mortgage and making regular contributions to your retirement fund will not only set you and your family up for a positive financial future, both will also pay off when it comes time to apply for financial aid since the federal formula takes neither the equity invested in your primary home nor the funds tied up in an IRA or 401(k) into consideration.

How to Start Saving

That's the million-dollar question...literally...and the answer depends entirely on your family's financial circumstance and where you feel comfortable placing your cash. Kids, grab your parents. The rest of this chapter pertains to them. In Virginia, families have a wide array of options on where to put their money now so they'll have more of it later when Junior's ready for school. Most financially-savvy parents adopt one of three long-term strategies for paying for college – they pay for tuition credits as the child grows up (The Prepaid Plan), they make a series of investments that fluctuate with the current economic market (The Investment Plan), or they diversify their investments by combining the two strategies (The All-Inclusive Plan). If played right, each of these strategies can pay off handsomely.No matter what you choose, the most important thing to remember is **DO NOT STORE ANY COLLEGE MONEY IN AN ACCOUNT OWNED BY YOUR CHILD UNLESS YOU HAVE NO OTHER CHOICE.** If the huge font and bold letters didn't tip you off, I'll just come out and say it–this is important, tremendously important if you have any hope of scoring financial aid. So important, in fact, that it's going to be written at the bottom of every page for the rest of the chapter. Accounts owned by students are assessed at a much higher rate on financial aid than money stored in an account owned by a parent. Because dependent students probably aren't making mortgage, gas, water, electric, telephone, or car payments, the federal government assumes that college-bound kids can afford to put a higher percentage of their hard earned cash (20%) towards higher education. That means for every dollar stored in a student-owned savings vehicle, $.20 will be lost in financial aid money. Since parents hold an array of financial responsibilities, Uncle Sam assesses their savings at a much lower rate (5.64%). That's a huge difference. Keeping savings plans in a parent's name, or better yet in a relative's name where it won't be assessed at all!) is one of the easiest and most effective ways to increase your check from the feds. Choosing the savings vehicle that best fits your family is another. Here's a quick breakdown of the pros and cons of each type of savings plan.

Strategy #1: The Prepaid Plan—How it works

Wouldn't it be nice to avoid all of that nasty tuition inflation? Now you can! Thanks to prepaid tuition plans, parents can purchase college credits at today's rates and have their children cash in on them five, ten, or even fifteen years down the road. The true benefit of prepaid plans is peace of mind. By buying college credits now, parents won't have to worry about whether their investments are increasing at the same rate as tuition inflation. Backed by a written guarantee, prepaid plans ensure that every dollar you invest will pay off manifold in years to come, so long as both the investor and the student comply with the plan's restrictions. Furthermore, all interest earned from prepaid tuition programs is exempt from federal income tax and in some cases from state income tax as well as long as the money is used for qualified higher education expenses. The final benefit is that any and everyone can get in on the red-hot prepaid tuition action. Parents, grandparents, friends, relatives, and even kind strangers can freely contribute to your prepaid tuition plan, allowing those who love you to give you the ultimate gift – a high-quality education at a blue-light special price. Thousands of tuition dollars can be saved without ever having to apply for a single scholarship, you won't feel the burn when tax season rolls around, and all of your loved ones can contribute their little hearts out. Hooray!

But wait, there's a catch! Prepaid tuition plans come with restrictions on how much you can contribute each year, what institutions you can use your newly bought tuition credits, and what expenses the plan will cover. Evaluate your options carefully and make sure you read the fine print several times before handing over your cash.

Your Prepaid Options—The 529 State Program

As a Virginia resident, you've got the benefit of having one of the nation's best prepaid savings plans at your fingertips. The Virginia Prepaid Education Program - VPEP for short - offers residents with children in the 9th grade or younger the ability to buy tuition credits that can be used at almost any accredited college or university in the good old U.S. of A. as well as certain technical and vocational schools. Parents can choose between opening a 1, 2, or 3-year Community College Plan or a University Plan, available in one, two, three, four, or five-year contracts. Both VPEP plans are based on the average price of one credit at an in-state two or four-year school respectively. If your student chooses to go to an in-state public college or university, no sweat, he or she can use the credits stashed away in your VPEP University Plan to pay for tuition and fees. Should your student choose a private school or venture out of state for college, your VPEP tuition credits will be subtracted from the cost of the school your kid will attend, leaving you to pay for the difference between the price of your child's school of choice and the average cost of a public Virginia school at the time. Because students are fickle and may change their minds several times before settling on a final higher education plan, VPEP credits can be used up to ten years after you child graduates high school or can easily be transferred into a different VPEP plan or into a Virginia Education Savings Trust plan. If, for example, you open a Community College Plan and your child decides instead to head directly to a four-year institution (or vice versa), you can roll your cash over into a University Plan and simply pay the difference between the average cost of an in-state four year school and an in-state two-year school. Should your student decide that higher education really isn't for them, VPEP plans can also be transferred to a sibling or cousin who is the same age as your child or younger. An added bonus to opening either a Community College or University Plan is that all VPEP account holders receive up to a $2,000 state income tax deduction per VPEP account each year (in addition to all earnings being federal income tax exempt) as a reward for contributing to their child's college savings plan.

VPEP Restrictions

Before you fork over the $25 application fee, know that VPEP is primarily designed for students who will use their tuition credits in-state. Although credits can be transferred to an out-of-state school, students who take this option will be left to fork over a hefty difference in price. Additionally, VPEP only covers tuition and mandatory fees. You're on your own to pay for lab fees, books, room and board, computer costs, club dues, and anything else you'll need to get through college. If your kid decides to attend an unaccredited school or certain foreign institutions, you may not be able to use your tuition credits at all. Also, VPEP is a long-term investment strategy designed to accrue interest over time. It's made for families who are prepared to make steady payments over a number of years, not those who want or need to pull their cash out at a moment's notice. VPEP requires account holders to:

A) Purchase all tuition credits up front. This is the least expensive method in the long run and great for big families where grandparents, aunts, uncles, and distant cousins all want to pitch in for the child's education. Thanks to federal gift tax law, contributing to your kid's educational fund works to everyone's advantage. Unlike other cash gifts (which in most cases are limited to $12,000 per year before the gift tax kicks in), individuals can contribute up to $60,000 (married couples can give up to $120,000) for your kid's educational fund over a 5-year period without paying a penny in gift tax. Get those wealthy aunts and uncles to pony up as soon as the account is opened and you'll get tuition credits at a cheaper rate, they'll have no financial repercussions, and everyone walks away feeling a little bit better about themselves.

And:

B) Stick to a monthly payment schedule, lasting either five years or however long it takes for your child to enter college.

Though account holders are welcome to overpay their monthly payments and reduce the overall length of their contract, missing a payment or paying late will result in a nasty $15 fee which can add up quickly if several payments are late. Once money is in VPEP, it stays in VPEP until your kid is ready to turn the tassel. Withdrawing your cash early for reasons other than death, disability, receipt of a generous scholarship package, or rolling funds over into a different state tuition program will cost you 10% of the interest earned on your VPEP money AND an administrative fee AND you'll have to repay any federal and state income tax deductions made while you held a VPEP account AND you'll have to pay additional income tax on interest gained on the money withdrawn. Yikes!

To take full advantage of the tuition savings, VPEP plans should be started as soon as your child is born. For more information on VPEP benefits and restrictions, contact the Virginia College Savings Plan toll-free at 1-888-567-0540 or check them out online at www.virginia529.com.

VPEP *Summary*

- Kicking tuition inflation to the curb.

- Federal, state, and gift tax advantages.
- Flexibility. If your long-term game plan changes, your cash can be rolled over into a different account.
- Anyone can contribute!
- Guaranteed return on your investment and a hedge against tuition inflation.

- Will detract from your financial aid package if the account owner is the student or a parent. Won't if the account is held in a grandparent or relative's name.

- Limited access and control over your funds.
- Age and residency limitations. The student or account holder must be a Virginia resident and the student must be in the 9th grade or younger.
- 10% penalty for using money for non-educational expenses.
- Only covers tuition and fees, everything else is on you.
- Only covers credit in-state. Go out of state or to a private school and you'll pay the difference, tuition inflation and all.
- Contribution maximum. The most you can purchase per account is a 5-year University Plan.

Prepaid Option #2: The Independant Program

If your child is determined to attend a private college, in-state or not, the Independent 529 Plan offers a prepaid tuition plan good at any of the 270+ member institutions across the nation, including 10 private schools based in Virginia. Because tuition varies wildly from college to college, the Independent 529 Plan allows parents to purchase certificates good for a fixed percentage of tuition at each member school. If, for example, you purchase a $25,000 certificate today, your student could redeem that years later for one full year's tuition at Sweet Briar College where the current undergrad tuition price is $24,740 or for 66% of one year's tuition at the University of Richmond where the current undergrad tuition price is $37,610 per year. By purchasing credits through the Independent 529 Plan, parents not only skip out entirely on paying tuition inflation, they also receive a discount on tuition overall. Each member school offers a reduced tuition rate, usually between 0.5% and 1% off the regular tuition price, to Independent 529 Plan holders, so that in buying now, you'll actually be getting more tuition for your money than students attending the school today.

College Savings Tip

Want to score more cash for your child's college education? Think carefully, very carefully, about who owns the account. Cash stored in prepaid tuition accounts as well as in 529 College Savings Accounts (see the next page) must be declared as an asset when it comes time to apply for federal financial aid. If held in the parent's name, approximately six cents for every dollar stored in the prepaid account will be added to your expected family contribution (EFC) thereby lowering the amount of federal aid you're eligible to receive. One way to get around losing potential scholarship money is to open the account in a relative's name. While the federal government will be watching mom and dad's assets like a hawk, they won't notice if gran and gramps are the ones holding your college cash.

Like VPEP, the Independent 529 Plan is backed by a guarantee, funds are only applicable to tuition and mandatory fees, and all interest earned on your prepaid plan is federal tax exempt; however, you won't receive a state income tax deduction. You also won't pay administrative fees at any time. The Independent 529 Plan is free to enter, free to maintain year after year provided you keep up with your monthly payments, and free to exit as long as you use the cash to pay for tuition and fees. If you don't, you'll have to pony up a penalty of 10% of your earnings as well as fork over an administrative fee and back federal income taxes you exempted before. You could also wind up losing cash, or rather not accruing cash, if your child decides not to go to a member school. While the Independent 529 Plan does allow you to roll your money over to a different savings program, you'll only be allowed to roll over you're the money you've put in, plus or minus 2% depending on market fluctuations. The major thing you're losing is time. While your money would have steadily gained interest over a number of years in other college savings plans, going to a school outside of your prepaid plan forces you to rely on the amount you've put in without receiving any interest or a discount on tuition.

For more information on the Independent 529 Plan, go to www.independent529plan.org or call 1-888-718-7878.

Independent 529 Plan *Summary*

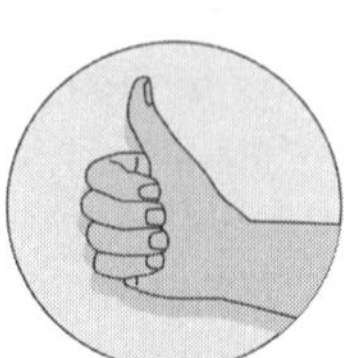

- Major league savings on tuition inflation.
- Reduced rate on tuition credits.
- Federal and gift tax advantages.
- Guaranteed return on your investment.
- Anyone can contribute!

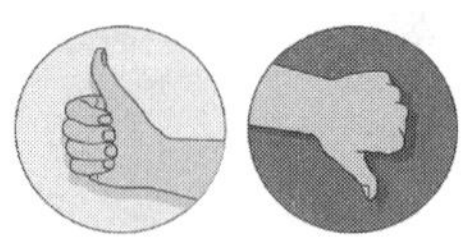

- Will detract from your financial aid package if the account owner is the student or a parent. Won't if held in a grandparent or relative's name.

- No state income tax deduction.
- Flexibility. If your child attends a non-member school, you forego your tuition discount AND your money doesn't gain any interest.
- Limited access and control over your cash.
- Only pays for tuition and fees.
- 10% penalty for using your money for non-educational expenses.
- Time limitations. Certificates must be held at least 36 months before being redeemed.
- Contribution limit of $171,000.

Strategy #2: The Investment Plan—How it Works

For families that want more control over their money, prepaid tuition plans simply won't work. Instead of buying college credits in advance, many families choose to save for school by spreading their funds out over a series of investments. Those who save for college using The Investment Plan have a higher earning potential, more options on where to store their cash, better access to their money, and fewer restrictions on how and where their money can be used than those who choose The Prepaid Plan. Additionally, prepaid plans only cover tuition and fees, but those who use The Investment Plan can save for tuition as well as all other college expenses in one place. The downside is that The Investment Plan offers limited security for your funds. How much money your plan makes depends entirely on how smartly you invest and on market fluctuations. While there is no ceiling on your investment returns, there's also no guarantee that you won't lose your savings. Choose carefully, diversify your investment portfolio, and enter at your own risk.

Your Investment Options—The 529 State Program

Should you opt for The Investment Plan, the easiest way to get started is through the Virginia Education Savings Trust (VEST). Acting like your personal money manager, VEST offers both in and out-of-state parents their choice of 11 investment packages, ranging in risk level from highly aggressive portfolios that have a high earning potential to stable, low risk options aimed at increasing your college savings steadily over several years. Parents may either select a package based on the risk level they're comfortable with or can opt for an age-based package in which a fixed percentage of money starts in high-yield accounts and funds automatically shift to stable, low-risk accounts as your student grows up. Start your age-based VEST account early, say when your child is between the ages of 0 and 3, and the majority of your cash (80%) will be stored in high-yield stocks and money-market funds with 20% getting stored in low-risk fixed-income investments. Start it later on when your child has reached middle school and half of your cash will be placed in stocks with the other half sitting safely in low-risk accounts. Because VEST accounts are designed to protect your savings against last-minute market crashes, a higher percentage of your money will be shifted to stable accounts every few years. By the time your kid reaches college age, 100% of your investments will be sitting in low-risk accounts, waiting for you and your child to blow it on any education-related expenses including tuition, books, room and board, and required miscellaneous supplies at almost any accredited community college, vocational school, four-year college or university, or graduate institution in the nation, in or out of state.

The three major benefits of investing through VEST are the flexibility, the low-cost financial help, and the tax advantages. A distinct departure from prepaid plans, VEST money can be withdrawn at any time for higher education expenses and can be used for almost anything your kid will need for school. To make sure you've got the money to cover all of those expenses, VEST financial advisors will work with you to help pick the investments that suit your family's needs best. Instead of blindly putting all of your money into a single stock or mutual fund, VEST packages spread you cash out over a series of mutual funds, fixed-income securities, and money market accounts, all hand-picked by a team of investment pros. Account holders pay a low annual fee (0.33% to 0.56% depending on what package you choose), may change packages from year to year, and are welcome to open several VEST accounts in order to truly diversify their investments. Additionally, VEST account holders also enjoy some significant tax benefits. While enrolled in VEST, account holders won't be responsible for paying any federal income tax on returns earned and state residents may also deduct up to $2,000 each year from their state income taxes per account just for contributing to their child's educational fund. Parents aren't the only ones who can get in on the steamy investment action. Grandparents, relatives, and friends may freely contribute to the VEST account, up to $60,000 per contributor per beneficiary over a five-year period without paying yucky gift tax and if opened in their name, contributions won't impact the students' financial aid eligibility at all.

VEST Restrictions:

The con to opening a VEST account is that like prepaid plans, VEST accounts are meant to be long-term investments used for accredited schools. Withdrawing your money for reasons other than educational expense, death, disability, receipt of an awesome scholarship package, or rolling funds over to another state-sponsored savings plan will cost you 10% of your earnings as well as an administrative fee and all the federal and state taxes you didn't pay while the account was open. Instead of pulling your cash out entirely, if an unexpected situation arises (like your kid doesn't want to attend college at all or insists on attending a non-accredited institution), you can always transfer the money in your account over to a relative or keep your account open just in case the situation changes.

VEST accounts cost $25 each to start and can be opened at any time year-round. For more information on VEST benefits and restrictions, contact the Virginia College Savings Plan toll-free at 1-888-567-0540 or check them out online at www.virginia529.com.

VEST *Summary*

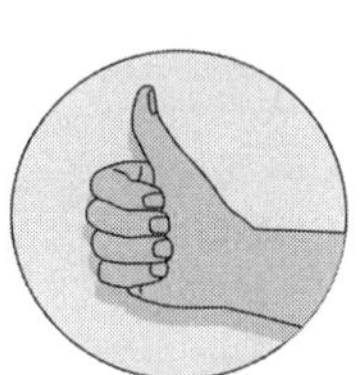

- Earn away. There's no limit to the amount you can earn!
- Federal, state, and gift tax advantages.
- No age or residency restrictions! Perfect for adults returning to the classroom.
- Greater control over how your money is invested.
- Can be used for any educational expense at any accredited school in the U.S.
- Anyone can contribute!
- Financial help provided.

- Security. If the market takes a dive, so could you.
- Withdrawal restrictions. Pull your cash out early for reasons other than death, disability, or receipt of a scholarship and you'll be forking over 10% of your earnings and an administrative fee and all of your federal and state income back taxes.

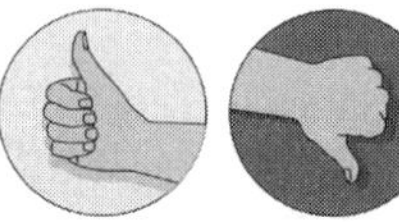

- Will detract from your financial aid package if the account owner is the student or a parent. Won't if held in a grandparent or relative's name.

Option #2: The CollegeAmerica 529 Savings Plan

The bigger, badder, and potentially better version of VEST, the CollegeAmerica program offers parents nearly twice the investment options as well as the ability to custom design their own personal portfolio. Like VEST, CollegeAmerica offers age-based and non-age-based investment options, funds can be used for any educational expense at almost any accredited school in the U.S., anyone of any age can open or contribute to an account, and all federal, state, and gift tax advantages apply. An additional plus CollegeAmerica provides is the ability to invest in several funds without opening a new account and students have three times as long (30 years after high school graduation) to use their CollegeAmerica cash. Parents have more options when it comes to their money, may switch funds once a year or roll the account over to another family member, and on-staff financial advisors will help you every step of the way. Many of the same restrictions and drawbacks apply as well. CollegeAmerica money spent on things other than qualified educational expenses or used to attend a non-accredited institution is subject to federal income tax as well as a penalty of 10% of the earnings and an administrative fee. Accounts held in either the students or parents name will affect need-based financial aid eligibility, so it's to your advantage to have a friend or relative open the account. Parents should also know that although CollegeAmerica accounts are cheaper to open (just $10 to start), the management fees are significantly higher than those required by VEST. Parents can open a CollegeAmerica account with just $250 starter cash. To get started, contact American Funds at (800) 421-0180 or read up about the CollegeAmerica program at www.americanfunds.com/college/index.htm.

CollegeAmerica *Summary*

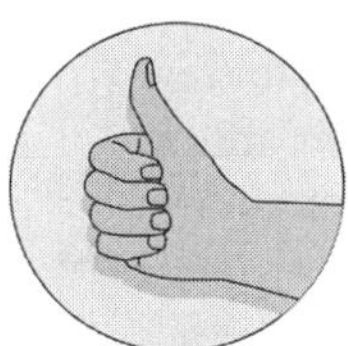

- No limit to the amount you can earn.
- Federal, state, and gift tax advantages.
- No age or residency restrictions!
- Greater control over how your money is invested.
- Can be used for any educational expense at any accredited school in the U.S.
- Anyone can contribute!

Financial help provided.

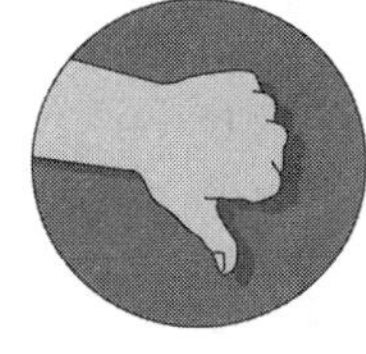

- No guarantee on your investment.
- Withdrawal restrictions. Pull your cash out early for reasons other than death, disability, or receipt of a scholarship and you'll be forking over 10% of your earnings and all of your federal and state income back taxes.

- Will detract from your financial aid package if the account owner is the student or a parent. Won't if held in a grandparent or relative's name.

Option #3: Coverdell Educational Savings Accounts (The Artist Formerly Known as Educational IRAs)

Armed with the look, the feel, and many of the benefits and drawbacks of a retirement account, Coverdell ESAs are accounts specifically for educational expenses (of all types) for kids ages 18 and under and special needs children. Whether you're looking to pay for four years of college or one year at a private elementary school, money stashed in Coverdell ESAs can grow tax-free and be withdrawn without penalty for educational expenses ranging from tuition and room and board to uniform fees and transportation costs. Like a retirement account, there are contribution limits - $2,000 total per student per year, no matter how many accounts are opened in the child's name - and going over that mark will result in a sharp slap on the wrist, namely a 6% penalty tax on all excess contributions. Using your money for things other than educational expenses will result in - you guessed it - a penalty as well, specifically 10% of your earnings as well as back federal income taxes you skipped for all those glorious, tax-free years. If your kid decides to blow off college entirely or attend a foreign or unaccredited school, your best bet is to roll the money over into an account for a relative's kid rather than cough up the fees. The major benefit of having a Coverdell ESA is that the account owner has complete control over the investments. Unlike 529 plans, Coverdell ESA owners can pick any stock, bond, or mutual fund they'd like to invest in, giving you absolute power over where you place your cash.

While Coverdell ESAs are definitely more flexible than both prepaid and 529 college savings plans, they also come with a boatload of restrictions. Catch number one (brace yourself, there are several to follow) is that due to the $2,000 per year contribution limit (which by the way, breaks down to a maximum contribution of less than $40 per week), Coverdell ESAs can really only be used to cover part of your educational expenses, not wipe them out completely. If you start an account when your child is born, the maximum you'll be able to contribute from day one until your kid reaches adulthood and the account can no longer legally accept contributions is $36,000. Even if the market skyrockets over that 18 year period and your returns are absolutely stupendous, you still won't have enough to pay for your kid's total cost of attendance. Restriction number two ties directly in with number one. Due to the low contribution limit, any maintenance or annual fees you'll pay could have a big impact

Across the Country

Because savings plans like VEST and CollegeAmerica have no residency requirements, in-state isn't your only option. In fact, 49 states nationwide offer similar 529 college savings plans open to anyone with the capital to start an account, but none will offer you a break on Virginia state income taxes. An out-of-state account could pay off big time for a distant relative whose into helping you foot those collegiate bills. Relative X can open a 529 plan in his or her home state, reap the sweet, sweet state income tax rewards then use the money to pay for your college expenses no matter where you go to school. A double benefit is that money held in a relative's name won't affect your federal financial aid eligibility at all. For the skinny on the ins and outs on out of state 529 programs, check out www.savingforcollege.com or www.finaid.org/savings.

on your returns. ESAs are offered through banks, brokerage firms, and mutual fund companies, each of whom set their own fees and regulations on the accounts. If you think that going Coverdell is right for you, it pays to do your homework and compare ESA packages before enrolling. Finally, not everyone qualifies to hold an educational savings account. Coverdell ESAs are only open to single parents with an income below $110,000 per year or married folks with a combined income below $220,000. An additional restriction is that only single parents with an income below $95,000 per year ($190,000 for the marrieds) can contribute the full $2,000 per year. To find out what types of ESAs are available and their fees and restrictions, contact your local bank, brokerage firm, or mutual trust manager.

Coverdell *Summary*

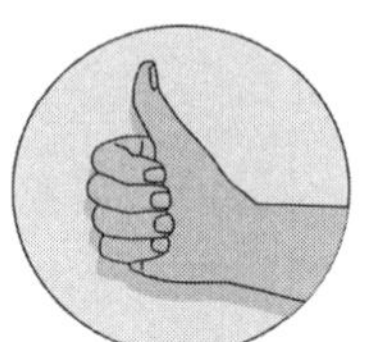

- No limit to the amount you can earn.
- Anyone can contribute!
- Federal tax advantages.
- Flexibility. Can be used for almost any educational expense.

- Age restrictions.
- No guarantee on your returns.
- Low contribution limit of $2,000 per student per year.
- Only available to single parents with an income below $110,000 per year or married folks with a combined income below $220,000.
- Withdrawal restrictions. Pull your cash out early for reasons other than death, disability, or receipt of a scholarship and you'll be forking over 10% of your earnings and an administrative fee and all of your federal income back taxes.

Option #4: UGMA AND UTMA Custodial Accounts

You never knew there were so many options, right? Providing even more flexibility than other college savings plans, an UGMA (Uniform Gift to Minors Act) or UTMA (Uniform Transfer to Minors Act) account is a custodial savings plan held by a parent until the student beneficiary becomes a legal adult. Operating like a mutual fund, UGMA and UTMA accounts allow parents to choose which funds their money gets placed in and change accounts as they see fit. What makes UGMA/UTMA accounts so different from every other college savings plan is that funds stored in these accounts can be used for any purpose, educational or not, after your child has reached the age of 18. That translates to no restrictions on where your kid can go to school, no limitations on where the funds can be applied, and no worries about paying a penalty if the money isn't used for qualified educational expenses. Where and how far your UGMA/UTMA money goes depends entirely on your student. After your child turns 18, the UGMA/UTMA cash legally becomes theirs and it can be used for anything from college courses to Caribbean cruises without penalty.

A few tax benefits also come with an UGMA account (although they pale in comparison to the benefits offered through other college savings plans). If your child is under the age of 18 and has no other income, you won't pay a penny of tax on the first $850 earned through the UGMA or UTMA account, you'll pay a reduced rate on the next $850, and you'll pay your regular federal rate on everything beyond. What you save in taxes, you may very well lose in financial aid. UGMA and UTMA accounts are considered student assets and subject to a much harsher assessment rate (20%!) than parental assets. To find out what types of ESAs are available and their fees and restrictions, contact your local bank, brokerage firm, or mutual trust manager.

UGMA/UTMA *Summary*

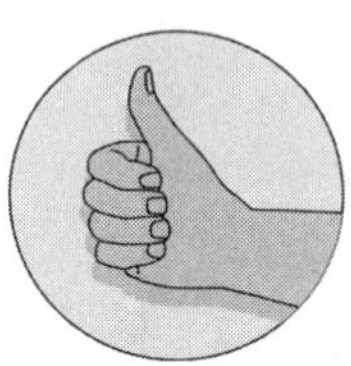

- No limit to the amount you can earn.
- Anyone can contribute!
- Limited tax advantages.
- Flexibility. Can be used for anything.

- Age restrictions.
- No guarantee on your returns.
- Significantly subtracts from your financial aid eligibility.
- Not transferable to another beneficiary.
- Significantly subtracts for your financial aid eligibility.

Option #5: Collegesure CDs and Everything Else (Savings Accounts, Mutual Funds, Money-market Funds, Bonds, and Trusts)

Of course standard savings vehicles work too, but you won't get any of the security or tax advantages that come with the aforementioned plans. The CollegeSure CD is the exception to that rule. Acting as a sort of halfway house between prepaid plans and 529 college savings plans, the CollegeSure CD is the only certificate of deposit in the country guaranteed to increase at the same rate as college tuition. Operating similar to the Independent 529 Plan, CollegeSure allows parents to buy certificates based on the current average cost of attendance at a four-year private college and use that tuition one to twenty-two years down the road at almost any school in the nation. In fact, even if tuition inflation stops entirely, your CollegeSure CD is guaranteed to increase at least 2% each year. An added bonus is that CollegeSure CDs can be combined with either Montana or Arizona's 529 college savings plan, giving you the ability to let your money grow without having to pay federal income tax on it as long as it's used for educational expenses. If not placed in a 529 account, CollegeSure is treated in the same way as any other investment and you'll be forced to pay income taxes on it.

If it sounds too good to be true, that's because it kind of is. The catch is that you'll pay for the plan's added security...literally. CollegeSure certificates are sold at a price that's higher than face value, so you won't get out of paying tuition inflation entirely, you'll just pay a portion of it up front. Also you can kiss your money goodbye, at least until you're ready to cash it in. CollegeSure accounts allow you to withdraw your interest at any time without penalty; however, if you touch your principal investment before your CD has matured, you'll pay a penalty of 1 to 10% of the funds withdrawn.

CollegeSure CDs can be started with just $250 starter cash. For more information, contact The College Savings Bank at www.collegesavings.com or by calling 1-800-888-2723.

Collegsure *SUMMARY*

- Erasing a big portion of your tuition inflation.
- Backed by a guarantee of up to $100,000.
- Federal and gift tax advantages.
- No age or residency restrictions.
- Anyone can contribute!
- Can be used for any educational expense at any accredited school in the U.S.

- Parents pay some tuition inflation up front.
- Must invest in an out of state 529 plan, no state tax advantages.
- Limited control over your funds.
- Withdrawal restrictions. Pull your cashout early and you'll fork over a penalty.

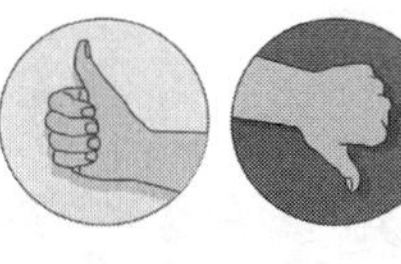

- Will detract from your financial aid package.

Strategy #3: Combining Forces—The All-Inclusive Plan

Parents who want both the safety of a prepaid plan and the investment returns of a non-prepaid plan can compromise by splitting their money and investing in both. Mixing and matching investment plans is a great way to diversify your college savings portfolio and take full advantage of programs that can pay off for your family. If you take this approach, think about opening a VPEP account to pay for tuition and a VEST account to pay for everything else in order to take full advantage of the tax benefits. If your kid is already in high school and none of these long-term plans seem to fit your short-term schedule, read on about short-term financial aid options in the next chapter.

6 Ways to Save Smart.

1. **Direct Deposit**–Out of sight, out of mind. Having a portion of your paycheck automatically sent to your kid's college fund will ensure that you will add to your kid's college savings fund on a regular basis without having to scrimp for it at the end of the month.

2. **Don't Forget the Holidays**–Many college savings plans allow friends and relatives to contribute, so take advantage! A contribution to the college savings account will do Junior a lot more good than a new video game anyway.

3. **Break It Down**–Making a payment of $150 each month sounds a lot harder than simply skipping your morning latte, but the truth is, they add up to the same thing. By breaking down your payments into daily increments and cutting down a little here and there, you can save for school without sacrificing the big stuff.

4. **Bank Your Bonus**–Looking for a way to spend unexpected gifts from the gods of green? Throw cash from income tax returns, holiday bonuses, or extra commissions in your child's college savings account.

5. **Make Them Work For It**–Paying for college is, or at least should be, a family affair. Requiring your kids to put a portion of their income into their college savings accounts will not only teach them financial responsibility, it will also increase your financial aid eligibility.

6. **Pay Off Credit Card Debt**–Earning 8% on an investment does nothing if you're simultaneously paying off a credit card with a 16% interest rate. If you really want your bank account to grow, pay off your high-interest debts as soon as possible and invest your leftover cash wisely.

Save While You Spend

These three rebate programs put a percentage of your purchase towards your child's college education. Spend away and save in the process.

1 **LittleGrad.com**—Get rewarded for shopping online! Parents who open a free LittleGrad account receive a rebate (anywhere from $0.25 to 50% of your purchase) that goes directly into your 529 college savings account every time you shop online at The Gap, Wal-Mart, Home Depot, Linens N' Things, T Mobile, eBay, Barnes and Noble, or any of the other 1,000+ affiliated online retailers. Get your friends and family on board and you get a percentage of their rebates as well.

2 **Upromise.com**—Designed for those who prefer shopping in the real, rather than virtual, world, Upromise offers rebates up to 10% just for shopping at any of the 40,000+ associated retailers. Who knew that some gas at Exxon, some groceries from Kroger, and booking your vacations through Expedia.com could pay for college?

3 **FutureTrust.com**—Forget frequent flyer miles, think college tuition instead. Every time you use a FutureTrust Mastercard, you'll have a 1% rebate deposited directly into your 529 college savings plan and even more if you shop through one of FutureTrust's retail partners.

5 Fast Financial Aid Resources

1. **This book**...duh...specifically Chapter Three which covers long-term savings strategies, Chapter Four which covers short-term financial aid programs, and the index of scholarships and grants available to Virginia students only. In fact, this book is chocked SO full of information, you may want to buy 5 or 6 or 42 copies for friends, relatives, or anyone else who wants to hold the unbridled power of free money in the palm of his or her hand. MUWHAHAHAHA!

2. **FinAid.org**–The alpha and omega of financial aid. You'll find absolutely everything from basic savings guides to information on tax credits, military aid, custodial accounts, and everything in between. If you have a question, this is the place to find the answer.

3. **Collegeboard.com**–While the site is most famous for being a bastion of all test-taking things, it also contains valuable information on applying for financial aid as well as a scholarship search.

4. **Bankrate.com**–Designed to serve the whole student, this site contains information on both scoring financial aid as well as how to pay it off after you've graduated.

5. **The Federal Student Aid Information Center**–Ready and willing to answer any of your FAFSA-related questions, this free phone service (1-800-4FED-AID) can help you get in good with the feds. If you prefer the online route, www.fafsa.ed.gov contains a wealth of FAFSA info as well. What's a FAFSA you ask? Find out in saucy Chapter Four.

Name of Plan	Virginia Prepaid Education Plan	Independent 529 Plan	Virginia Education Savings Trust	CollegeAmerica
Applicability	Pays for in-state tuition and fees only at in-state colleges and universities	Pays tuition and fees at 250+ private colleges	Any higher education expense	Any higher education expense
Guaranteed Return	Yes	Yes	No	No
Tax Advantages	Federal, state, and gift	Federal and gift	Federal, state, and gift	Federal and gift
Who Can Contribute?	Anyone	Anyone	Anyone	Anyone
Contribution Limits	One 5-year University Plan or one 3-year Community College Plan	$171,000	$250,000	$250,000
Age Restrictions	Students must be 9th grade or younger to start the account	Student must be high school sophomore or younger	None	None
Residency Restrictions	Student or account holder must live in VA	None	None	None
Transferability	Transferable to relatives of the same age or below	Transferable to relatives	Transferable to relatives	Transferable to relatives
Cost to Open an Account	$25 application fee	Free to open, $25 minimum contribution	$25 application fee, must deposit $250 in the first year	$10 application fee, $250 minimum balance
Withdrawal Restrictions	10% penalty if used for non-educational expenses plus back taxes	10% penalty if used for non-educational expenses plus back taxes	10% penalty if used for non-educational expenses plus back taxes	10% penalty if used for non-educational expenses plus back taxes
Financial Aid Impact	Up to 5.64% if the account owner is a parent, none if the account owner is a relative.	Up to 5.64% if the account owner is a parent, none if the account owner is a relative.	Up to 5.64% if the account owner is a parent, none if the account owner is a relative.	Up to 5.64% if the account owner is a parent, none if the account owner is a relative.

Name of Plan	Coverdell ESAs	UGMA/UTMAs	CollegeSure CD
Applicability	Any educational expense	Any expense	Any higher education expense
Guaranteed Return	No	No	Yes
Tax Advantages	Federal	Limited federal	Federal and gift
Who Can Contribute?	Anyone	Anyone	Anyone
Contribution Limits	$2,000 per student per year	None	$304,000
Age Restrictions	Student must be 18 or under or have special needs	Student must be 18 or under	None
Residency Restrictions	None	None	None
Transferability	Transferable to relatives	Not transferable	Transferable to relatives
Cost to Open an Account	Varies from bank to bank	Varies from bank to bank	No application fee, $250 minimum balance
Withdrawal Restrictions	10% penalty if used for non-educational expenses plus back taxes	None	10% penalty if used for non-educational expenses plus back taxes, 1 - 10% penalty if withdrawn before plan matures.
Financial Aid Impact	Up to 5.64% if the account owner is a parent, none if the account owner is a relative.	20% assessment rate	Up to 5.64% if the account owner is a parent, none if the account owner is a relative.

Chapter Four

Paying For It All–The Short-Term Plan

Sure, you could sweat it out and pay off all of your tuition bills, but why do that when you could go for free...or at least closer to free? From federal grants to work-study programs to educational tax credits, there's tons of free money available for students motivated enough to go get it. Before we jump into the ins and outs of the free dough, let's discuss what kinds of financial aid are out there and who gives it out.

Free Money 101

There are two basic types of financial aid–gift aid such as scholarships and grants that you'll never, ever in a million years have to pay back and self-help aid such as student loans, service awards, and work-study jobs that you'll either have to work for or pay back at some point. As a student, your goal is to score as much free gift aid as you can and then cover your leftover college expenses by ponying up the money yourself (the preferable option!) or relying on self-help aid which, in most cases, involves paying your expenses plus hefty interest (boooo!!!!!!). Both gift aid and self-help aid can come from a wide variety of sources ranging from the federal and state governments to your specific college, private corporations, community-based organizations, national service programs, local and national award competitions, and your high school clubs, just to name a few. While some organizations award funds based on financial need, others make that decision based on merit, how well you perform academically, creatively, athletically, rhetorically, and the list goes on. Although it may seem like any and everyone is handing out financial aid (if you don't believe me, take a peek at the amazing number of scholarships listed on Fastweb.com), the truth is that most financial aid comes from a few key players. In order to land the most money you can get your greedy paws on before you head off to school, it's essential to prioritize where you are most likely to get the fattest check and apply there first. Luckily, this book has already done that for you.

The Top Four Sources of Financial Aid

1 **Federal Government**—The largest provider of financial aid in the country, Uncle Sam passes out a cool $94+ billion in financial aid each year. All you have to do is fill out a FAFSA and send it in by as close to January 1 of your senior year as possible.

2 **State Government**—On top of federal aid, Virginia shells out scholarships and grants for state residents only. State financial aid is offered through an array of programs which vary in terms of deadlines and eligibility requirements. Specifics on state-funded scholarship and grant programs for undergrads are listed in the appropriately-titled Index of Scholarships and Grants for Virginia Students in the back of this sultry book.

3 **Your Future School**—Colleges and universities themselves provide nearly 20% of all need-based financial aid out there. After you've handed in the FAFSA, give your school's financial aid office a call to find out how to apply for school-based aid.

4 **Everywhere Else**—Corporate, faith-based, community, and other private organizations only account for a small percentage of the gift aid given out each year. The bright side is that private agencies offer financial aid to students who might not otherwise qualify. A little research could land you some cash.

Section One: Tapping into Uncle Sam

Pell Grants, Stafford Loans, and work-study gigs, oh my! The federal government is a veritable explosion of money waiting to be claimed. The icing on the proverbial cake is that you won't have to be the track star or valedictorian to land this cash. Most of the free money, low-interest loans, and student jobs Uncle Sam hands out are based on how much you need them. Should you be lucky enough to receive a financial aid offer from the government, it will consist of one or several of the following:

- **Pell Grant**—The motherload of federal money for undergrads, the Pell Grant offers undergrad students with established financial need up to $4,050 per year to help pay for school. The Pell Grant is tied to your financial need as well as how long you intend to stay in school (one semester vs. the entire academic year) and your courseload, so bumping yourself into the "fulltime student" category may work to your advantage.

- **SEOG Grant**—Like the Pell Grant, Supplemental Educational Opportunity Grants (SEOG if you're nasty) all depend on how much you need them. Up to $4,000 per year goes to the undergrads who demonstrate the lowest expected family contribution combined with the highest cost of attendance. The difference is that this money isn't guaranteed. SEOG cash is handed out early, yet another reason to get your FAFSA in as soon as you've rung in the New Year.

- **Academic Competitiveness Grant**—It even sounds smart doesn't it? The newest addition to the federal financial aid family, ACG's are based on both need and merit. ACG's are only available to full-time freshmen and sophomores who are eligible for a Pell Grant AND who have already survived a rigorous high school curriculum, whether it be through an Advanced Studies Diploma, an AP or IB-intensive curriculum, or a technical education-heavy program of study. Students are eligible to receive up to $750 for the first year of undergrad study and $1,300 for the second year. Students are also expected to maintain at least 3.0 GPA while they're in college. Kiss the idea of sleeping through your first class goodbye.

- **National SMART Grant**—Chill out arts and business majors. SMART grants are only offered to full-time undergrad juniors and seniors with a 3.0 or above who are majoring in science (specifically a physical, life, or computer science), math, technology, engineering, or foreign language critical to national security. Oh yeah, you've got to demonstrate enough financial need to be eligible for the Pell Grant and be a U.S. citizen as well. Students who meet these criteria will be rewarded with up to $4,000 for each of their upperclassmen years. For a full list of eligible majors, head here: www.ifap.ed.gov/dpcletters/attachments/GEN0606A.pdf.

Add that up and you're looking at a grand total of up to $42,250 of free money available to students who need it the most. Beyond scholarships and grants, the feds also offer the following programs for students with less financial need:

- **Stafford Loan**—Available in either the unsubsidized (you pay the interest) or subsidized (the government pays the interest until you graduate) varieties, Stafford loans allow students to borrow up to $23,000 for undergraduate education ($3,500 for freshmen, $4,500 for sophomores, and $5,500 for juniors on up) and $65,500 for graduate ed. In borrowing from the government, you can avoid getting squeezed by private lenders. Stafford loans are fixed at a 6.8% interest rate, charge a small loan fee, and give students up to ten years to pay the money back.

- **Perkins Loan**—This is the first-come, first-serve, subsidized-only version of the Stafford Loan. The Perkins Loan provides up to $40,000 for undergraduate and graduate study (about $4,000 per year). Although technically considered federal funds, Perkins money is disbursed by individual schools, meaning not all schools will have the same amount of Perkins cash to dole out, and is limited so not all qualified applicants can expect to receive a check. If you are one of the lucky ones, expect a low 5% interest rate (a figure WAY lower than that of most private student loans) and the freedom to pursue your studies without having to pay a dime until after you graduate. Students may also have a chance to turn Perkins money into scholarship cash. Educational award programs such as Teach for America, Americorps, and the Peace Corps as well as outside loan forgiveness programs are aimed at getting rid of your Perkins debt. Give back to your country and your country will give back to your student loan.

- **PLUS Loan**—Those truly strapped for cash can get the whole family involved. The PLUS Loan allows ready, willing, and eager moms and dads to take out a cash for their kids up to the student's total cost of attendance. Not just for undergrads anymore, PLUS loans can now be taken for students pursuing an undergraduate, grad, or professional degree; however, the parents, not the students, will be responsible for making sure the loan is paid. A radical departure from other federally-funded loan programs, the PLUS Loan isn't based on need, it's based on credit. As long as parents have reasonable credit, they may take out as much cash as they wish provided it's spent on legitimate educational expenses. PLUS Loans have a comparable interest rate (fixed at 8.5%) and loan fees (4%) as the Stafford Loan; however, the rules change when it comes to paying the loan back. Payments on PLUS loans start just two months after the money is taken out, making this type of loan significantly less attractive than other federal loan programs, but still better than the rates and conditions of most private lenders.

- **Work-Study** —If you want to go to college bad enough, here's one way to subsidize your education. Students who financially qualify for this program and who attend a school where there are available work-study positions will be set up with a paid part-time job for their college or university. Most work study gigs require 10 to 15 hours per week and it's one of the few programs where none of your earnings will affect your financial aid eligibility. In addition to the paycheck, work-study positions will also give you work experience while you're in school and an opportunity to beef up your resume.

The first step to getting your hands on the funding (well, all funding except for the PLUS Loan) is to ace the FAFSA (Free Application for Federal Student Aid), the federal government's way of measuring how much money you'll need to get through school. The FAFSA boils you and your parents' incomes, assets, and financial resources down to an estimate of how much your family can contribute to your education. Remember that fantastically clever financial aid equation used in the last chapter:

Cost of Attendance – Expected Family Contribution = Your Financial Aid Package

This is where it gets used. Unfortunately, conquering FAFSA isn't as simple as filling out one form. To make sure that you receive the maximum amount of aid, you and your parents need to start preparing for the FAFSA during your sophomore year in high school and make sure to get that application in as soon as possible after January 1st of your senior year.

Preparing for FAFSA

How much federal aid you receive will be determined by your family's income and assets as of the tax year before you apply for aid. That means it's to your fiscal advantage to help your parents organize their finances before you hit your junior year. Little things such as the account owner on your college savings plan, how your family handles their stock portfolio, and how your family fills out the FAFSA form can make a HUGE impact on the size of your financial aid award. Successfully organizing your money breaks down to three basic rules: (1) Use the Right Name, (2) Spend in the Right Places, and (3) Report the Right Figures.

1. A Savings Program By Any Other Name

If you've been financially savvy so far, your college money should be stored in some sort of savings program (check out the College Savings Comparison Chart in Chapter Three to review your options) held in a parent or relative's name. If your college dough is somewhere else, you could be in trouble. As mentioned in Chapter Three, students are expected to pitch in a much higher portion of their income and savings to college tuition bills than their parents. For every dollar held in an account owned by a student, the government subtracts a walloping $0.20 from your total financial aid package. For every dollar held in an account owned by mom and/or dad, the government only subtracts about $0.06. That means moving $10,000 from your account to a parent's account could add $1,400 extra in financial aid. Ideally you should save in an account owned by a relative. College money held in an account owned by a relative is one of FAFSA's most fantastic loopholes. Have an aunt, uncle, grandparent, or benevolent cousin open a savings account for you and any cash stored there won't count at all on the FAFSA

If you are saving your college cash in an account that you own, get rid of it if you can. Money stored in regular checking and savings accounts can be transferred directly into an account owned by a parent or relative. If you're locked into an UGMA or other non-transferrable savings plan, consult your accountant to see how and if your funds can be changed around. UGMA and custodial accounts can be liquidated; however, your parents may have to pay back taxes. Depending on how much money is in the account and whether your family is eligible to apply for need-based aid at all, it may not be worth it. An alternative route is to simply start spending (music to your ears right?). Blowing your college cash on things you'll need for school such as dorm supplies or a new computer is an easy way to get rid of money in your account while still saving for college. While you're watching your savings, watch your earnings too. Students can earn up to $3,000 per year without penalty; however, anything over 3 grand will be assessed at a...brace yourself...fifty percent rate. Make $3,500 in a year and you'll lose $250 in financial aid. The exception to this rule is money earned through federal work-study programs, Americorps, Peace Corps, and Teach for America. Who says giving back doesn't pay?

FAFSA Secrets—How to Make the Government Work for You

You can't doctor the numbers on your FAFSA form, but you can control how and when you apply. Here are four ways to squeeze a bigger chunk of change out of the federal government.

1. **Time It Right**—What are siblings good for if they can't help you out when you need it? The more students your family has in college at once, the more financial aid you'll receive. Timing your education to be in sync with your brothers and sisters means a cheaper college ride for everyone.

2. **Send the 'Rents to School**—No siblings? No problem. The same rule applies when mom and/or dad return to school as well. If your parents see a new degree in their future, now's the time to get it.

3. **Postpone the Bonus**—The amount of need-based aid your family receives is directly tied to the amount of money the head(s) of the household earn each year. Postponing your bonus until after you've applied for aid could land you a larger check.

4. **Think Outside the Raise**—To reduce your income during the year before you apply for aid, push for non-monetary perks like better insurance, more vacation time, or tuition reimbursement, particularly if your combined household income is near the $50,000 mark. Households under the $50,000 income line have a much better shot at scoring aid than those over, so if you're on the border, it's possible that you could earn more aid just by taking a pay cut, perks, or an unpaid leave of absence.

2. Spend Smart, Sell Smart

There are places your parents can invest money that will never affect your aid eligibility. Their house and their retirement funds are the two major ones. The FAFSA does not count the value of your family's primary residence when calculating your aid package, so putting family money towards the mortgage can actually pay off for you in the long run. Likewise, the FAFSA doesn't assess money stored in a 401(k). Encouraging your parents to maximize their yearly retirement contributions and discouraging them from pulling money from their retirement accounts to pay for your education could result in a bigger check from the government. Additionally, funds invested in a small family-owned business with fewer than 100 full-time employees also aren't taken into account on the FAFSA. Investing in a much-needed copy machine, phone service, or any other business-related expenses could pay off.

Paying off lingering debt is another way to liquefy assets that may count against you. While the FAFSA will consider the $10,000 your parents could have stashed in a savings account, it won't consider the fact that your parents intended to use that money to pay off a car loan or credit card bill. Using that money to eliminate your family's outstanding debt is an easy way to boost your aid eligibility and improve your family's credit score. If your family is looking for extra cash to throw into a mortgage, IRA, or outstanding debt, try selling off some stock. Every dollar of capital gains earned through your stock portfolio subtracts from your aid eligibility. Encouraging your parents to sell stocks off during your sophomore year in high school then redistributing that cash into a financial aid-exempt fund can significantly help boost your aid eligibility.

3. Report the Right Figures

Break out the tax returns, it's FAFSA time. How you fill out the FAFSA form and when you turn it in are crucial in determining how much aid you receive. Grab your parents (and their financial information) and pay close attention, this handy dandy book will tell you how to fill out those forms to maximize your aid.

Step One: Get the Forms

Head to www.fafsa.ed.gov to download this year's form or simply pick one up from your high school career office or your future college's financial aid office. If you're already in school and you filed FAFSA last year, you'll need to download a FAFSA Renewal Form from www.fafsa.ed.gov/FOTWWebApp/complete004.jsp. If you can, fill out the forms online – 80% of the country does. Online FAFSA forms are typically processed faster than paper applications, giving you the best opportunity for first-come, first-serve money. Before you touch a FAFSA form, you'll need a PIN to get started. Head to www.pin.ed.gov to get your FAFSA PIN.

Step Two: Mark Your Calendar

To make sure you are in the running for all first-come, first-serve aid, write down your deadline, in several places around your house if necessary. Your FAFSA form should be turned in as soon as possible after January 1 of the year before you apply for school (typically during your senior year in high school) as you can.

Step Three: Organize the Paperwork

If you're a complete type A, this step should be a breeze. Everybody else hold on. Grab your parents, pull out those financial records, and get to work. Before you take pen to paper, you'll need to have following on hand:

- Both of your parent's federal income tax returns as well as IRS forms 1040, 1040A, 1040 EZ, and any foreign tax returns they filed this year or the previous year
- Both of your parent's W-2 forms and any IRS 1099 forms
- Records of any untaxed income (e.g. welfare checks, veterans benefits, social security, etc.)
- Your bank statements for the past 6 months
- Your driver's license
- Any investment records for both this year and the previous year. This includes (but isn't limited to) stock and/or bonds portfolio statements, mortgage statements, and home business records
- Records of any child support paid or received this year or last year
- Permanent residence card (if applicable)

Step Four: Read the Instructions and Get to Work

Once you've got your materials in front of you, filling out FAFSA is just a matter of plugging in numbers. The majority of the financial information on FAFSA will come directly from your tax returns, so you won't have to worry about doing many calculations...that is, if you actually have your tax returns in front of you. One of the most common problems families encounter is the fact that FAFSA is due long before most people receive their tax returns for that year. Getting around this is fairly simple – fake it...well, fake it intelligently. Families that haven't received their tax returns are advised to make educated estimations then file a correction once they receive their tax returns.

The key to filling out a successful FAFSA form – one that will land you the biggest aid check possible – is to read carefully and keep your eyes peeled (ew!). That means be aware of which sections are asking for information about the student and which are looking for information about the parent(s). [NOTE: In cases of divorce, the FAFSA will only ask for information about the parent that the student has lived with for the past 12 months; however, single parents are required to report any child support they've either given or received]. Families are also required to report any living allowances they currently receive as well as any cash payments made to the student by friends and relatives. When asked if the student would like to be considered for federal student loans and work-study, always say yes. This will qualify you for the maximum amount of aid and if you

Stuff Happens

And unfortunately there's not always a place on the FAFSA to tell your tale. If your family has experienced extenuating circumstances such as divorce, death, unexpected medical expenses, or loss of employment the year before you head off to college, a financial aid officer may be able to help you. Aid officers are like the barons of the free money world, lording a tremendous amount of power over the serfs' (that's you) financial aid packages. If your family has had tough times, put it in writing and make an appointment to speak with your school's financial aid counselor. Request a "professional judgment" review (sometimes called a "special circumstances" review) and bring along copies of third-party documentation of the circumstance.

Make it Simple

Low on cash? That could be to your benefit. Households with combined incomes of under $50,000 may be eligible to file a Simplified Needs Test along with the FAFSA form. In order to help middle to low-income families get the maximum amount of federal aid, the Simplified Needs Test totally ignores any financial assets (such as savings accounts, mutual funds, stocks, and bonds) your family may hold, thus making your Expected Family Contribution plummet. The lower your EFC, the bigger the financial aid check you can expect. Talk to your family's accountant or tax preparer to find out if your family qualifies for Simplified Needs.

Baby Bucks!

When it comes to financial aid, the bigger your family, the better. When filling out FAFSA, make sure to count unborn children in your final tally.

are offered a loan or position you simply don't want, you can always turn it down. The last thing to remember is just to be honest. FinAid.org reports that colleges are required to verify at least 30% of all FAFSA forms and many choose to verify all. Any little white lies that work their way onto your form could mean losing your entire aid package.

If you need additional help with FAFSA or have any further questions, the government provides a line-by-line breakdown of the FAFSA as well as answers to the most common FAFSA questions at http://studentaid.ed.gov/ students/publications/completing_fafsa/index.html.

Other Gifts From the Government: Tax Credits

Monetary treats from the federal government aren't limited to scholarships, grants, loans, and work-study jobs. If your family income is low enough and your educational bills are high enough, the federal government will grant your family up to $7,300 worth of tax breaks during your undergraduate tenure. Families with combined incomes of under $110,000 ($55,000 for single filer households) are eligible for not one, but two - count them, two - educational tax credits. The first and easiest to land is the Hope Scholarship, good for up to a $1,650 tax break per student per year for the first two years of higher education. To prevent families on full scholarships from cashing in, the Hope Scholarship is limited to families that are paying at least $2,200 out of pocket per year for educational expenses. The second, more elusive tax break is the Lifetime Learning Credit which provides up to a $2,000 deduction per household per year for families that shell out up to $10,000 or more per year in educational expenses. Families who pay less out of pocket for college will receive a prorated deduction (see why we said that this was the trickier one?). The same income phase-out rules apply; however, the Lifetime Learning Credit won't expire like the Hope Scholarship. You can claim it as long as you are pursuing a degree, whether it's a bachelor's degree or a doctorate. Families may not claim both tax credits in a single year. If your family is paying off a student loan, the deal keeps getting sweeter. In addition to the Hope Scholarship and the Lifetime Learning Credit, families may deduct up to $2,500 in student loan interest, provided that the combined income of the household is under $135,000 ($65,000 for single filers). Like everything else the IRS does, these tax credits are plagued with red tape and fine print. Www.irs.gov/publications/p970 and www.finaid.org/otheraid/tax.phtml will give you the skinny on educational tax credits or consult your accountant.

Military Aid

An easy way to pay for college is to give your body to the government. High school students looking to gain leadership training, a guaranteed job after college, and more financial aid than they can shake a stick at should check out their school's The Reserve Officers' Training Corps, ROTC for short. In exchange for completing military science courses and drilling requirements while in school as well as fulfilling a service obligation lasting anywhere from three to ten years after you graduate,the armed forces will pay all of your tuition, fees, and living expenses for all four years of college. The ROTC comes in three basic flavors - Army, Navy, and Air Force - and each branch has its own set of course and service requirements. The Coast Guard also offers a similar program called the College Student Pre-Commissioning Initiative, available to sophomores and above. Upon graduation, students in both programs enter the armed service as commissioned officers and get to skip the laborious process of working their way up the chain from being Privates. Students thinking of joining the ROTC should heavily consider whether they want to spend their first four years after college in the military. If you're thinking of jumping in, arrange a visit with at least one ROTC program and interview a couple of current ROTC students. For more info, contact the U.S. Air Force ROTC at www.afrotc.com or 1-866-423-7682, the Navy ROTC at www.nrotc.navy.mil or 1-800-NAV-ROTC, the Army ROTC at www.goarmy.com/rotc/ or 1-800-USA-ROTC, or the Coast Guard Pre-Commissioning Initiative at www.gocoastguard.com/cspi.html or 1-877-NOW-USCG.

For soldiers returning to the classroom either during or after completing active duty, the armed forces provides a wealth of educational benefits, most notably tuition reimbursement programs such as the Montgomery GI Bill (worth up to $1,075 per month for educational assistance), the Montgomery GI kicker (which can almost double the value of the GI Bill itself), and the Armed Forces Tuition Assistance Program (worth up to $4,500 per year). Additional educational benefits include student loan repayment programs and free access to higher educational testing such as CLEP exams. Specifics on what your branch offers can be found at Military.com.

Section Two: Virginia is For Lovers
(Of Cold, Hard, No Strings Attached Money)

Compared to most of the other 49 states, Virginia gets a fat A+ complete with a smiley face sticker when it comes to providing for their college-bound students. Not only does the state offer two state tax-exempt savings programs, it also doles out more than $160 million each year to fiscally help those who live in-state or who attend in-state schools. The good news about state aid is that Virginia offers both need and merit-based scholarship programs that are significantly less competitive than national awards. The downside is that applying for state aid is a bit more complicated than the federal aid application. Because Virginia offers more than 20 different scholarship and grant programs, each with their own eligibility requirements, students must apply to each program separately. What the state and the feds have in common is that both require students to submit a completed FAFSA form when applying for need-based aid (and you thought you could get out of the joy that is FAFSA). Students may also have to submit additional requirements such as residency documentation or a separate state aid application. Requirements for non-need based aid vary significantly from program to program. A list of Virginia scholarship and grant programs available to undergrad students as well as eligibility requirements and information on how to apply can be found in the Virginia Scholarships and Grants index of this book.

Watch the Market

By far the most underhyped aid program in the state, the Academic Common Market allows students to attend school out-of-state without getting financially punished for it. The Academic Common Market is a tuition reciprocation agreement between 16 southern states, Virginia being one of them. If you're interested in studying a subject that isn't offered by a public school in Virginia (underwater basket weaving not included), the ACM will allow you to attend a public school in another member state that does offer your major without charging you out-of-state tuition. Because the South offers a huge range of esoteric programs you won't find at the typical university (Agricultural Aviation, Polymer and Fiber Engineering, Jewish Studies, and Equine Administration for example), the Academic Common Market is your ticket to saving thousands on tuition. Of course some restrictions do apply. A few member schools only allow students to take advantage of the ACM discount after they have completed introductory courses in their program of study and some institutions limit the number of out-of-state students admitted. For all students, the Academic Common Market benefits only apply after the student has been admitted to an out-of-state school. After the student has received their acceptance letter, they may submit an ACM application. To get a full list of ACM's rules and restrictions and to download the application, head to www.schev.edu/Students/AcademicCommonMkt.asp?from=students.

6 Ways to Cut College Costs Without Federal or State Finacial Aid

1. **Make a Difference—**Either at home or abroad. Americorps, the Peace Corps, and Teach for America offer service rewards up to $9,450 to help pay for educational expenses as well as a 15% reduction on qualified student loans.

2. **Prepare Early—**Thanks to AP, IB, dual enrollment, and CLEP credits, students can enter college with a fistful of credits before they hand over that first tuition check. The Virginia Early College Scholars Program is a great way to start. Head to www.pen.k12.va.us/VDOE/senioryearplus/earlycollegescholars.shtml for more info.

3. **Market Yourself—**If you have to go out of state for school (ugh!), check out the Academic Common Market to see if your intended major will allow you to attend school out-of-state but pay in-state prices.

4. **Don't Forget Your Taxes—**Between the Hope Scholarship and the Lifetime Learning credit, you can claim up to $7,300 in tax credits without ever picking up a single scholarship application.

5. **Get a Job—**Specifically one at the college or university you'd like to attend. Schools such as the University of Richmond, UVA, and the College of William and Mary offer free courses to those who work on staff.

6. **Leave Town—**For those dead set on leaving the fine, fine state of Virginia for school, deferring your admittance for a year or two and moving to the state of your future school immediately could save you thousands. Spending the year before you attend school establishing residency could qualify you for in-state prices. Read up on each state's residency requirements here: ww.collegeboard.com/about/association/international/residency.html.

Section Three: Getting Institutionalized

Outside of the government, your college or university is your number one source for college funding, especially if you don't quality for need-based aid. Because schools create and operate on their own individual budget, the amount of financial aid available varies tremendously from institution to institution. In general, the more expensive the school, the more financial aid they have available for their students. In fact, the most expensive school in the state, the University of Richmond (a walloping $44,810 each year including room and board), offers full tuition scholarships to one out of every fifteen incoming freshmen and meets the demonstrated financial need of 100% of its applicants. Less than 40 schools across the country do that! Students looking to sip from the overflowing fountain of institutional money will need to complete a FAFSA and may need to submit a CSS PROFILE available at https://profileonline.collegeboard.com. Designed to get a little more personal with your financial situation than the FAFSA, the CSS PROFILE calculates financial need differently, taking things such as your home equity assets into consideration. The other major difference is that it'll cost you $5 just to fill out the CSS PROFILE and $18 to send it to a specific school or scholarship program. Pony up.

Section Four: Finding Funds Everywhere Else

Once you've exhausted the government, the state, and you're school, you'll have no choice but to turn elsewhere. Thankfully, there are a lot of elsewheres that offer money to college-bound kids. After filling out the FAFSA and PROFILE, most students turn their attention to the thousands and thousands of private scholarships offered in nearly every corner of the country. While sites such as Fastweb.com, Collegeboard.com, and Petersons.com will allow you to sift through the hoards of scholarships offered by nonprofits, corporations, faith-based organizations, and community programs; however, you'll be competing for these funds against the best and brightest students from across the country. Statistically, your best chance of landing any college money is to think locally then globally. Virginia offers a cornucopia of scholarships, grants, fellowships, and tuition reimbursement programs that are reserved for in-state students only. Let those out-of-state kids fend for themselves. A list of Virginia-only aid programs is available in Index #2 of this book. Head there first. After you've exhausted that list, search for scholarships in your own community then dip into the pool of national awards.

Fellowships, Assistantships, Internships, Practicums, and Co-ops: Earn While You Learn

There's more than one way to earn money while in school. Jobs offered in your major are fantastic ways to earn some cash, build up professional contacts, gain real-world work experience, and boost that resume all while earning credit. While some schools simply don't offer in-major positions, others offer deals from summer research stipends to grants for independent projects. The best place to find out more information about available positions is through an academic advisor in your major. Another potential cash route is seeking outside paid internships, cooperative learning programs, and private fellowships. Idealist.org, Internjobs.com, Fastweb.com, and Princeton Review's online internship search at www.princetonreview.com/cte/search/internshipAdvSearch.as p will help you find paid positions in your area of study. You'll also want to check out national chapters of professional associations and major companies in your field. Corporations and nonprofits alike (including the American Physiology Society, the National Institutes of Health, the U.S. Department of Energy, AT&T, and the Social Science Research Council) offer paid fellowships and research positions to eager undergrads willing to work for a buck.

Educational Awards, Loan Forgiveness, and Tuition Reimbursement Programs, OH MY!

If you've got a fever and the only cure is doing good for others, you may as well get paid for it. Teach for America, Americorps, VISTA, and the Peace Corps will give you a living stipend and work experience, an educational reward of up to $9,450 that can only be applied towards students loans or educational expenses, and the opportunity to knock 15% off of your Perkins Loan before you even start paying on it, all for the low, low cost of your blood, sweat, tears, and time. Besides the warm fuzzy feelings that come with working for a good cause, students who participate in any of the above programs also receive on-the-job training, the opportunity to experience new places, and an eye-catching addition to their resumes. The added bonus to working with these programs is that any money you receive won't subtract from your financial aid eligibility.

Educational awards programs aren't the only way to turn your debt into a scholarship. The federal government as well as private organizations throughout the country offer loan forgiveness programs aimed at drawing new post-grads into high-demand professions. How it works is simple. Young professional post-grads agree to work for a certain amount of time (usually two to five years) in an area where there's a critical labor shortage in exchange for a chunk, potentially all, of their student loans getting dismissed. The list below will give you an idea of how much loan forgiveness money is out there and who's handing it out.

Increasingly, employers are picking up the tuition slack as well. According to a survey conducted by Mercer Human Resource Consulting, 84% of all employers offer some form of tuition assistance or reimbursement. With tuition reimbursement programs, the catches are aplenty. Drawback number one is that you have to land the job first, a difficult task for students without a bachelor's degree, but great for adults returning to the classroom and post-grads eyeing graduate school. Secondly, most firms limit your options and will only reimburse you for coursework directly related to your current job. If you're a computer programmer, you'll have a much easier time scoring reimbursement money to brush up on your Vi-

Smells Like a Scam

Not all scholarship programs are made equal, or even legal for that matter. Thanks to the invention of the world wide web, scholarship scams have exploded in recent years, taking the hard-earned money of eager scholars across the country. To make sure you don't fall into the scholarship scam trap, here are four ways to spot a rat.

1 **Fees**—You should never have to pay for free money. Period. If your scholarship requires an entry, application, or registration fee, file that sucker straight in your trash can. The exception, of course, is the CSS Financial Aid PROFILE.

2 **Guarantees**—The cardinal rule of financial aid is that NOTHING is guaranteed. In fact, this book about financial aid could self-destruct in your hands at any second. THAT'S how precarious financial aid is. Organizations that make grandiose guarantees are most likely setting you up for a financial fall.

3 **Seminars and Consultations**—If you're offered a free financial aid consultation along with a scholarship application, be wary, but don't trash your application immediately. While some organizations like College Goal Sunday USA do offer legitimate consultations, most simply want to sell you something you don't need. Make some phone calls before you go to save yourself some stress.

4 **Credit Card Requirements**—If they need your credit card to process the application, you need to rip up that application immediately.

Before you send in any scholarship, grant, fellowship, or student loan application, do your research to make sure the agency and the award are legitimate. If you need a little scholarship-savvy help, consult your local librarian, college counselor, or financial aid officer.

sual Basic than you will to learn metal sculpting. Finally, tuition reimbursement programs are simply riddled with stipulations. Few firms will pay for all of your education, some companies will only provide reimbursement money after you've been with the organization for a certain number of years, and a few firms even require a written promise, stating that you will stay with the firm for a certain number of years after you've earned your new credential. Still, free money is free money and if you can earn a new degree on someone else's tab, it's a program worth checking out.

Private School Loans and Home Equity Lines of Credit

If you can't find free cash anywhere, take out a government loan. If that's not an option or if the government will only lend you cash to cover part of your expenses, you'll have to resort to private student loans and/or home equity lines of credit. Of the two, home equity lines of credit usually offer lower interest rates than private lenders and interest paid on a home equity loan is typically fully tax deductible, whereas you can only deduct up to $2,500 for interest paid on a student loan. A home equity line of credit is only possible if you own a home, meaning the loan would be in your

7 Jobs that ~~Pay~~ Cancel the Bills

Can't decide on a major? Consider these. The following professions offer loan forgiveness programs to post-grads going into the field.

1. **Clinical Researchers**—Whether you're into pediatric, infertility, or HIV research, the National Institutes of Health wants to help you pay off those student loans. Offering up to $70,000 in exchange for a two-year commitment, NIH's loan forgiveness programs are open to working pros, Ph.D.s, and grad students.

2. **Teachers**—Teachers who work in low-income, high-need areas are eligible to have up to 100% of their Perkins Loan and up to $17,500 of their Stafford Loan cancelled just for putting in 5 years of service. Head to www.tcli.ed.gov/CBSWebApp/tcli/TCLIPubSchoolSearch.jsp for a list of qualified low-income schools across the country.

3. **Health Care**—Calling all physical, mental, and behavioral health care professionals. The National Health Service Corps will foot all of your federal, state, and commercial student loans so long as you're willing to work in areas where there are health care shortages. Http://nhsc.bhpr.hrsa.gov/publications/faq-index.cfm is where you can get your specific questions answered or by calling (800) 221-9393.

4. **Military Careers**—Thanks to the Army National Guard, a sweet $20,000 student loan discount can be yours if you're willing to sport that camo. For more info, check out www.1800goguard.com or toll free at 1-800-Go-Guard.

5. **Nursing**—60% off of your student loans in exchange for working two years in hospitals, clinics, and nursing homes affected by nursing shortages. Tack on a third year and you could get an extra 25% on top of that! Http://bhpr.hrsa.gov/nursing/loanrepay.htm has the scoop.

6. **Social Workers**—Those with a passion for helping children are eligible for an awesome reward. Students with a BSW or higher that gain employment at a child welfare agency are eligible to have up to 90% of their Stafford loans forgiven. Ask your local agency if they qualify.

7. **Law Enforcement or Corrections Officer**—Forget paying off that pesky Perkins Loan. Up to 100% can be forgiven if you're up for putting in 5 years in a high-need area. 1-800-4-FED-AID has all the details.

parent's name and they would legally be responsible for making sure it gets paid. You would literally be indebted to them. Private lenders are another option; however, not all student loans are made equal. Finding a loan is easy (they're offered through all major banks as well as Sallie Mae, Nelnet, and other specialty finance firms), but to get the best deal, you'll have to do some serious shopping around, paying close attention to hidden charges such as origination, loan, and administrative fees as well as penalties that could be incurred for missing a payment or paying the loan back early. To save you a few phone calls and several headaches, head to Estudentloan.com to compare price tags or for a complete list of lenders, go to:
www.finaid.org/loans/privatestudentloans.phtml.

Offers on the Table

Congratulations! Both the application and the financial aid paperwork is done! WOO HOO! Now all you have to do is wait it out until April when you'll receive your aid offers. If you receive multiple aid offers, the key to picking the most lucrative package is to make sure you're comparing apples to apples. First figure out the total cost of attendance for each school. This number should include your tuition, room and board, books, transportation, computer and lab fees, club dues, fun money, the works, all multiplied by four for the number of years you'll be in school. To factor in tuition inflation, add in an extra $2,500 if you're attending an in-state public school or $5,000 if you're attending an out-of-state or private school. The mammoth number you're looking at is the amount you'll be expected to fork over to attend that school for four years. Once you've got your four-year total cost of attendance, add up the amount of free aid (not counting loans!) you've been offered from that school. Check to see if your scholarships, grants, fellowships, and work-study money is renewable (if so, multiply it by four or the number of years it may be renewed) and subtract your gift aid from the total cost of attendance.

Things You Should Know About Your Student Loan

1. **Federal or private**—Federal loans usually offer better interest rates, more flexible payment plans, and more opportunities to get your loan forgiven than private lenders.
2. **Subsidized or Un**—Are you responsible for all of the interest or will the government foot some of the bill while you're in school?
3. **In Case of Slip-Ups** – What happens if you miss a payment...or two...or twenty?
4. **The impact of your grades**—Many loans are tied to a students' enrollment status (full vs. part-time) and in some cases may also require a certain GPA. Ask before you deposit the cash.
5. **Payback Time** – How long will you have upon graduation to pay the total loan back?
6. **What's covered** – While some loans will only cover your tuition and fees, others will pay for your entire cost of attendance and then some.
7. **In case of emergency**—If you need to drop out or take a semester off, you'll need to know what happens to your student loan. Save yourself some stress and find out now.
8. **Start time** – When do you have to start making payments? Some loans require payment immediately while others give you a grace period after graduation.
9. **Your interest rage** – Is your interest rate fixed or variable depending on market conditions? – Answer this question and you'll have a much easier time planning your payments.
10. **The fees** – Hidden administrative and loan fees and financially kill you. To avoid getting hit with a surprise price tag, ask your loan officer to calculate the total amount you'll need to pay back before signing on the dotted line.
11. **Flexibility**—Can you increase the amount you can borrow in case of emergency?

Let's have a quick review. In case you're stumped on one, use the cost estimates listed below:

<table>
<tr><td>
Tuition: ________
Room and Board: ________
Books: ~$600 per year
+ Fees: ~$200 per year
Transportation: ~$200 per year
Club dues: ~$75 per year
Fun Money: ~$1,000 per year
</td><td>
Scholarships Offered: ________
Grants Offered: ________
+ Fellowships Offered: ________
Work-Study Offered: ~$3,000 per year
</td></tr>
<tr><td>Cost of Attendance for 1 Year: ________ X 4 years</td><td>Gift Aid for 1 Year: ________ X 4 years (if renewable)</td></tr>
<tr><td>Cost of Attendance for 4 Years ________
+ Tuition Inflation: ~$2,500 or ~$5,000</td><td rowspan="2">Total Gift Aid for 4 Years: ________</td></tr>
<tr><td>Total Cost of Attendance for 4 Years: ________</td></tr>
</table>

Total Cost of Attendance: ______ - Total Gift Aid: ________

=

How Much You'll Owe: ________

Now that you're left with the amount that will have to come from your own pocket, you can see if the loan package your school is offering truly is as appealing as it looks on paper. Repeat this delightful exercise for all schools that offered you moolah and you'll see who's willing to cough up the most for your presence. If you'd like a little help in the calculation department, check out FinAid's financial aid award comparison tool at www.finaid.org/calculators/awardletter.phtml.

Your Financial Aid Arsenal

The fight for financial aid is a war of knowledge. These three tools will help you figure out exactly how much money your family will need, how much you're eligible for, and how to financially brace yourself for the road ahead.

1. *The College Cost Calculator*—How much will you need? Find out here. The College Cost Calculator at www.finaid.org/calculators/howmuchtoborrow.phtml will help you estimate how much your family should be able to cover and how much you'll need.

SUMMER SAVINGS STRATEGY

A semester of college at one-third of the cost? Sign you up, right? The dream of saving pocketfuls of money can be your reality if and only if you plan your college tenure right. Almost all Virginia colleges and universities have some sort of transfer agreement with local community and two-year colleges, giving you the power to knock a few general education requirements out during the summer at a community college where the price is right, or at least right-er, than at most four-year schools. If you take just two courses per summer at a two-year school starting after your freshman year, that's 18 credits or one full college semester you can transfer in. An added bonus is that the state could pick up your community college tab. The Virginia Part-Time Assistance Grant offers students who have demonstrated financial need the opportunity to take 3 to 5 hours of community college for free. Before you high-tail it to your local community college, do your research and find out where your school has transfer agreements. An added bonus is that you may be eligible to get your community college classes paid for by the state. The Virginia Part-Time Assistance Grant offers students who have demonstrated financial need the opportunity to take 3-5 hours of community college credit on the state's tab. Before you high-tail it to your local community college, you'll have to ask your academic advisor which two-year schools your college accepts credits from, what exact courses will transfer in, and what paperwork you'll have to fill out before you enroll.

2. *The Expected Family Contribution Calculator*—Now that you know how much money you need, find out how much money your family is eligible for. Head to http://apps.collegeboard.com/fincalc/efc_welcome.jsp to get an estimate of how much the government expects your family to pitch in for college. Anything outside of this amount you can expect to take out in loans.

3. *The Student Loan Calculator*—Loans aren't the end of the world. The Student Loan Calculator at www.finaid.org/calculators/ loanpayments.phtml will help you figure out what your monthly payments will cost.

Lifestyles of the Rich and Strangest

You don't have to be the top student, the fastest athlete, or the most creative kid in class, to get free college cash.

Check out ten of the strangest scholarships available

1. Stuck at Prom Contest www.stuckatprom.com– Students who really want to show their fashion (and financial) sense can win college cash by wearing Duct Tape to prom. The couple that creates the coolest outfit and accessories out of the sticky stuff wins $3,000 each to blow on the college of their choice. Who knew adhesive could look this good?

2. The Kor Memorial Scholarship kli.org/scholarship– Designed to promote language study, the Klingon Language Institute offers a sweet $500 scholarship to students dedicated to promoting crosscultural (perhaps even intergalactic) communication.

3. Lillian and Arthur Dunn Scholarship www.dar.org–If your mother is a direct descendent of a patriot who fought in the American Revolution, you could bank big. Each year the Daughters of the American Revolution hands out $2,000 (renewable for up to four years) for children of current DAR members. Strap on your bayonet and get ready to cash in.

4. Excellence in Predicting the Future Award www.cenimar.com/contest/award.jsp–Luck in the markets translates to a slightly lighter tuition bill. Students who ace the Troy Studios stock market game can win $400 for higher education. While the pot is noticeably smaller than the other scholarships listed, Troy Studios picks a new winner every two months year-round, giving you a better shot at scoring loot.

5. The Patrick Kerr Skateboard Scholarship – www.skateboardscholarship.org - $5,000 could be yours if you can grind, carve, and ollie your way past the competition. Applicants must be "skateboarding activists that promote the sport in their community."

6. TCI Foundation Scholarship www.tcifoundation.org/scholarships.cfm– Short for Tall Clubs International, TCI offers up to $1,000 to female members over 5'10" and male members over 6'2". Just don't hit your head on the door frame on the way to collect your prize.

7. College Inventors Competition www.invent.org–On your mark, get set, invent! College students with a knack for building high-tech gadgets can win up to $25,000 as well as a trip to Washington D.C. and bragging rights to last a lifetime.

8. Make It Yourself With Wool Contest www.sheepusa.org–Those long hours spent perfecting your knit are about to pay off. Make an original garment that's both functional and fashionable and you could earn yourself up to $2,000 of college dough.

9. Ayn Rand Institute Essay Contest http://www.aynrand.org–Can't get enough of that sweet, sweet 20th century literature? Who can? Ayn aficionados can try their hand at scoring a slice of $70,000 in cash and prizes. Get ready to get literary.

10. Galaxy Music Scholarship www.spaacse.org–If you love music, specifically the type of music inspired by the beauty of our intricate universe, look no further. SPAACE, the Society of Performers, Artists, Athletes, and Celebrities for Space Exploration, offers $1,000 each year to the graduating high school senior who can write and perform the best original ambient space music. Far out man.

Chapter Five

Virginia College and University Guide

Your search for schools starts here. The next chapter will provide you with a snapshot of all 41 regionally accredited colleges and universities in Virginia. Although there are far more than 41 higher ed institutions in the state, the schools featured in this book are the only ones that come with a stamp of approval from the Southern Association of Colleges and Schools, the premier accrediting agency in the region. Before you delve any further, keep in mind that this is just a statistical snapshot designed to provide you with a general idea of what each school offers. Here's how each profile is broken down:

The Basics

In this section, you'll find logistical information about the size and location of each school as well as a few highlights on what each school has to offer. The average math/verbal SAT score for admitted students is also listed; however, this is only to give you a general idea of each school's selectivity level.

Admission Stats

Your guide to getting in. This section will provide you with a list of materials you'll need to apply as well as information on where you can go to obtain the necessary paperwork and when you should plan on mailing in that app. The average math/verbal SAT score for students admitted to each school is also listed; however, this is only provided to give you a general idea of how selective the school is. If your scores are lower than the figure listed, keep in mind that SAT scores are only one part of your application packet.

Life Off-Campus

Get info on the varsity sports and ROTC programs as well as a cross-section of clubs offered on campus. The percentage of students living on campus should give you an idea of whether you can expect a bustling residential campus community or a more commuter-based campus.

Financial Stats

The dirt on how much each school costs for both full and part-time students. If the school seems out of your price range, look beyond the sticker price at the percentage of students receiving financial aid. Even if the tuition tag is high, the school may be able to offer a generous financial aid package that compensates.

Extra Credit

Like what you see? Here's a list of other Virginia schools that have comparable admissions criteria and offer similar academic programs.

Academic Life On-Campus

Kicks off with an alphabetical list of each school's majors with concentrations for those majors listed in parentheses. If you're planning on graduate or professional school after the undergrad life, the list of pre-professional programs will give you an idea of how well the school profiled can cater to your career aspirations. While the average class size and faculty/student ratio will give you a glimpse of how classes work on campus, the retention rate will tell you what percentage of students return after their freshman year.

The Art Institute of Washington

www.artinstitutes.edu/arlington

1820 North Fort Myer Drive, Arlington, VA 22209 Admissions Office: (703) 358-9550, aiwadm@aii.edu

The Basics

Type of School: Private

Type of Campus: Urban

Size: 1,616

Male/Female Ratio: 57/43

Diversity: 75%

Out of State Students: 60%

FYI: Don't let the name fool you. Based in Arlington, VA, The Art Institute of Washington is the artistic hub of the state. Providing mind-blowingly awesome facilities (the full-scale Television Studio and Sound Stage for example) as well as an urban location perfect for interning and meeting future employers, AI Washington gives its enrollees the opportunity to explore their creative sides and gain practical industry experience. To help you build a portfolio of work that can land you jobs in the post-grad world, the school offers the Community Arts Resource Exchange program which pairs art students up with nonprofit organizations and community groups in need of a little design help. After the project is over, students walk away with a bit of real-world experience under their belts and something to show future employers.

Admission Stats:

Admissions Deadlines: Rolling

How to Apply: Apply online at: https://www.applyweb.com/apply/aiw/ or call (703) 358-9550 to obtain a paper application.

Accepts the Common Application: No

Application Requirements: Online or paper application, $50 application fee, high school transcript and profile, SAT or ACT scores, essay, admissions interview, portfolio of work required for scholarship applicants.

Average SAT Score: Information Not Available

Academic Life on Campus:

Honors program: No

Majors Offered: Advertising, Audio Production, Digital Filmmaking and Video Production, Fashion and Retail Management, Game Art and Design, Graphic Design, Interactive Media Design, Interior Design, Media Arts and Animation, Photographic Imaging, Visual and Game Programming

Pre-professional Programs:

None

Teacher Licensure Program: No

Retention Rate: 56%

Student/Teacher Ratio: 20:1

Average Class Size: Information Not Available

Cool Programs: Upperclassmen mentoring program, student leadership program, study abroad, independent studies courses, Community Arts Resource Exchange program.

Distance Learning Options: Yes

Financial Stats:

Undergraduate In-State Tuition: $20,070 full time, ($18,223 for Visual and Game Programming Majors), $418 per credit hour ($375 for Visual and Game Programming Majors)

Room and Board Fees: $9,500

Yearly Cost of Attendance: $31,564

% Receiving Financial Aid: Information Not Available

Life Off-Campus:

Living on campus: Information Not Available

ROTC Programs: None

Varsity Sports: None

Sports level: N/A

Cool Clubs: Culinary Club, Comic Book Club, Video Game Club, Sculpture of Animation club, Design Theory club.

Extra Credit: Shenandoah University, Virginia Commonwealth University, James Madison University

Averett University www.averett.edu

420 West Main Street, Danville, VA 24541
Admissions Office: (434) 791-4996, 1-800-AVERETT, admit@averett.edu

The Basics

Type of School: Private
Type of Campus: Suburban
Size: 800 traditional undergrads, 2,467 total

Male/Female Ratio: 51/49
Diversity: 28% minority
Out of State Students: 32%

FYI: Averett defies the one size fits all mentality. Designed to fulfill the needs of a wide demographic of students, this Christian university offers undergraduate programs for traditional students as well as statewide accelerated degree programs for working adults. No matter where you're located or how you learn, Averett has something to accommodate everyone. The school's IDEAL program allows adult learners to develop their own personal academic plan with the help of Averett advisors. Combining on-campus courses, correspondence courses, classes at other accredited universities, and independent studies courses, adults can earn their degree from almost anywhere on Earth.

Admission Stats:

Admissions Deadlines: Rolling Admissions

How to Apply: Apply online at:
http://www.averett.edu/admissions/entrance-requirements.html
or request a paper application at:
http://www.averett.edu/admissions/form/paperform.php

Average GPA: 3.14

Accepts the Common Application: No

Application Requirements: Online or paper application. High School transcript, SAT or ACT scores. TOEFL required for International students.
Average SAT Score: 988

Academic Life On-Campus:

Honors program: Yes

Majors Offered: Aeronautics (Aerospace Management, Aerospace Management/Criminal Justice, Aviation Business, Aviation Maintenance Operations, Aviation Technical Systems Flight Operations), Art (Studio), Biology (Biomedical Sciences, Ecology/Environmental Biology, Radiologic Technology), Business (Accounting, Global Marketing Management, Finance, Management Science, Business Administration), Chemistry (Biochemistry, General, Chemistry), Computer Information Systems, Computer Science, Criminal Justice, English (English, General, English with Teaching 6-12, English/History, English/Theatre), Environmental Sciences, Equestrian Studies (Equestrian Studies: Dressage, Equestrian Studies: Eventing, Equestrian Studies: Management, Equestrian Studies: Business Administration), History History, General, History & Politics), Human-Computer Interaction, Journalism, Mathematics (Mathematical Decision Sciences, General Mathematics), Medical Technology, Music (Choral Music, Music Performance), Physical Education (Athletic Training, Sport Management, Wellness/Sports Medicine), Political Science, Pre-Law (English/History), Psychology (Biological Psychology, Counseling and Clinical, Cognitive Science, Industrial/Organizational), Religion, Sociology (General Sociology, Sociology/Criminal Justice), Theatre (Theatre Arts)

Pre-professional Programs:

Law

Teacher Licensure Program: Yes

Retention Rate: 62%

Student/Faculty Ratio: 12:1

Average Class Size: 13

Cool Programs: Study abroad, independent studies courses, IDEAL program for adult learners, non-traditional program for working adults

Distance Learning Options: Yes

Financial Stats:

Undergraduate In-State Tuition: $19,512 full time (12-21 credits), $650 per credit hour for less than 9 hours.

Room and Board Fees: $7,100

Yearly Cost of Attendance: $28,612

Receiving Financial Aid: 95%

Averett Continued

Life Off-Campus:

Living On-Campus: 53%

ROTC: None

Varsity Sports: Baseball, basketball (m/w), cross country (m/w), football, golf (m), lacrosse (w), soccer (m/w), softball, tennis (m/w), volleyball (w)

Sports level: NCAA Division III

Cool Clubs: The Ember literary magazine, Fellowship of Christian Athletes, Habitat for Humanity, Writer's Folio Club

Extra Credit: Hampton University, Old Dominion University, Norfolk State University

Bluefield College

www.bluefield.edu
3000 College Drive, Bluefield, VA 24605
Admissions Office: (800) 872-0175, admissions@bluefield.edu

The Basics

Type of School: Private
Type of Campus: Small Town
Size: 775 undergrads

Male/Female Ratio: 40/60
Diversity: 11% minority
Out of State Students: 6%

FYI: Looking for a college where everybody knows your name? This is the place. With only 775 students on campus, Bluefield College is more like an academic family than a large, impersonal campus. Don't worry about falling through the cracks here. Bluefield caters to students from a wide variety of backgrounds and provides undergraduate programs as well as distance learning programs designed specifically for adult learners. Students looking for a Christ-centered education will have fantastic opportunities here. Bluefield offers programs in Christian Studies, Christian Drama, and Church Music.
Notable Names: Nobel Prize-winning economist John F. Nash, Jr.

Admission Stats:

Admissions Deadlines: Rolling Admissions

How to Apply: Apply online or download an application at: www.bluefield.edu/applynow

Accepts the Common Application: No

Application Requirements: Online or paper application, $30 application fee, high school transcript, SAT or ACT scores
Optional: Essay or personal statement, letters of recommendation

Average SAT Score: 920

Academic Life On-Campus:

Honors program: Yes

Majors Offered: Behavioral Science, Biology (Biological Studies, Pre-Health Professions), Business (Accounting, Information Technology, Management), Chemistry, Christian Drama, Christian Studies, Communications (Mass Communications, Print Journalism), Criminal Justice (Law Enforcement/Corrections/Probation, Pre-Law track), English (Literature, Writing), Exercise and Sport Sciences (Physical Education, Sport Management/Recreation, Sports Medicine), Graphic Communication, History, Mathematics, Music (Applied Music, Church Music, General Music, Music Education), Organizational Management and Leadership, Psychology, Social Studies, Theatre Arts, Visual Art

Pre-professional Programs:

Health Professions, Law

Teacher Licensure Program: Yes

Retention Rate: 58%

Student/Faculty Ratio: 14:1

Average Class Size: 20

Cool Programs: Study abroad, Student exchange program in Somerset, England, community fine arts school on campus

Distance Learning Options: Yes

Bluefield Continued

Financial Stats:

Undergraduate In-State Tuition: $12,550 full time, $410 per credit hour

Room and Board Fees: $6,294

Yearly Cost of Attendance: $20,844

Receiving Financial Aid: 94%

Life Off-Campus:

Living On-Campus: 26%

ROTC: None

Varsity Sports: Baseball, basketball (m/w), golf (m), soccer (m/w), softball, volleyball (w)

Sports level: National Association of Intercollegiate Athletics

Cool Clubs: Appalachian Trail Hiking Club, Bluefield College Art Club, Student Ambassadors, Fellowship of Christian Athletes, Intramural Billiards teams

Extra Credit: Ferrum College, Radford University, Bridgewater College

Bridgewater College www.bridgewater.edu

402 East College Street, Bridgewater, VA 22812
Admissions Office: (800) 759-8328, admissions@bridgewater.edu

The Basics

Type of School: Private
Type of Campus: Small Town
Size: 1,514 undergrads

Male/Female Ratio: 44/56
Diversity: 13% minority
Out of State Students: 22%

FYI: Bridgewater aims to educate the whole student, not just the academic side. To make sure you're getting a well-rounded liberal arts education, all students are required to create a personal development portfolio that reflects your academic, cultural, service learning, career, and co-curricular accomplishments for each year of enrollment. Consider this encouragement to get involved with an on-campus play, start your own student organization, or put in a few volunteer hours with a local charity. You'll meet new people, try new things, and learn a little something all while making the grade.
Notable Names: Supreme Court of Virginia Justice G. Steven Agee

Admission Stats:

Admissions Deadlines: Rolling

How to Apply: Apply online or download an application at: http://www.bridgewater.edu/index.php?id=19

Accepts the Common Application: No

Average SAT Score:1014

Application Requirements: Online or paper application, $30 application fee (waived for electronic applicants and those that attend Bridgewater's Open House), high school transcript, SAT or ACT scores, letter of recommendation from guidance counselor or principal, letter of recommendation from other source, health record
Optional: Essay or personal statement

Academic Life On-Campus:

Honors program: Yes

Majors Offered: Allied Health Sciences, Athletic Training, Art (Graphic Design Digital Media, Photography Digital Media, Studio), Biology (General Biology, Pre-Medicine, Medical Technology, Veterinary Medicine), Business Administration (Accounting, Finance, International Commerce, Marketing, Organizational Management), Chemistry, Communication Studies (General Communication Studies, Media Studies, Public Relations), Computer Science, Economics (Business, Government Policy, Pre-graduate School), English (Language and Literature, Literary Studies, Writing), Environmental Science, Family and Consumer Sciences, Foreign Language (French, Spanish), Health and Exercise Science, Health and Physical Education, History (General History, History and Political Science), Information Systems Management, International Studies, Liberal Studies, Mathematics, Music (Applied Music, Music Education), Nutrition and Wellness, Philosophy and Religion, Physics (Applied Physics, General Physics, Physics and Mathematics), Political Science, Psychology, Sociology

Bridgewater Continued

Pre-professional Programs:

Law, Medicine, Veterinary Medicine

Teacher Licensure Program: Yes

Retention Rate: 73%

Student/Faculty Ratio: 14:1

Average Class Size: 19

Cool Programs: Study abroad, joint degree programs, personal development portfolio program, independent studies courses, transitional college course for first-year students, student leadership program, Intersecting With the Past study abroad program in Athens, Greece

Distance Learning Options: No

Financial Stats:

Undergraduate In-State Tuition: $21,490 full time, $716 per credit hour

Room and Board Fees: $9,310

Yearly Cost of Attendance: $33,470

Receiving Financial Aid: 99%

Life Off-Campus:

Living On-Campus: 81%

ROTC Programs: None

Varsity Sports: Baseball, basketball (m/w), cross country (m/w), equestrian (m/w), field hockey, football, golf (m), lacrosse (w), soccer (m/w), softball, tennis (m/w), track and field (m/w), volleyball (w)

Sports level: NCAA Division III

Cool Clubs: Equitation Club, Outdoorsmen Club, Forensics and Debate Team, Interdistrict Youth Cabinet, International Club, Students in Free Enterprise

Extra Credit: Christopher Newport University, Mary Baldwin College, Bluefield College

Christendom College www.christendom.edu

134 Christendom Drive, Front Royal, VA 22630
Admissions Office: (800) 877-5456, admissions@christendom.edu

The Basics

Type of School: Private
Type of Campus: Rural
Size: 400 undergrads

Male/Female Ratio: 48/52
Diversity: 5% minority
Out of State Students: 75%

FYI: Christendom College is taking it back to the old school...the really old school. Rooted in Roman Catholic tradition and the teachings of St. Thomas Aquinas, Christendom students follow a classic liberal arts curriculum, kicking off their college tenure by focusing on theology, philosophy, and language (specifically Hebrew, Latin, or Greek), then moving into one of the school's six majors. By the time students hit their junior year, they'll be ready to see the hub of Western tradition first-hand. Christendom's Junior Semester in Rome provides an opportunity for all students to get up close and personal with Western thought in the making and still graduate on time.

Admission Stats:

Admissions Deadlines: Early Action – Dec. 1, Regular and Transfer Admissions – March 1, (Jan. 15 for priority consideration)

How to Apply: Apply online or download an application at: http://www.christendom.edu/admissions/index.shtml

Accepts the Common Application: No

Average SAT Score:1130

Application Requirements: Online or paper application, $25 application fee, high school transcript, SAT or ACT scores, two letters of recommendation, preferably one from a teacher, essay Optional: SAT II test scores

Christendom Continued

Academic Life On-Campus:

Honors program: No

Majors Offered: Classical and Early Christian Studies, English Literature, History, Philosophy, Political Science and Economics (Political Science and Economics track, Politics track), Theology

Pre-professional Programs:

Seminary

Teacher Licensure Program: No

Retention Rate: 90%

Student/Faculty Ratio: 12:1

Average Class Size: 20

Cool Programs: Study abroad, senior capstone courses, Great Books curriculum, Junior Semester in Rome, Extensive Speakers program offered on campus every year

Distance Learning Options: No

Financial Stats:

Undergraduate: $17,270 full time, $715 per credit hour

Room and Board Fees: $6,370

Yearly Cost of Attendance: $26,090

Receiving Financial Aid: 52%

Life Off-Campus:

Living On-Campus: 95%

ROTC Programs: None

Varsity Sports: Baseball, basketball (m/w), soccer (m/w), softball, volleyball (w)

Sports level: United States Collegiate Athletic Association

Cool Clubs: Intramural Wallyball, Oratory group, Christendom Literary Club, St. Genesius Society Players

Extra Credit: Hollins University, Randolph College, Emory and Henry College

Christopher Newport University www.cnu.edu

1 University Place, Newport News, VA 23606 Admissions Office: (800) 333-4CNU, admit@cnu.edu
Instant Message Name: Askcnu on AIM or Yahoo

The Basics

Type of School: Public
Type of Campus: Suburban
Size: 4,622 undergrads, 4,793 total

Male/Female Ratio: 46/54
Diversity: 16% minority
Out of State Students: 3.5%

FYI: Kiss rote memorization goodbye. Christopher Newport classes are tiny and more than 90% are taught in a seminar style, meaning you can count on eye-opening discussions. Learning here doesn't stop when class is over. In addition to the 100+ student organizations you'll find on campus, CNU also hosts the annual Ella Fitzgerald Music Festival which brings in internationally-recognized performers such as Andrea Bocelli, David Copperfield, and B. B. King

Admission Stats:

Admissions Deadlines: Early Action – Dec. 1, Regular and Transfer Admissions – March 1

How to Apply: Apply online or download an application at http://admissions.cnu.edu/undergraduateAdmissions/applyAsAFreshman.cfm; Transfers apply on-line at: http://registrar.cnu.edu/transferguide/tg_home.html

Accepts the Common Application: No

Average SAT Score:1165

Application Requirements: Online or paper application, $45 application fee, high school transcript, SAT or ACT scores, In-state Tuition Form for VA residents
Optional: letters of recommendation, resume of activities, personal statements, portfolio, or other relevant material

Christopher Newport Continued

Academic Life On-Campus:

Honors program: Yes

Majors Offered: Accounting, Biology, Chemistry, Communication Studies, Computer Engineering, Computer Foundations (Applied Physics, Computer Science), Economics, English (Creative Writing, Journalism, Language Arts, Literature, Technical Writing, Writing), Environmental Science, Finance, Fine Arts (Studio Art, Art History), Foreign Language (French, German, Spanish), History, Information Science, Interdisciplinary Studies, Management, Marketing, Mathematics, Music (History/Literature, Music Ed/Instrumental, Music Ed/Choral, Performance, Theory/Composition), Philosophy (Critical Thinking, General, Indic Studies, Pre-Seminary Studies, Religious Studies, Values and Professions), Ornamental Horticulture, Political Science, Psychology, Sociology (Anthropology, Criminology, Culture & Society, General), Social Work, Theatre Arts (Acting, Arts Administration, Design/Technology, Directing/Dramatic Literature, Music/Dance)

Pre-professional Programs:

Dentistry, Law, Medicine, Optometry, Pharmacy, Physical Therapy, Seminary Studies, Veterinary Medicine

Teacher Licensure Program: Yes

Retention Rate: 79%

Student/Faculty Ratio: 17:1

Average Class Size: 25

Cool Programs: Study abroad, undergraduate research opportunities, independent study courses, first-year residential learning communities, upperclassmen mentoring program, student-designed majors, first year seminars, member of the Virginia Tidewater Consortium along with the College of William and Mary, Norfolk State University, Old Dominion University, and Virginia Wesleyan College

Distance Learning Options: No

Financial Stats:

Undergraduate: $7,050 full time, $294 per credit hour

Room and Board Fees: $8,700

Yearly Cost of Attendance: $17,750

Receiving Financial Aid: 58%

Life Off-Campus:

Living On-Campus: 60%

ROTC Programs: Army

Cool Clubs: Irish Culture Club, Disc Golf Club, Ice Hockey Club, Pershing Rifles (Professional Rifles Fraternity), Young Constitutionalists

Varsity Sports: Baseball (m), basketball (m/w), cheerleading, cross country, field hockey, football, golf, lacrosse (m/w), rugby, sailing, soccer (m/w), softball, tennis (m/w), track and field, volleyball

Sports level: NCAA Division III

Extra Credit: Longwood University, Old Dominion University, University of Mary Washington

College of William & Mary www.wm.edu

P.O. Box 8795, Williamsburg, VA 23187-8795
Admissions Office: (757) 221-4223, admiss@wm.edu

The Basics

Type of School: Public
Type of Campus: Small City
Size: 5,500 undergrads, 7,500 total

Male/Female Ratio: 46/54
Diversity: 31.5% minority
Out of State Students: 34%

FYI: Harvard Schmarvard, William and Mary is the only school in the country deemed a "Public Ivy," giving you all of the academic opportunities afforded by an Ivy League school at one-quarter of the price. The equation is simple – top-ranking professors (89% of whom hold their terminal degrees) plus small classes (12:1 student-faculty ratio) plus phenomenal academic programs (like summer field school in archaeology, student exchange programs from Australian to Taiwan, and seminars specially designed for first year students) equals powerhouse alumni well prepared for the world ahead.
Notable Names: George Washington, James Monroe, Thomas Jefferson, John Tyler, Henry Clay, Winfield Scott, Jon Stewart, Gateway, Inc. founder J. Edward Coleman, Glenn Close, and designer Perry Ellis, U.S. Secretary of Defense Robert Gates

William & Mary Continued

Admission Stats:

Admissions Deadlines: Early Decision – Nov. 1, Regular Admissions – Jan. 1, Transfer Admissions – Feb 15 (fall semester), Nov. 1 (spring semester)

How to Apply: Apply online or download an application at http://www.applyweb.com/apply/wm/

Accepts the Common Application: Yes

Average SAT Score: 1355

Application Requirements: Online or paper application, $60 application fee, high school transcript, SAT or ACT scores, recommendation from guidance counselor, In-state Tuition Form for VA residents, the William and Mary Supplement to The Common Application (if applicable)
Optional: SAT II Subject Tests, teacher recommendations, photo, creative or performing arts submissions

Academic Life On-Campus:

Honors program: Yes

Majors Offered: American Studies, Anthropology, Applied Science, Biology, Black Studies, Business Administration (Individualized Program of Study), Chemistry, Classical Studies (Latin, Greek, Hebrew), Computer Science, Economics, English, Environmental Science, Film Studies, Fine Arts (Studio Art, Art History), Geology, Global Studies, Government, History, International Relations (International Relations and separate concentrations in African, East Asian, European, Latin American, Middle Eastern and Russian Studies), Kinesiology, Linguistics, Literary and Cultural Studies, Mathematics, Medieval and Renaissance Studies, Military Science, Modern Languages (Arabic, Chinese, French, German, Hispanic Studies, Italian, Japanese, Russian), Music, Neuroscience, Philosophy, Physics, Psychology, Public Policy, Religious Studies, Sociology, Theatre, Speech, and Dance, Women's Studies

Pre-professional Programs:

Law, Medicine

Teacher Licensure Program: Yes

Retention Rate: 95%

Student/Faculty Ratio: 11:1

Average Class Size: 30

Cool Programs: Study abroad, first-year seminars, undergraduate research opportunities, independent studies courses, themed housing for students with common interests, student-designed majors, independent studies courses, paid summer independent research opportunities, first-year service learning projects, member of the Virginia Tidewater Consortium along with Christopher Newport University, Norfolk State University, Old Dominion University, and Virginia Wesleyan College

Distance Learning Options: No

Financial Stats:

Undergraduate: $9,164 full time, $208 per credit hour

Room and Board Fees: $8,134

Yearly Cost of Attendance: $19,298

Receiving Financial Aid: 51%

Life Off-Campus:

Living On-Campus: 76%

ROTC Programs: Army

Varsity Sports: Baseball, basketball (m/w), cheerleading, cross country (m/w), football field hockey, football, golf (m/w), gymnastics (m/w), lacrosse (w), soccer (m/w), swimming and diving (m/w), tennis (m/w), track and field (m/w), volleyball (w)
Sports level: NCAA Division I

Cool Clubs: Capture the Flag Team, Ballroom Dancing Club, Composer's League, Global Village Project, Dance Dance Revolution Club, Independent Filmmakers Club, Metal Club, Shakespeare in the Dark

Extra Credit: University of Virginia, Hollins University, University of Richmond

Eastern Mennonite University www.emu.edu

1200 Park Road, Harrisonburg, VA 22802
Admissions Office: (800) 368-2665, admiss@emu.edu

The Basics

Type of School: Private
Type of Campus: Small City
Size: 900 undergrads, 1,660 total

Male/Female Ratio: 40/60
Diversity: 20% minority
Out of State Students: 52%

FYI: Getting involved is what EMU students do best. The school prides itself on giving enrollees a global, socially-conscious education. All EMU students are required to participate in some form of cross-cultural study, whether it be trekking the Himalayas on a study abroad trip or spending a semester interning in our nation's capital. Each semester, EMU also offers community learning courses that combine in-class coursework with service learning opportunities through local organizations. If the opportunity you're looking for doesn't exist, make it. EMU's service learning mini-grants allow students to make an impact any way they see fit.

Admission Stats:

Admissions Deadlines: Rolling Admissions, January 1st for best shot at scholarships

How to Apply: Apply online or download an application at: http://www.emu.edu/admissions/apply/

Accepts the Common Application: No
Average SAT Score: 1101

Application Requirements: Online or paper application, $25 application fee, high school transcript, SAT or ACT scores, letter of recommendation

Academic Life On-Campus:

Honors program: Yes

Majors Offered: Accounting, Art (Art Education, Studio Art), Biology (Biochemistry, Environmental Science, General Biology, International Agriculture, Medical Technology, Pre-Med), Business Administration, Chemistry, Communication, Computer Information Systems, Computer Science, Digital Media, Economics, English, Foreign Language (French, Spanish), History (General History, History and Social Science, Pre-Law), International Business, Justice, Peace, and Conflict Studies, Liberal Arts, Mathematics (Applied Mathematics, Pre-Engineering), Music (Church Music, Music Education, Music Performance), Nursing, Photography, Physical Education, Psychology, Theatre

Pre-professional Programs:

Dentistry, Engineering, Health Sciences, Law , Medicine, Seminary, Veterinary Medicine

Teacher Licensure Program: Yes

Retention Rate: 74%

Student/Faculty Ratio: 11:1

Average Class Size: 25

Cool Programs: Study abroad, student-designed majors, independent studies courses, undergraduate research opportunities, Semester in Washington program, EMU Shenandoah Valley Bach festival

Distance Learning Options: Yes

Financial Stats:

Undergraduate: $21,860 full time, $915 per credit hour

Room and Board Fee: $6,900

Yearly Cost of Attendance: $30,860

Receiving Financial Aid: 97%

Life Off-Campus:

Living On-Campus: 44%

ROTC Programs: None

Varsity Sports: Baseball, basketball (m/w), cross country (m/w), field hockey, soccer (m/w), softball, tennis (m/w), track and field (m/w), volleyball (m/w)

Sports level: NCAA Division III

Cool Clubs: Cycling Club, Future Leaders of Equality & Diversity, Peace Fellowship, Table Tennis Club, Social Work is People club

Extra Credit: George Mason University, Bridgewater College, Randolph-Macon College

ECPI College of Technology www.ecpi.edu

Locations in Virginia Beach, Newport News, Manassas, Richmond, Glen Allen, and Roanoke, VA
Admissions Office: (888) 526-4654

The Basics

Type of School: Private
Type of Campus: Varies
Size: Varies From Campus to Campus

Male/Female Ratio: Varies
Diversity: Varies
Out of State Students: Varies

FYI: This is where tech-heads come to get career training. Ditching liberal arts curriculums entirely, ECPI only provides technology-based degree and certificate programs. Catering to working adults, the school offers online as well as night courses to fit your schedule. ECPI's flexible class times and reasonable price tag have become a hit among those seeking better credentials. Community College Week magazine reports that ECPI awards more Computer, Information Sciences, and Support Services associate's degree graduates than any other institution in the country.

Admission Stats:

Admissions Deadlines: Rolling

How to Apply: Call (888) 526-4654 to obtain an application

Accepts the Common Application: No

Average SAT Score: Not required

Application Requirements: Admissions test, proof of high school diploma or GED

Academic Life On-Campus:

Honors program: No

Majors Offered: Information Systems, Network and Security Management, Simulation and Game Programming, Web Design

Pre-professional Programs:

None

Teacher Licensure Program: No

Retention Rate: Varies

Student/Faculty Ratio: Day campuses approximately 20:1; Evening classes approximately 14:1

Average Class Size: Varies

Distance Learning Options: Yes

Financial Stats:

Undergraduate: $4,950 including books and fees

Room and Board Fees: None

Yearly Cost of Attendance: Averages $9,900 including books and fees

Receiving Financial Aid: Varies

Life Off-Campus:

Living On-Campus: None

ROTC Programs: None

Varsity Sports: None

Sports level: N/A

Cool Clubs: None Offered

Emory and Henry College www.ehc.edu

PO Box 947, Emory, VA 24327
Admissions Office: (800) 848-5493, ehadmiss@ehc.edu

The Basics

Type of School: Private
Type of Campus: Rural
Size: 1,000 undergraduates

Male/Female Ratio: 50/50
Diversity: 20% minority
Out of State Students: 70%

FYI: E&H expects a lot out of its students from the day they step foot on campus. All E&H enrollees complete a four-year writing-intensive Liberal Arts Foundation curriculum, designed to provide the student with a solid background in Western thought and tradition. Students are expected to complete their chosen major plus a minor or second major. Additionally, the school also boasts 9 study abroad programs, an extensive undergraduate research program, service-learning opportunities (complete with community service scholarships), and nearly 100 cultural programs every year. It's like a knowledge buffet. Hope you're hungry.
Notable Names: Dr. Jack Roper, winner of the 2005 Carnegie Foundation Virginia Professor of the Year Award. E&H has had more VA Professors of the Year than any other school in the state.

Admission Stats:

Admissions Deadlines: Early Decision - Nov. 1, Regular Admissions - Rolling

How to Apply: Apply online or download an application at: http://www.ehc.edu/admissions/howtoapply.html

Accepts the Common Application: No

Average SAT Score: 1065

Application Requirements: Online or paper application, $30 application fee, high school transcript, SAT or ACT scores, letter of recommendation
Optional: Admissions interview

Academic Life On-Campus:

Honors program: Yes

Majors Offered: Anthropology, Art (Art Education, Graphic Design, Studio), Biology, Business Administration, Chemistry, Computer Information Management, Economics, English (Interdisciplinary English, Literature, Literature and Creative Writing), Foreign Language (French, Spanish), Geography (Geography, Social Sciences), History (General History, Public History, Social Sciences), Management (Accounting, General Management), Mass Communication (Corporate Communication, Electronic Media, General Media Studies, Print Communication, Visual Communication), Mathematics, Music (Church Music, Instrument Performance, Music Education, Piano, Vocal Performance), Philosophy, Physical Education (Athletic Training, Physical Education, Sport Management), Political Science (American Politics, Comparative and International Politics, Interdisciplinary Political Science, Law and Politics), Psychology, Religion, Sociology, Theatre

Pre-professional Programs:

Engineering, Law, Medicine

Teacher Licensure Program: Yes

Retention Rate: 70%

Student/Faculty Ratio: 11:1

Average Class Size: Information Not Available

Cool Programs: Study abroad, undergraduate research opportunities, first-year curriculum, student-designed majors, independent studies courses, peer mentoring program

Distance Learning Options: No

Financial Stats:

Undergraduate: $22,320 full time, $930 per credit hour

Room and Board Fees: $7,670

Yearly Cost of Attendance: $31,990

Receiving Financial Aid: 98%

Emory & Henry Continued

Life Off-Campus:

Living On-Campus: 65%

ROTC Programs: None

Varsity Sports: Baseball, basketball (m/w), cross country (m/w), field hockey, football, golf, soccer (m/w), softball, tennis (m/w), swimming (w), volleyball (w)

Sports level: NCAA Division III

Cool Clubs: Dance Team, Ecology Club, Lions Club, Outdoor Leadership Program, Ultimate Frisbee Team, WEHC-FM radio station

Extra Credit: Sweet Briar College, Mary Baldwin College, Roanoke College

Ferrum College www.ferrum.edu

P.O. Box 1000, Ferrum, VA 24327
Admissions Office: (800) 868-9797, admissions@ferrum.edu

The Basics

Type of School: Private
Type of Campus: Rural
Size: 1,060 undergraduates

Male/Female Ratio: 58/42
Diversity: 38% minority
Out of State Students: 15%

FYI: Get ready to E-xpress yourself at Ferrum. All Ferrum students are required to complete two E-terms (short for Experiential Terms) prior to graduation. Designed as a break from the normal classroom routine, E-terms are intensive three-week courses offered in a variety of majors that focus on providing students with a hands-on education. In addition to in-class assignments, E-term students find themselves conducting research alongside faculty mentors, traveling the world, creating independent artistic works, volunteering in their local community, or hitting the road to do a service learning project in a far corner of the country. Wherever your E-terms take you, you can E-xpect and unforgettable E-xperience.

Admission Stats:

Admissions: Rolling

How to Apply: Apply online or download an application at: http://www.ferrum.edu/admissions/application_intro.htm

Accepts the Common Application: No

Average SAT Score: 850

Application Requirements: Online or paper application, $25 application fee, high school transcript, SAT or ACT scores. Optional: Letters of recommendation, essay

Academic Life On-Campus:

Honors program: Yes

Majors Offered: Accounting, Agriculture, Art (Art Education, Studio Art), Biology, Business (Decision Support Systems, Finance, Management, Marketing), Chemistry, Computer Information Systems, Computer Science, Criminal Justice, Dramatic and Theatre Arts, English (General English, Professional Communication), Environmental Science, Foreign Language (Russian, Spanish), Health Sciences, History, Horticulture, International Studies, Liberal Arts, Mathematics, Parks, Recreation, and Tourism (Community Leisure Services, Hospitality and Tourism Management, Outdoor Recreation), Performing and Visual Arts, Philosophy, Physical Education (Exercise Science, Health Education, Sports Medicine), Political Science, Psychology, Religious Studies (Christian Ministries, General Religion), Social Studies, Social Work, Sports Management (Sports Information and Journalism, Sports Management, Sports Marketing)

Ferrum Continued

Pre-professional Programs:

Dentistry , Forensic Science, Medicine, Seminary, eterinary Medicine

Teacher Licensure Program: Yes

Retention Rate: 53%

Student/Faculty Ratio: 12.7:1

Average Class Size: 18

Cool Programs: Independent studies courses, student-designed majors, undergraduate research opportunities, peer mentoring program, study abroad, first year college transitional course, E-term program, interdisciplinary humanities courses, Holocaust Private College Consortium member (provides special events and study abroad programs focused on Holocaust education)

Distance Learning Options: No

Financial Stats:

Undergraduate: $20,840 full time, $420 per credit hour up to six hours, $580 per credit hour for anything over six hours

Room and Board Fees: $ 6,500

Yearly Cost of Attendance: $6,700

Receiving Financial Aid: $29,540

Life Off-Campus:

Living On-Campus: 82%

ROTC Programs: None

Varsity Sports: Baseball, basketball (m/w), cross country (m/w), football, golf (m), lacrosse (w), soccer (m/w), softball, tennis (m/w), volleyball (w)

Sports level: NCAA Division III

Cool Clubs: The Jack Tale Players, Handbell ensemble, Big Buddy/Little Buddy club, Environmental Action Coalition, Wildlife Club, Intramural Ping Pong teams, FerrumRadio.com, Blue Ridge Dinner Theatre

Extra Credit: Virginia State University, Virginia Intermont College, Averett University

George Mason University www.gmu.edu

4400 University Drive, Fairfax, VA 22030-4444
Admissions Office: (703) 993-2400, admissions@gmu.edu

The Basics

Type of School: Public
Type of Campus: Suburban
Size: 18,221 undergrads, 29,889 total

Male/Female Ratio: 45/55
Diversity: 33% minority
Out of State Students: 21%

FYI: George Mason University offers the connections and excitement of Washington, D.C. with the comfort and student life of a modern residential campus. You may be attending school in Virginia, but you'll be getting a global education. Besides an array of globally-minded majors and study abroad programs, the school also operates the U.S.'s only campus in Ras-Al-KhaiMah in the United Arab Emirates.
Notable Names: Current U.S. Treasurer Anne E. Cabral, CNN anchors Hala Gorani and Susan Rook, The Weather Channel President Debora Wilson, and Olympic athletes Mike Kohn and Rob Muzzio

Admission Stats:

Admissions: Early Action – Nov. 1, Regular Admissions – Dec. 1 for scholarship consideration, Jan. 15 for final freshman deadline, Transfer Admissions – April 15 (fall semester), Oct. 15 (spring semester)

How to Apply: Apply online or download an application at: http://admissions.gmu.edu/common/onapps.asp

Accepts the Common Application: No

Average SAT Score: Information Not Available

Application Requirements: Online or paper application, $50 application fee for online applications, $70 for mail-in applications, high school transcript, SAT or ACT scores, Secondary School report filled out by guidance counselor, In-state Tuition Form for VA residents.
Optional: SAT II Subject Tests, additional recommendations

George Mason Continued

Academic Life On-Campus:

Honors program: Yes

Majors Offered: Accounting, Administration of Justice, Anthropology , Art and Visual Technology, Art History, Astronomy, Assisted Living, Athletic Training, Biology, Chemistry, Civil and Infrastructure Engineering, Communication, Computer Engineering, Computer Science, Conflict Analysis and Resolution, Dance, Decision Sciences and Information Management, Earth Science, Economics, Electrical Engineering, English, Exercise Science, Finance, Foreign Languages (French, Spanish), Geography, Geology, Gerontology, Global Affairs, Government and International Politics, Health and Physical Education, Health Promotion, Health Sciences, Health, Fitness, and Recreation Resources, History, Individualized Studies, Information Technology, Integrative Studies, Interdisciplinary Studies, Latin American Studies, Management, Marketing, Mathematics, Medical Technology, Music, Nursing, Parks and Outdoor Recreation, Philosophy, Physical Education, Physics, Psychology, Public Administration, Religious Studies, Russian Studies, Social Work, Sociology, Sport Management, Systems Engineering, Theatre, Tourism and Events Management

Pre-professional Programs:

Dental, Law, Medical, Pharmacy, Seminary, Veterinary

Teacher Licensure Program: Yes

Retention Rate: 86%

Student/Faculty Ratio: 16:1

Average Class Size: Information Not Available

Distance Learning Options: Yes

Cool Programs: Study abroad, on-campus day care, student-designed majors, undergraduate research opportunities, independent studies courses, residential learning communities, Consortium of Universities of the Washington Metropolitan Area member (member schools include University, Catholic University of America, Gallaudet University, Georgetown University, The George Washington University, Howard University, Southeastern University, Trinity University, University of the District of Columbia, and University of Maryland at College Park)

Financial Stats:

Undergraduate: $6,408 full time, $285 per credit hour

Room and Board Fees: $6,890

Yearly Cost of Attendance: $15,730

Receiving Financial Aid: 52%

Life Off-Campus:

Living On-Campus: 23% (65% of all first-year students)

ROTC Programs: Army, Air Force, Navy

Cool Clubs: Anarchist Society, Independent Arts Collective, Game Analysis and Design Interest Group, New Century College Student Leadership Group

Varsity Sports: Baseball, basketball (m/w), cross country (m/w), golf (m), lacrosse (w), rowing (w), soccer (m/w), softball, swimming and diving (m/w), tennis (m/w), track and field (m/w), volleyball (m/w), wrestling

Sports level: NCAA Division I

Extra Credit: James Madison University, Virginia Commonwealth University, Old Dominion University

Hampden-Sydney College www.hsc.edu

PO Box 667, Hampden-Sydney, VA 23943
Admissions Office: (800) 755-0733, admissions@hsc.edu

The Basics

Type of School: Private
Type of Campus: Rural
Size: 1,060 undergraduates

Male/Female Ratio: 100/0
Diversity: 9% minority
Out of State Students: 36%

FYI: Active is the only way to describe Hampden-Sydney students. Despite its small student body, Hampden-Sydney students participate in more than 100 study abroad programs, complete research projects each summer, intern in Washington D.C., complete coursework at 12 different exchange institutions, and more than 80% of the campus participates in intramural sports. Staying active may be the secret to Hampden-Sydney's success. Almost half of all HSC grads go on to graduate or professional schooling and one out of every ten runs their own company.
Notable Names: Former U.S. President William Henry Harrison, Comedian Stephen Colbert, U.S. Deputy Secretary of Education Eugene Hickok, William Mullens CEO Julius P. Smith, Jr.

Admission Stats:

Admissions: Early Decision – Nov. 15, Early Action – Jan. 15, Regular Admissions – March 1, Transfer Admissions – July 1 (fall semester), Dec. 1 (spring semester)

How to Apply: Apply online at http://www2.hsc.edu/admissions/apply/personal_info.html or download a paper application here: http://www2.hsc.edu/admissions/apply/pdfs/apply.pdf
Accepts the Common Application: Yes

Average SAT Score: 1120

Application Requirements: Online or paper application, $30 application fee, high school transcript, essay, SAT or ACT scores, letter of recommendation from a teacher
Optional: Admissions interview, personal reference, photograph

Academic Life On-Campus:

Honors program: Yes

Majors Offered: Biology, Chemistry, Classical Studies, Computer Science, Economics (Economics and Commerce, General Economics), Engineering (Dual degree program with the University of Virginia), English, Foreign Language (French, German, Greek, Latin, Spanish), History, Humanities, Interscience (Biology/Chemistry, Biology/Physics, Mathematics/Physics, Mathematics/Natural Science), Mathematics (Applied Mathematics, General Mathematics, Mathematical Economics), Philosophy, Physics, Political Science, Pre-Medicine (BS/MD program with Eastern Virginia Medical School and George Washington University), Psychology, Religion (General Religion, Religion and Philosophy)

Pre-professional Programs:

Dentistry, Engineering, Law, Medicine, Veterinary Medicine

Teacher Licensure Program: No, but students may gain licensure at Longwood University.

Retention Rate: 66%

Student/Faculty Ratio: 11:1

Average Class Size: 18

Cool Programs: Study abroad, paid summer research program, joint degree programs, independent studies courses, Seven College Exchange member, cooperative tuition program with Longwood University, student leadership program, marine science exchange with Duke University

Distance Learning Options: No

Financial Stats:

Undergraduate: $26,676 full time, $854 per credit hour

Room and Board Fees: $8,713

Yearly Cost of Attendance: $37,398

Receiving Financial Aid: 85%

Hampden-Sydney Continued

Life Off-Campus:

Living On-Campus: 96%

ROTC Programs: Army through Longwood University

Varsity Sports: Baseball, basketball, cross country, football, golf, lacrosse, soccer, tennis

Sports level: NCAA Division III

Cool Clubs: Animation Society, Hampden-Sydney Rifle Association, Fencing Club, Film Club, Rugby Club, Clay Target Club

Extra Credit: Roanoke College, Virginia Wesleyan College, Randolph-Macon College

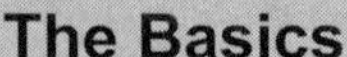

Hampton University www.hamptonu.edu

Hampton University, Hampton, VA 23668 Admissions Office: (800) 624-3328

The Basics

Type of School: Private
Type of Campus: Suburban
Size: 5,468 undergrads, 6,152 total

Male/Female Ratio: 35/65
Diversity: 89% minority
Out of State Students: 63%

FYI: One of the oldest and most prestigious historically black universities in the country, Hampton University maintains a reputation for being a pioneer institution. Currently the school is home to one of four Physics Frontier Centers in the country, one of the top marine sciences programs on the east coast, and a full-scale radio production studio that plays host to the nationally syndicated radio show, "The Doug Banks Show." Hampton University is also one of the few schools in the state to offer majors in Air Traffic Control, Aviation Electronics, and Flight Education and the only institution to offer a major in Professional Tennis Management.

Notable Names: Booker T. Washington, Comedienne Wanda Sykes, former Good Morning America correspondent Spencer Christian, Oracle Corporation President Charles Phillips, NBA player Devin Green, National Teacher of the Year Kimberly Oliver

Admission Stats:

Admissions: Deadlines: Early Action – Dec. 1, Regular Admissions – March 1 (fall semester), Nov. 1 (spring semester)

How to Apply: Apply online or download an application here: http://www.hamptonu.edu/studentservices/admissions/apply.htm

Accepts the Common Application: No

Average SAT Score: 1062

Application Requirements: Online or paper application, $35 application fee, high school transcript, SAT or ACT scores, letter of recommendation, essay

Optional: Admissions Interview

Academic Life On-Campus:

Honors program: Yes

Majors Offered: Accounting, Architecture, Art (Graphic Art, Studio Art), Aviation (Aviation Administration, Air Traffic Control, Aviation Computer Science, Aviation Electronics, Flight Education), Banking and Finance (Banking track, Finance track), Biological Sciences (Cellular/Molecular Biology, Organisms/Ecology/Biodiversity), Business Administration, Chemical Engineering, Chemistry (Forensic Chemistry, General Chemistry), Communication Sciences and Disorders, Communications (Advertising, Broadcast Journalism, Print Journalism, Public Relations), Computer Engineering, Computer Science (Computer Information Systems, General Computer Science), Economics, Electrical Engineering, English, Entrepreneurship, Health and Physical Education (Health Education, Recreation Programming, Sport Management), History (History Education, General History), Management (General Management, Management Information Systems), Marine and Environmental Sciences, Marketing (General Marketing, Professional Tennis Marketing), Mathematics, Music (Music Education, Music Engineering Technology, Music Performance), Nursing, Physics, Political Science, Psychology, Sociology, Spanish (Business, Culture, Language, Medical Spanish), Theatre (Technical Theatre, Theatrical Performance)

Hampton Continued

Pre-professional Programs:

Forensic Science, Law, Medicine, Pharmacy, Physical Therapy

Teacher Licensure Program: Yes

Retention Rate: 85%

Student/Faculty Ratio: 16:1

Average Class Size: 22

Cool Programs: Study abroad, student leadership program, undergraduate research opportunities, Semester in DC program, Aquatic Sciences undergraduate research program for minority students, upperclassmen mentoring program, independent studies courses

Distance Learning Options: Yes

Financial Stats:

Undergraduate: $14,026 full time, $350 per credit hour

Room and Board Fees: $7,084

Yearly Cost of Attendance: $23,694

Receiving Financial Aid: 70%

Life Off-Campus:

Living On-Campus: 42%

ROTC Programs: Army, Navy

Varsity Sports: Basketball (m/w), bowling (w), cross country (m/w), football, golf (m/w), sailing (m/w), softball, tennis (m/w), track and field (m/w), volleyball (w)

Sports level: NCAA Division I

Cool Clubs: Underwater Explorers Club, Debate Team, Students In Free Enterprise, Math Club, WVOH-FM radio station

Extra Credit: Roanoke College, Virginia Wesleyan College, Randolph-Macon College

Hollins University

PO Box 9707, Roanoke, VA 24020

www.hollins.edu

Admissions Office: (800) 456-9595, huadm@hollins.edu

The Basics

Type of School: Private
Type of Campus: Suburban
Size: 850 undergrads (single-sex), 1120 total (co-ed)

Male/Female Ratio: 0/100 undergrad
Diversity: 13% minority
Out of State Students: 48%

FYI: Coming in first is what Hollins University students do best. The first chartered women's college in the state, Hollins has a reputation for producing sharp, successful female powerhouses. Taking a look at the academics, it's no wonder. The school offers a solid liberal arts general education curriculum and several nationally-recognized academic programs, including the Batten Leadership Program and a creative writing program deemed "the most productive writing program in America." An education here isn't all textbook learning though. The school's month-long January Short Term allows students to take a study abroad trip, complete an internship, complete a research or independent studies project, take an extra course on-campus, or start a volunteer project.

Notable Names: Pulitzer Prize winner Annie Dillard, ABC News White House Correspondent Ann Compton, Pumping Iron director George Butler, Ten Indians author Madison Smartt Bell, U.S. Ambassador to Mongolia Pamela Slutz, Charlotte Fox, the first woman to climb Mount Everest

Admission Stats:

Admissions: Early Decision – Dec. 15, Batten Scholar Applicants – Jan. 10, Regular Admissions – Feb. 1, Transfer Admissions – Rolling Admissions.

How to Apply: Apply online at https://www.applyweb.com/apply/hollinsu/ or download a paper application here: https://www.applyweb.com/apply/hollinsu/

Application Requirements: Online or paper application, $35 application fee, high school transcript, essay, SAT or ACT scores, letter of recommendation

Optional: Admissions interview, SAT II tests (English composition highly recommended)

Accepts the Common Application: Yes

Average SAT Score: 1140

Hollins Continued

Academic Life On-Campus:

Honors program: Yes

Majors Offered: Art (Arts Management, Studio Art), Art History, Biology, Business (Business Communication and Technology, Finance, General Business, International Business), Chemistry (Business Chemistry, Biochemistry, General Chemistry), Classical Studies (Ancient Studies, Classical Philology), Communication Studies, Computational Sciences (General Computational Sciences, Mathematics/Statistics Computational Sciences), Computer Science, Dance, Economics (General Economics, International Economics), English (Creative Writing, General English), Environmental Studies, Film and Photography, Foreign Language (French, German, Spanish), History, Interdisciplinary Studies, International Studies, Mathematics and Statistics, Music, Philosophy (Ethics, General Philosophy), Physics, Political Science, Psychology, Religious Studies, Sociology (Cultural Sociology and Anthropology, General sociology, Social Psychology, Social Work and Social Policy), Theatre, Women's Studies

Pre-professional Programs:

Dental, Law, Medicine, Pharmacy, Physical Therapy, Seminary, Veterinary Medicine

Teacher Licensure Program: Yes

Retention Rate: 76

Student/Faculty Ratio: 10:1

Average Class Size: 15

Cool Programs: Student leadership program, study abroad, Seven College Exchange member, student-designed majors, January Short Term, undergraduate research opportunities, independent studies courses, extensive pre-college summer program for high school students, Hollins Outdoor Program

Distance Learning Options: No

Financial Stats:

Undergraduate: $25,110 full time, $785 per credit hour

Room and Board Fees: $9,140

Yearly Cost of Attendance: $36,785

Receiving Financial Aid: 98%

Life Off-Campus:

Living On-Campus: 80%
ROTC: None
Varsity Sports: Basketball, equestrian, golf, lacrosse, soccer, swimming, tennis
Sports level: NCAA Division III

Cool Clubs: AIDS Awareness Coalition, Colleges Against Cancer, Foundation 42 (for sci-fi, fantasy, or horror enthusiasts), Global Interest Association, Students for Environmental Action

Extra Credit: College of William and Mary, Sweet Briar College, Christendom College

James Madison University

www.jmu.edu

800 South Main Street, Harrisonburg, VA 22807
Admissions: (540) 568-5681, admissions@jmu.edu

The Basics

Type of School: Public
Type of Campus: Small City
Size: 15,653 undergrads, 17,393 total

Male/Female Ratio: 39/61
Diversity: 11% minority
Out of State Students: 29%

FYI: Involvement is the name of the game at James Madison University and you'll have more than enough opportunities to get in on the action. Home to 200+ student organizations, 20 nationally-recognized Greek organizations, 23 varsity sports teams, an extensive intramural sports program, and a service learning department that provides domestic and international volunteer opportunities, JMU is known for attracting passionate students who contribute to their campus and community...and their contributions are being heard. In 2003, the school was named one of the top ten most activist campuses in the nation by Mother Jones magazine.

Notable Names: Former NFL players Scott Norwood, Gary Clark, and Ed Perry, Joan of Arcadia creator Barbara Hall, Hoop Dreams Director Steve James, Ten Things I Hate About You and Legally Blonde writer Karen McCullah-Lutz

JMU Continued

Admission Stats:

Admissions: Early Action – Nov. 1, Regular Admissions – Jan. 15, Transfer Admissions – March 1 (fall semester), Jan 15 (summer semester), Oct. 15 (spring semester)

How to Apply: Apply online or download an application at http://www.jmu.edu/admissions/apply/

Application Requirements: Online or paper application, $40 application fee, high school transcript, SAT or ACT scores, Secondary School report filled out by guidance counselor, one letter of recommendation, In-state Tuition Form for VA residents

Optional: Personal Statement

Accepts the Common Application: No

Average SAT Score: 1140

Academic Life On-Campus:

Honors program: Yes

Majors Offered: Accounting (Public Administration), Anthropology (Archeology, Biological Anthropology, Cultural Anthropology), Art (General Fine Arts, Graphic Design, Interior Design, Studio Art, Industrial Design), Art History, Athletic Training, Biology, Biotechnology, Business and Marketing Education, Chemistry (Biochemistry, Chemical Education, Chemistry and Materials Chemistry) Chemistry/Business, General Chemistry], Communication Sciences and Disorders, Communication Studies (Conflict Analysis and Intervention, Cultural Communication, Health Communication, Interpersonal Communication Studies, Organizational Communication Studies, Political Communication, Public Communication Studies, Public Relations Studies), Computer Information Systems, Computer Science, Dietetics (Nutrition), Earth Science, Economics (Environmental and Natural Resource, Financial, International, Socioeconomics), English, Finance, Foreign Languages (French, German, Italian, Spanish), Geographic Science (Environmental Studies, Geographic Information Science, Geography, Global Studies), Geology (Earth Science Education), Health Sciences (Health Assessment and Promotion, Health Studies, Occupational Studies, Public Health Education, Substance Abuse Intervention), Health Services Administration, History (Public History), Hospitality and Tourism Management, Individualized Study, Integrated Science and Technology (Biotechnology, Energy, Engineering and Manufacturing, Environment, Environmental Information Systems, Health Systems, Information and Knowledge Management, Technology Education, Telecommunications), Interdisciplinary Liberal Studies, Interdisciplinary Social Science (Social Studies), International Affairs (Comparative Study, International Politics), International Business (Finance, Marketing), Justice Studies, Kinesiology (Coaching Education, Exercise Leadership, Exercise Science and Leadership, Physical and Health Education Teacher Education, Sport Communication, Sport and Recreation Management), Management (Technology, Innovation and Entrepreneurship, General Management, Human Resource Management), Marketing (Business to Business Marketing, Business to Consumer Marketing, Marketing Information Systems, European Marketing, Retail Merchandising) , Mathematics (Computational Sciences), Media Arts and Design (Cinema Studies, Corporate Communication, Digital Video, Interactive Media, Print Journalism), Music (Composition, Jazz Studies, Music Education, Music Industry, Music Theatre Emphasis, Performance, Piano, Accompanying/Coaching), Nursing, Philosophy and Religion (Interdisciplinary Philosophy, Interdisciplinary Religion, Philosophy, Religion), Physics (Applied Physics, Astronomy, Fundamental Studies, Individual Option, Physics/Engineering Combined Program), Political Science (Political Communication), Psychology,P ublic Policy and Administration (Political Communication, Political Science), Quantitative Finance, Social Work, Sociology (Applied Sociology, Deviance and Criminology, Diverse Cultural Experiences, Family and Lifestyles, Occupations and Bureaucracy, Social Psychology, Sociology of Education),S tatistics, Technical and Scientific Communication (Online Publications, Publications Management, Technical and Scientific Communication in the Public Sector), Theatre and Dance (Dance, Musical Theatre, Theatre)

Pre-professional Programs:

Dentistry, Forensic Studies, Law, Medicine, Occupational Therapy, Optometry, Pharmacy, Physical Therapy, Physician Assistant, Seminary, Veterinary Medicine

Teacher Licensure Program: Yes

Retention Rate: 92%

Student/Faculty Ratio: 16:1

Average Class Size: 30

Cool Programs: Study abroad, undergraduate research opportunities, independent studies courses, themed housing for students with common interests

Distance Learning Options: Yes

JMU Continued

Financial Stats:

Undergraduate: $6,666 full time, $662 per credit hour

Room and Board Fees: $6,836

Yearly Cost of Attendance: $15,562

Receiving Financial Aid: 98%

Life Off-Campus:

Living On-Campus: 37%

ROTC: Army

Sports level: NCAA Division I

Varsity Sports: Archery, baseball, basketball (m/w), cross country (m/w), fencing (w), field hockey, football, golf (m/w), gymnastics (m/w), lacrosse (w), soccer (m/w), softball, swimming and diving (m/w), tennis (m/w), volleyball (w), wrestling

Cool Clubs: Cartoon Satire Club, Madison Motorcycle Club, Living Buddhism Club, Science Fiction Fantasy Guild, Roller Hockey Club, Ski Club, Breakdance Club

Extra Credit: George Mason University, Emory and Henry Colleg, Virginia Commonwealth University

Liberty University www.liberty.edu

1971 University Boulevard, Lynchburg, VA 24502
Admissions Office: (800) 543-5317, admissions@liberty.edu

The Basics

Type of School: Private
Type of Campus: Small Town
Size: 9,500 on campus, 22,500 total

Male/Female Ratio: 47/53
Diversity: 21% minority
Out of State Students: 63%

FYI: The poster child for fundamentalist, faith-based education, Liberty University trains students to be academically as well as spiritually strong. The Liberty curriculum focuses on a strong, Christ-centered liberal arts education. In addition to completing a diverse regimen of general education courses, Liberty students also complete one full year of Christian community service learning and are required to attend chapel three times each week. Outside of class, Liberty brings internationally-renowned business, political, and spiritual leaders to campus, giving students access to some of the world's most influential people.
Notable Names: Liberty President Jerry Falwell, NFL players Dwayne Carswell, Eric Green, and Sam Gado, WNBA player Katie Feenstra, DC Talk members Toby McKeehan, Michael Tait, and Kevin Max, World Help founder Vernon Brewer, author Angela Elwell Hunt

Admission Stats:

Admissions Deadlines: Rolling Admissions, May apply as early as the end of your junior year in high school

How to Apply: Apply online at http://www.liberty.edu/index.cfm?pid=1000&CFID=921658&CFTOKEN=76236487 or download a paper application at http://www.liberty.edu/media/1241/ShortTermAppSource.pdf

Application Requirements: Online or paper application, $35 application fee, essay, high school transcript, SAT or ACT scores (not required for students ages 22 or older)

Accepts the Common Application: No

Average SAT Score: 1017

Academic Life On-Campus:

Honors program: Yes

Majors Offered: Accounting, Athletic Training, Aeronautics (Commercial Aviation, Military Aviation, Missions Aviation), Biology (Environmental Sciences, General Biology, Molecular Biology, Pre-Medicine track), Biochemistry, Business (Economics, Finance, General Business, International Business, Management, Marketing), Communication Studies (Advertising and Public Relations, Broadcasting, General Communication, Graphic Design, Journalism, Speech), Computer Science, Criminal Justice, English, Family and Consumer Sciences, Foreign Language (Spanish), General Studies, Interdisciplinary Studies, Government (Administration of Justice, International Studies, Politics and Policy, Pre-Law track), Health Promotion (Clinical track, General Health Promotion), History (General History, International Studies), Interdisciplinary Studies, Interiors and Fashion Merchandising, Kinesiology (Exercise Science, Fitness Specialist, Health and Physical Education), Management Information Systems, Mathematics, Music (Choral, Instrumental), Nursing, Philosophy and Religion (Biblical Studies, General Philosophy), Psychology (Adult Development, Child/Adult Development, Clinical/Experimental, Human Services Counseling), Religion (Biblical Studies, Cross-Cultural Studies, Pastoral Ministries, Women's Ministries, Youth Ministries), Social Sciences, Sports Management, Teaching English as a Second Language, Theatre (Acting, Drama Ministry, Musical Theatre, Production), Visual Communication Arts, Web, Technology, and Design, Worship and Music Ministry

Pre-professional Programs:

Law, Medicine, Seminary

Teacher Licensure Program: Yes

Retention Rate: 74.5%

Student/Faculty Ratio: 25:1

Average Class Size: 29

Cool Programs: Study abroad, student-designed majors, Christian community service requirement, student leadership program, annual Winterfest Christian music festival, domestic and international mission trips

Distance Learning Options: Yes

Financial Stats:

Undergraduate: $14,850 full time, $495 per credit hour

Room and Board Fees: $5,600

Yearly Cost of Attendance: $22,450

Receiving Financial Aid: 100%

Life Off-Campus:

Living On-Campus: 63.5%

ROTC: Army

Varsity Sports: Baseball, basketball (m/w), cross country (m/w), football, golf (m), soccer (m/w), softball, tennis (m/w), track and field (m/w), volleyball (w), wrestling

Sports level: NCAA Division I

Cool Clubs: Club hockey team, Debate team, Intramural Dodgeball, Bridging the Gap Urban Ministries, Huntin' & Fishin' Club, Jiu Jitsu Club, Paintball Club

Extra Credit: Regent University, Lynchburg College, Virginia Wesleyan College

Longwood University

www.longwood.edu

201 High Street, Farmville, VA 23909
Admissions Office: (800) 281-4677, admit@longwood.edu

The Basics

Type of School: Public
Type of Campus: Small City
Size: 3,750 undergrads, 4,380 total

Male/Female Ratio: 35/65
Diversity: 11% minority
Out of State Students: 10%

FYI: Beginning as a teacher's college 1839, Longwood is still home to one of, if not the best, teacher training programs in the state. In recent years, the school has placed a heavy emphasis on training graduates for the real world and helping them find positions once they've turned the tassel. Longwood is currently the only school in the state to require all students to complete at least one internship, extended field experience, or research project in order to graduate. Studies show that the hands-on training pays off for Longwood grads in the end. LU has the highest job placement rate among public institutions in Virginia with more than 90% of all alum finding work within three months of graduation.

Notable Names: Ghost Recon 2 video game designer Rafael Chandler, NBA player Jerome Kersey, former New York Mets player Michael Tucker, Hostage actor Ransford Doherty

Admission Stats:

Admissions Deadlines: Early Action – Dec. 1, Regular Admissions – March 1 (fall semester), Oct. 15 (spring semester), Transfer Admissions – March 1 (fall semester), Dec. 1 (spring semester)

How to Apply: Apply online or download an application at http://whylongwood.com/applynow/index.htm

Application Requirements: Online or paper application, $40 application fee, high school transcript, SAT or ACT scores, personal statements, In-state Tuition Form for VA residents
Accepts the Common Application: No

Average SAT Score: 1075

Longwood Continued

Academic Life On-Campus:

Honors program: Yes

Majors Offered: Anthropology, Art (Crafts, Drawing and Printmaking, Education, Graphic Design, History, Painting, Photography) , Biology, Business Administration (Accounting, Business Education, Computer Information Management Systems, Economics, Finance, Management, Marketing, Real Estate, Retailing), Chemistry, Communication Sciences and Disorders, Communication Studies (Mass Media, Organizational and Strategic Communication), Computer Science, Criminology/Criminal Justice, Economics (Business Economics, International Economics, Public Policy), English, Foreign Language (French, German, Spanish) , History, Kinesiology (Athletic Training, Exercise Science, Physical Education Teaching), Liberal Studies, Mathematics, Music (Education, Performance, Piano Pedagogy), Physics, Political Science, Psychology, Social Work, Theatre, Therapeutic Recreation

Pre-professional Programs:

Clinical Studies,Law, Forensic Science, Medicine

Teacher Licensure Program: Yes

Retention Rate: 76%

Student/Faculty Ratio: 18:1

Average Class Size: 25

Cool Programs: Study abroad, required internship program, undergraduate research opportunities, independent studies courses, residential learning communities for first-year students, upperclassmen mentoring program, joint degree programs with the University of Virginia, Virginia Tech, Virginia Commonwealth University, Old Dominion University, Christopher Newport University, Georgia Institute of Technology, and the University of Tennessee

Distance Learning Options: Yes

Financial Stats:

Undergraduate In-State Tuition: $8,058 full time, $269 per credit hour

Room and Board Fees: $6,267

Yearly Cost of Attendance: $16,334

Receiving Financial Aid: 77%

Life Off-Campus:

Living On-Campus: 70%

ROTC: Army

Varsity Sports: Baseball, basketball (m/w), cross country (m/w), field hockey, golf (m/w), lacrosse (w), soccer (m/w), softball, tennis (m/w)

Sports level: NCAA Division I

Cool Clubs: Student Organization for Disability Awareness, In-Line Hockey Club, Synchronized Swimming Club, Flag Football Intramurals, Habitat for Humanity, annual Oozeball Tournament

Extra Credit: Bridgewater College, Mary Baldwin College, Roanoke College

Lynchburg College www.lynchburg.edu

1501 Lakeside Drive, Lynchburg, VA 24501
Admissions Office: (800) 426-8101, admissions@lynchburg.edu, AIM name: LCQuestions

The Basics

Type of School: Private
Type of Campus: Small City
Size: 2,050 undergrads, 2,400 total

Male/Female Ratio: 41/59
Diversity: 15% minority
Out of State Students: 37%

FYI: Get ready to get dirty. Lynchburg College's extensive science and health majors are only for those who don't mind a hands-on education. Lynchburg students learn about the world around them by studying body parts in the cadaver lab, researching plant species in the 470-acre Claytor Nature Study Center, and completing coursework in the school's 10 health-related pre-professional programs. Whether or not their academic experience includes corpses, all students participate in the Lynchburg College Symposium Readings Program, a full semester of interdisciplinary lectures and student-led discussions on current hot-button topics.

Lynchburg College Continued

Admission Stats:

Admissions Deadlines: Early Action – Oct. 15, Early Decision – Nov. 15, Regular Admissions – Rolling, Transfer Admissions – July 31 (fall semester), Nov. 30 (spring semester), April 1 (summer semester)

How to Apply: Apply online or download an application at: http://www.lynchburg.edu/x2116.xml

Application Requirements: Online or paper application, $30 application fee (fee waived for online applicants), high school transcript, SAT or ACT scores

Optional: Admissions interview, essay, letter of recommendation

Accepts the Common Application: Paper version only

Average SAT Score: 1031

Academic Life On-Campus:

Honors program: Yes

Majors Offered: Accounting, Art (Graphic Design, Studio Art), Athletic Training, Biology , Biomedical Science, Business Administration, Chemistry, Communication Studies (Communications and Social Influence, Electronic Media, General Communication Studies, Public Relations and Journalism), Computer Science, Economics (Financial Economics, General Economics), English (Literature, Writing), Environmental Science, Exercise Physiology, Foreign Language (French, French Global Commerce, Spanish, Spanish Global Commerce), Health and Physical Education, Health Promotion, History, Human Development and Learning (Elementary, Special Education), International Relations, Management, Marketing, Mathematics, Music (Instrumental Education, Performance, Music Theory/Composition, Vocal Education), Nursing, Philosophy (General Philosophy, Philosophy/Political Science, Philosophy/Religious Studies), Physics, Political Science, Psychology , Religious Studies, Sociology (Criminology, General Sociology), Sport Management, Theatre

Pre-professional Programs:

Art Therapy, Dentistry, Chiropractic, Forestry/Wildlife Programs, Law, Library Science, Medicine, Museum Studies, Occupational Therapy , Optometry, Pharmacy, Physical Therapy, Physician's Assistant, Seminary, Veterinary Medicine

Teacher Licensure Program: Yes

Retention Rate: 87%

Student/Faculty Ratio: 13:1

Average Class Size: 18

Cool Programs: Student-designed majors, study abroad, upperclassmen mentoring program, college transition course for first year students, undergraduate research opportunities, student l74dership program, independent studies courses, first year learning communities

Distance Learning Options: No

Financial Stats:

Undergraduate In-State Tuition: 26,360 full time, $365.00 per credit hour for 7 hours or less, $703 per credit hour for 8 hours or more

Room and Board Fees: $6,970

Yearly Cost of Attendance: $35,330

Receiving Financial Aid: 98%

Life Off-Campus:

Living On-Campus: 87%

ROTC: None

Varsity Sports: Baseball, basketball (m/w), cross country (m/w), equestrian (m/w), field hockey, golf (m), lacrosse (m/w), soccer (m/w), softball, tennis (m/w), track and field (m/w), volleyball

Sports level: NCAA Division III

Cool Clubs: One Step Up Dance Team, Lynchburg College Recycling Club, Anime Society, Shotokan Karate Club, Ski and Snowboard Club, Arena Flag Football intramurals, Playstation Football tournament teams

Extra Credit: Radford University, Bluefield College, Hampton University

Mary Baldwin College www.mbc.edu

Mary Baldwin College, Staunton, VA 24401
Admissions Office: (800) 468-2262, admit@mbc.edu

The Basics

Type of School: Private
Type of Campus: Small Town
Size: 800 undergrads, 2,200 total
Male/Female Ratio: 0/100 (undergrad)
Diversity: 35% minority
Out of State Students: 40%

FYI: A women's college, gifted education facility, leadership institute, and adult education program all rolled into one, Mary Baldwin offers something for any motivated young woman. The school's undergraduate program, the Residential College for Women, provides one of the strongest liberal arts curriculums in the state. All undergrads are required to develop their own four-year education plan that incorporates both in and out of class experiences as well as an Individualized Wellness Plan that incorporates spiritual experiences as well. During their four years, MBC ladies have exposure to a strong network of experiential education courses, service learning opportunities, study abroad programs, living/learning programs, on-campus cultural programs from far reaches of the world, and a team of faculty and student mentors ready to help them every step of the way. If you simply can't wait until you're finished with high school, MBC's Program for the Exceptionally Gifted accepts students as young as 9th grade.

Admission Stats:

Admissions Deadlines: Early Decision and Transfer Applications – Nov. 15, Regular Decision – April 15

How to Apply: Apply online at http://www.mbc.edu/ssl/forms_admit/apply_trad_ol.asp or get a paper application by contacting the admissions office at (800) 468-2262 or admit@mbc.edu

Application Requirements: Online or paper application, $35 application fee, high school transcripts, SAT or ACT scores

Optional: Admissions interview

Accepts the Common Application: No

Average SAT Score: 1065

Academic Life On-Campus:

Honors program: Yes

Majors Offered: Art (Art History, Arts Management, Studio Art), Asian Studies, Biology (Biochemistry, General Biology), Business Administration (General Business Administration, Marketing Communication), Chemistry (Biochemistry, Chemistry), Clinical Laboratory Science (Biology or Chemistry emphasis), Communication, Computer Information Systems (Computer Science/Mathematics, General Computer Information Systems), Economics, English (Creative Writing, General English), Foreign Language (French, Spanish), Health Care Administration, History (Historic Preservation, General History, Public History), Mathematics (Applied Mathematics, General Mathematics), Philosophy (General Philosophy, Philosophy and Religion), Physics, Political Science (General Political Science, International Relations), Psychology, Religion (General Religion, Philosophy and Religion), Sociology (General Sociology, Sociology/Social Work),Theatre

Pre-professional Programs:

Law, Medicine , Seminary

Teacher Licensure Program: Yes

Retention Rate: 83%

Student/Faculty Ratio: 10:1

Average Class Size: 17

Cool Programs: Program for the Exceptionally Gifted, Individual Wellness Plan program, first year transition to college program, four-year portfolio project, study abroad, upperclassmen mentoring, senior capstone projects, independent studies courses, residential learning communities, themed housing, student leadership program, student-designed majors
Distance Learning Options: Yes

Financial Stats:

Undergraduate In-State Tuition: $22,530 full time, $380 per undergrad credit hour

Room and Board Fees: $6,470

Yearly Cost of Attendance: $31,000

Receiving Financial Aid: 99%

Mary Baldwin College Continued

Life Off-Campus:

Living On-Campus: 36%

ROTC: Air Force, Navy, Marines, Army

Varsity Sports: Basketball, cross country, field hockey, soccer, softball, swimming, tennis, volleyball

Sports level: NCAA Division III

Cool Clubs: Fencing club, African Student Kollective, Colleges Against Cancer club. Kuumba Players, T.E.A.R. (Together for the Earth and Animal Rights), Riding club

Extra Credit: Longwood University, Lynchburg College, Marymount University

Marymount University www.marymount.edu

2807 North Glebe Road, Arlington, VA 22207
Admissions Office: (800) 548-7638, admissions@marymount.edu

The Basics

Type of School: Private
Type of Campus: Suburban
Size: 2,300 undergrads, 3,600 total

Male/Female Ratio: 26/74
Diversity: 50% minority
Out of State Students: 40%

FYI: Students come first at Marymount. On this tiny campus of just 2,300 undergrads, you can expect to have your questions answered, to get to know your teachers on a personal level, and to become a valuable part of campus. Marymount seeks to provide a nurturing academic atmosphere chock full of educational opportunities you'll be pressed to find anywhere else (such as the school's undergraduate programs in Fashion Merchandising and Forensic Computing). Recognized by the John Templeton Foundation as a College of Character, Marymount students contribute more than 8,000 community service hours per year and make a tremendous impact on their community.

Admission Stats:

Admissions Deadlines: Rolling

How to Apply: Apply online at https://www.applyweb.com/apply/marymu/menu.html or download a paper application here: http://www.marymount.edu/application/xxunderapp.pdf

Application Requirements: Online or paper application, $40 application fee, two high school transcripts, SAT or ACT scores, letter of recommendation from your guidance counselor or dean of students

Accepts the Common Application: No

Average SAT Score: 996

Academic Life On-Campus:

Honors program: Yes

Majors Offered: Art (Art Management, Pre-Art Therapy), Biology (General Biology, Molecular and Cellular Biology, Pre-Medicine track), Business Administration (Accounting, Business Law and Paralegal Studies, Finance, General Business, International Business, Management, Marketing), Communications, Computer Science, Criminal Justice (Forensic Science, General Criminal Justice), Economics in Society, English (Dramatic Arts, Literature, Writing), Fashion Design, Fashion Merchandising, Graphic Design, Health Sciences (Health Promotion, Pre-Physical Therapy), History, Information Systems, Interior Design, Liberal Studies, Mathematics, Nursing, Philosophy, Politics, Psychology, Sociology, Theology and Religious Studies

Marymount University Continued

Pre-professional Programs:

Art Therapy, Law, Medicine, Physical Therapy

Teacher Licensure Program: Yes

Retention Rate: 68%

Student/Faculty Ratio: 13:1

Average Class Size: 20

Cool Programs: Study abroad, undergraduate research opportunities, independent studies courses, upperclassmen mentoring program, Consortium of Universities of the Washington Metropolitan Area member (member schools include University, Catholic University of America, Gallaudet University, George Mason University, Georgetown University, The George Washington University, Howard University, Southeastern University, Trinity University, University of the District of Columbia, and University of Maryland at College Park)

Distance Learning Options: Yes

Financial Stats:

Undergraduate In-State Tuition: $20,190 full time, $655 per credit hour

Room and Board Fees: $8,705

Yearly Cost of Attendance: $31,465

Receiving Financial Aid: 77%

Life Off-Campus:

Living On-Campus: 18%

ROTC: Army through Georgetown University

Varsity Sports: Basketball (m/w), cross country (m/w), golf (m), lacrosse (m/w), soccer (m/w), swimming (m/w), volleyball
Sports level: NCAA Division III

Cool Clubs: Students in Free Enterprise (SIFE), 12 Point (Graphic Design Club), Blue Harmony (singing group), Fashion Club, International Club, Marymount Dance Team, Science Club, Theatre One2One

Extra Credit: Mary Baldwin College, Regent University, Bluefield College

Norfolk State University www.nsu.edu

700 Park Avenue, Norfolk, VA 23504
Admissions Office: (757) 823-8396, admissions@nsu.edu

The Basics

Type of School: Public
Type of Campus: Urban
Size: 5,403 undergrads, 6,238 total
Male/Female Ratio: 36/64
Diversity: 86% minority
Out of State Students: 23%

FYI: One of the largest predominantly African-American institutions in the nation, Norfolk State prides itself on giving students an academically rigorous curriculum combined with an educationally supportive environment. If you've got your eye on a math or science-related major, this is the place to get your degree. The school's DNIMAS honors program provides minority students in certain math and science majors with a four-year scholarship, research internships, field trips, projects, peer mentoring and tutoring, career counseling, and a four-week summer session to get them ahead of the learning curve.
Notable Names: Nathan McCall, author of the New York Times best-selling book Makes Me Wanna Holler: A Young Black Man in America, television and movie actor/producer Tim Reid, Black Enterprise Magazine editor Derek Dingle, Omniplex World Services CEO Julien Patterson

Admission Stats:

Admissions Deadlines: Early Admissions – Not offered, Regular Admissions – May 31 (Fall semester), Oct. 1 (Spring semester)

How to Apply: Apply online or download an application at http://www.nsu.edu/applyonline

Application Requirements: Online or paper application, $25 application fee, high school transcript, SAT or ACT scores, two letters of recommendation, In-state Tuition Form for VA residents

Accepts the Common Application: No

Average GPA: 2.68

Average SAT Score: 897

Norfolk State University Continued

Academic Life On-Campus:

Honors program: Yes

Majors Offered: Accounting, Biology (Biology General, Biotechnology), Building Construction Technology, Business (Entrepreneurship, Finance, Management Information Systems, Manufacturing and Service Management, Management and Total Quality, Marketing, Economics), Business Education, Chemistry (Chemistry General, Food Science and Nutrition, Materials Science, Pre-Medicine), Communication Sciences and Disorders, Computer Science (Computer Science General, Computer Engineering, Informational Systems), Computer Technology, Electrical Engineering (Microelectronics, Communications, Computer), Electronics Technology, English (African-American Literature, Creative Writing, French Literature, Speech Communication, Spanish Literature, Theatre Performance and Technology), Exercise Science and Education (Exercise Science General, Food Science and Nutrition), Fine Arts (Fine Arts, Fine Arts Education), Foreign Languages (French, German, Spanish), Graphic Design, Health Information Management, Health Services Management, History (African and African Diaspora Studies, History, Social Science History, Military Science History), Interdisciplinary Studies, Journalism, Mass Communications, Mathematics (Applied Mathematics, Mathematics Education), Medical Technology, Music (Music Education, Music Media), Nursing, Optical Engineering, Physics, Political Science, Psychology, Social Work, Sociology, Tourism and Hospitality Management

Pre-professional Programs:

Law, Medicine

Teacher Licensure Program: Yes

Retention Rate: 68%

Student/Faculty Ratio: 17:1

Average Class Size: 18

Cool Programs: Study abroad, undergraduate research opportunities, upperclassmen mentoring program, preparatory courses available only to first-year students, independent studies courses, first-year residential learning communities, cooperative education program, joint degree program with Old Dominion University, student-designed majors, DNIMAS program, member of the Virginia Tidewater Consortium along with Christopher Newport University, the College of William and Mary, Norfolk State University, Old Dominion University, and Virginia Wesleyan College

Distance Learning Options: Yes

Financial Stats:

Undergraduate In-State Tuition: $5,322 full time, $234.60 per credit hour

Room and Board Fees: $6,909

Yearly Cost of Attendance: $14,231

Receiving Financial Aid: 92%

Life Off-Campus:

Living On-Campus: 36%

ROTC: Army, Navy

Varsity Sports: Baseball, basketball (m/w), bowling (w), cross country (m/w), football, softball, tennis (m/w), track and field (m/w), volleyball (w)

Sports level: NCAA Division I

Cool Clubs: Athletes in Action, Political Science Association, Pre-Alumni Club, Students in Free Enterprise (SIFE), Tae Kwon Do Club

Extra Credit: Old Dominion University, Ferrum College, UVA-Wise

Old Dominion University www.odu.edu

5115 Hampton Boulevard, Norfolk, VA 23529
Admissions Office: (800) 348-7926, admit@odu.edu

The Basics

Type of School: Public
Type of Campus: Urban
Size: 14,209 undergrads, 20,802 total
Male/Female Ratio: 46/54
Diversity: 26% minority
Out of State Students: 10%

FYI: 3 Virginia Outstanding Scientists, 3 U.S. Professors of the Year, 38 Fulbright Award winners, 8 American Physical Society Fellows, 1 Truman Fellow, 1 Rhodes Scholar, and 3 USA All-Academic team members have called ODU home. When they're not earning accolades, ODU students participate in more than 200 student organizations, volunteer in the community, and create their own independent research projects. If being stateside just isn't your thing, ODU's study abroad programs can help. From Marketing the NBA in China to Commerce and Culture in Brazil, the school's innovative summer break programs offer a gateway to the world.
Notable Names: Astronaut Michael Bloomfield, former NBA players Cal Bowdler, Kenny Gattison, and Chris Gatling, Delirious writer Tom Dicillo, Olympic Silver Medalist Nancy Lieberman

Admission Stats:

Admissions Deadlines: Early Action and Scholarship Applicants – Dec. 1, Regular and Transfer Admissions – March 15

How to Apply: Apply online at http://admissions.odu.edu/home.php

Application Requirements: Application, $40 application fee, high school transcript, essay, Resume, Essay, SAT or ACT scores

Accepts the Common Application: No

Average SAT Score: 1064

Academic Life On-Campus:

Honors program: Yes

Majors Offered: Accounting, Art (Art History, Studio Art), Biochemistry(graduate), Biology (General Biology, Marine Biology), Chemistry (General Chemistry, Pre-Pharmacy Track, Civil Engineering, Civil Engineering Technology (Construction Management, Structural Design, Surveying/Site Development), Communication (Corporate Communications, International and Intercultural Communications, Interpersonal and Small Group Communications, Mass Media, Persuasion and Critical Thinking, Public Relations, Theatre), Computer Engineering, Computer Science, Criminal Justice, Decision Sciences (Accounting, Economics, Finance, Insurance, Management, Marketing, Operations Management, Real Estate), Dental Hygiene, Economics, Electrical Engineering, Electrical Engineering Technology (Computer Engineering Technology, Computer and Network Operations, Electrical Systems Technology, Electromechanical Systems, General Electrical Engineering Technology, Geomatics and GIS, Technical Operations), English (Creative Writing, Journalism, Linguistics, Literature, Professional Writing), Environmental Engineering, Environmental Health, Finance (Insurance, Real Estate), Fine Arts (Drawing and Design, Fibers, Graphic Design, Metalsmithing and Sculpture, Painting, Print and Photo Media), Foreign Language (French, German, Spanish), Geography, Health Sciences (Cytotechnology, Ophthalmic Technology), History, Human Services Counseling, Information Systems and Technology, Interdisciplinary Studies (Education, Individualized Studies, Professional Writing, Work and Professional Studies, Zoological Parks Management), International Business, International Studies, Management, Maritime Supply and Management, Marketing, Mathematics (Applied Mathematics, Statistics/Biostatistics), Mechanical Engineering,Mechanical Engineering Technology (Manufacturing Systems, Mechanical Systems Design, Nuclear Engineering Technology), Medical Technology, Music (Music Composition, Music Education, Music Performance), Nuclear Medicine Technology, Nursing, Occupational and Technical Studies (Fashion, Industrial Technology, Marketing Education, Technology Education, Training Specialist), Ocean and Earth Sciences, Philosophy (Political/Legal Studies, Religious Studies), Physical Education (Exercise Science, Physical Education, Sport Management), Physics, Political Science, Psychology, Recreation and Tourism Studies (Recreation and Tourism Management, Therapeutic Recreation), Sociology (Anthropology, Social Welfare), Speech Language Pathology and Audiology, Theatre and Dance, Women's Studies

Old Dominion Continued

Pre-professional Programs:

Law, Medicine, Pharmacy

Teacher Licensure Program: Yes

Retention Rate: 77%

Student/Faculty Ratio: 18:1

Average Class Size: 30

Cool Programs: Study abroad, undergraduate research opportunities, upperclassmen mentoring program, specialized workshops available only to first-year students, independent studies courses, cooperative education program, student-designed major

Distance Learning Options: Yes

Financial Stats:

Undergraduate In-State Tuition: $6,300 full time, $211 per credit hour

Room and Board Fees: $6,834

Yearly Cost of Attendance: $15,134

Receiving Financial Aid: 64%

Life Off-Campus:

Living On-Campus: 23%

ROTC: Army, Navy

Varsity Sports: Baseball, basketball (m/w), field hockey, football, golf (m/w), lacrosse (w), sailing, soccer (m/w), swimming and diving, tennis (m/w), wrestling. The university will start a football program in 2009

Sports level: NCAA Division I

Cool Clubs: African Caribbean Association, Rock Climbing Club, Artificial Intelligence Initiative, Aviation Club, Rhythms Tap Association, Hip Hop Summit Action Network

Extra Credit: Radford University, Virginia Intermont College, Virginia Wesleyan College

Radford University

www.radford.edu

East Main Street, Radford, VA 24141
Admissions Office: (800) 890-4265, ruadmiss@radford.edu

The Basics

Type of School: Public
Type of Campus: Rural
Size: 8,155 undergrads, 9,220 total

Male/Female Ratio: 40/60
Diversity: 11% minority
Out of State Students: 8%

FYI: Armed with strong teachers (83% of whom hold their terminal degrees and seven of whom have won Fulbright Scholarships), unique academic programs (including majors in Music Therapy and Fashion Design and Merchandising), and a full roster of on-campus clubs, speakers, performing arts groups, musical productions, cultural events, and guest lecturers, Radford strives to bring a well-rounded education directly to your door. Students from 35 states and 35 countries flock to this Blue Ridge campus to take advantage of the school's 140 degree programs and 200+ student organizations. If you can make it through Radford's rigorous academic programs, you'll be handsomely rewarded in the end. 93% of RU grads find work or graduate school acceptance letters within eight months of leaving campus.

Admission Stats:

Admissions Deadlines: Early Action – Dec. 1, Regular Admissions – Feb. 1, Transfer Admissions – June 1 (fall semester), Nov. 1 (spring semester)

How to Apply: Apply online or download an application at: http://www.radford.edu/admissions/ruinfo/applyru.html

Application Requirements: Online or paper application, $50 application fee, high school transcript, SAT or ACT scores, In-state Tuition Form for VA residents

Accepts the Common Application: No

Average SAT Score: 1000

Radford University Continued

Academic Life On-Campus:

Honors program: Yes

Majors Offered: Accounting, Anthropology, Art (Studio Art, Art Education, Art History, and Museum Studies, Three Dimensional Art, Two Dimensional Art, Biology (Biotechnology, Environmental Biology, General Biology, Chemistry Communications (communications studies, organizational, public communication, public relations) Communication Sciences and Disorders, Computer Science and Technology (Computer Science, Database, Networks, Software Engineering) English (general English, Technical and Business Writing)Exercise, Sport and Health Education (Athletic Training, Exercise and Sport Science, Health Education and Health Promotion, Physical and Health Education, Sport and Wellness Leadership), Finance, Foreign Language (French, German, Spanish), Geography (Environmental Studies, General Geography, Planning, Technical), Geology (General Geology, Environmental and Engineering Geoscience), History, Information Science and Systems (Enterprise Systems and Development, Information Systems, Web Development, Sports Administration, Sports Medicine), Media Studies (Advertising, Journalism, Production Technology, Web Design), Medical Technology, Music (General Music, Composition, Music and Technology, Music Business, Music Education, Music Therapy), Nursing, Philosophy, Physics, Political Science (General Political Science, American Government, Comparative Government, Political Theory, Public Administration), Psychology, Recreation, Parks, and Tourism (Outdoor Recreation, Recreation Management, Therapeutic Recreation), Religious Studies, Social Science, Social Work, Sociology, Theatre

Pre-professional Programs:

Dentistry, Medicine, Forensic Studies, Pharmacy

Teacher Licensure Program: Yes

Retention Rate: 74%

Student/Faculty Ratio: 20:1

Average Class Size: 35

Cool Programs: Study abroad, undergraduate research opportunities, first-year residential learning communities, first-year intro to college course, independent studies courses, student-designed majors

Distance Learning Options: Yes

Financial Stats:

Undergraduate In-State Tuition: $5,746 full time, $257 per credit hour

Room and Board Fees: $6,218

Yearly Cost of Attendance: $13,964

Receiving Financial Aid: 66%

Life Off-Campus:

Living On-Campus: 32%

ROTC: Army

Varsity Sports: Baseball, basketball (m/w), cross country (m/w), golf (m/w), soccer (m/w), softball, swimming and diving (w), tennis (m/w), track and field (m/w), volleyball (w)

Sports level: NCAA Division I

Cool Clubs: Motorcycle Club, Habitat for Humanity, Ski and Snowboarding Club, American Red Cross, Rugby Club

Extra Credit: Old Dominion University, Bridgewater College, Mary Baldwin College

Randolph College *(formerly Randolph-Macon Woman's College)* www.rmwc.edu

2500 Rivermont Avenue. Lynchburg, VA 24503
Admissions Office: (800) 745-7692, admissions@rmwc.edu

The Basics

Type of School: Private
Type of Campus: Suburban
Size: 730 undergrads

Male/Female Ratio: Enrolling men this fall
Diversity: 30% minority
Out of State Students: 27%

FYI: Planning and prioritizing are the keys to making it at Randolph College. Starting in year one, students create a Macon Plan, a step-by-step educational guide that incorporates in as well as out of class experiences. By sitting down with an academic advisor and planning out which courses, extracurricular activities, volunteer projects, internships, research projects, and study abroad trips best fit your educational and career goals, Randolph College students know exactly how to take advantage of everything their campus offers. This year the boys will have a chance to. In 2007, RC officially went co-ed.
Notable Names: Nobel Prize winner Pearl S. Buck, U.S. Senator Blanche Lincoln, CNN Senior Political Correspondent Candy Crowley, Anne Tucker (named "America's Best Curator" by Time Magazine)

Admission Stats:

Admissions Deadlines: Early Decision – Nov. 15, Presidential Scholars Admissions – Dec. 10, Regular Admissions – March 1, Transfer Admissions – May 15 (fall semester)

How to Apply: Apply online or download a paper application at http://www.rmwc.edu/admissions/apply.asp

Application Requirements: Online or paper application, $35 application fee (fee waived if applying online or with The Common Application), high school transcript, SAT or ACT scores, letter of recommendation from your high school counselor, principal, or one of your senior year teachers, essay

Accepts the Common Application: Yes

Average SAT Score: 1178

Academic Life On-Campus:

Honors program: Yes

Majors Offered: American Culture, Anthropology, Art (History, History/Museum Studies, Studio), Biology, Chemistry, Classics (Archeology, Civilization, Languages), Communication Studies, Curricular Studies (Teaching Program Students only), Dance, Economics (General Economics, International Economics), Engineering Physics (dual degree program in conjuction with Virginia Commonwealth University, Vanderbilt University,Washington University St. Louis, and the University of Virginia), English (American Literature, British and American Literature, British Literature, Creative Writing, Reading and Writing of Fiction), Environmental Studies, Foreign Language (French Civilization, French for Commerce, German, Russian, Spanish), Global Studies, Health Services, History, Independently Designed Major, International Studies, Mathematics, Music (History, Performance, Theory), Philosophy, Physical Education and Health, Physics, Political Science (American Politics, Comparative Politics), Psychology, Religious Studies , Sociology, Sport and Exercise Studies, Theatre

Pre-professional Programs:

Business, Health Professions, Law , Medicine

Teacher Licensure Program: Yes

Retention Rate: 61%

Student/Faculty Ratio: 9:1

Average Class Size: 12

Cool Programs: Study abroad, independent studies courses, undergraduate research opportunities, summer research program, student-designed majors, upperclassmen mentoring program, residential leadership program, joint degree programs, first-year interdisciplinary seminars, Seven College Exchange member

Distance Learning Options: No

Financial Stats:

Undergraduate In-State Tuition: $25,350 full time, $1,060 per credit hour

Room and Board Fees: $9,000

Yearly Cost of Attendance: $36,350

Randolph College Continued

Life Off-Campus:

Living On-Campus: 95%

ROTC: None

Varsity Sports: Basketball, field hockey, riding, soccer, softball, swimming, cross country, tennis, volleyball
Sports level: NCAA Division III

Cool Clubs: Frozen Turkey Bowling intramurals, Classic Movie Club, Dollars and Sense Club, Food and Justice Club, Pan World Club, Sock and Buskin club, Student Global AIDS Campaign

Extra Credit: Sweet Briar College, Hollins University, Emory and Henry College

Randolph-Macon College www.rmc.edu

P.O. Box 5005, Ashland, VA 23005
Admissions Office: (804) 752-7305, admissions@rmc.edu

The Basics

Type of School: Private
Type of Campus: Suburban
Size: 1,150 undergrads

Male/Female Ratio: 46/54
Diversity: 14% minority
Out of State Students: 31%

FYI: Small classes, a small student body, and a high faculty-student ratio mean student success at Randolph-Macon. Here you can expect to receive individualized attention from professors eager to answer your questions. Randolph-Macon also offers a number of hands-on learning programs including summer research opportunities for undergrads and both domestic and international internship opportunities. That personal touch is proven to help Randolph-Macon students succeed both in and after college. Since 1920, Randolph-Macon has produced a higher percentage of future Ph.D. candidates than any other independent school in the state. This is where three state governors, four United States ambassadors, and 12 college or university presidents got their start.

Notable Names: Dollar Tree Founder Macon Brock, Congressmen Randy Forbes and Hugh Scott, International Youth Advocates founder Gregory Smith (also the youngest person in the U.S. to graduate from college. He completed a mathematics degree and two minors by the age of 13).

Admission Stats:

Admissions Deadlines: Early Decision – Nov. 15, Early Action – Dec. 1, Presidential Scholars Admissions – Feb. 1, Regular Admissions – March 1, Transfer Admissions – March 1 (Fall Semester), Jan. 1 (Spring Semester)

How to Apply: Apply online or download a paper application at http://www.rmc.edu/apply

Application Requirements: Online or paper application, $30 application fee, high school transcript, SAT or ACT scores, letter of recommendation from your guidance counselor
Optional: SAT II test scores, additional recommendations

Accepts the Common Application: Yes

Average SAT Score: 1086

Academic Life On-Campus:

Honors program: Yes

Majors Offered: Accounting, Art (Studio), Art History, Arts Management, Biology, Chemistry, Classical Studies, Computer Science, Drama, Economics (Business Economics, General Economics), English, Environmental Studies, Foreign Language (French, German, Greek, Latin, Spanish), History, International Relations, Mathematics, Music, Philosophy, Physics, Political Science, Psychology, Religious Studies, Sociology, Women's Studies

Pre-professional Programs:

Engineering, Law, Medicine

Teacher Licensure Program: Yes

Retention Rate: 76%

Student/Faculty Ratio: 11:1

Average Class Size: 16

Cool Programs: Study abroad, undergraduate research opportunities, summer research program, independent studies courses, student-designed majors, upperclassmen mentoring program, residential learning communities, themed housing, first-year cross-disciplinary seminars, Seven College Exchange member

Distance Learning Options: No

Randolph-Macon College Continued

Financial Stats:

Undergraduate In-State Tuition: $26,195 full time, $2,910 for one to two credits. Taking 3 or ore credits qualifies as full time.

Room and Board Fees: $7,685

Yearly Cost of Attendance: $35,880

Receiving Financial Aid: 96%

Life Off-Campus:

Living On-Campus: 74%

ROTC: Army in conjunction with the University of Richmond

Varsity Sports: Baseball, basketball (m/w), field hockey, football, lacrosse (m/w), soccer (m/w), softball, swimming (w), tennis (m/w), volleyball (w)

Sports level: NCAA Division III

Cool Clubs: Children's Miracle Network Dance Marathon Committee, Macon Peer Response, Macon Outdoors Club

Extra Credit: Christopher Newport University, Hampton University, Hampden-Sydney College

Regent University www.regent.edu

1000 Regent University Drive, Virginia Beach, VA 23464
Admissions Office: (800) 210-0060, undergrad@regent.edu

The Basics

Type of School: Private
Type of Campus: Small City
Size: 1,123 undergrads, 4,343 total

Male/Female Ratio: 34/66
Diversity: 30% minority
Out of State Students: 46%

FYI: The brainchild of Pat Robertson himself, Regent University is committed to turning out dedicated Christian leaders. Regent classes are short, lasting only eight weeks each, giving students more control over their schedules. Whether you're taking courses in the classroom or through the school's extensive online learning program, all undergrad students start their college career off by taking a Contemporary Problems for Christian Leaders course. Regent is perhaps best known for its School of Communications. Home to Academy Award-winning producers, nationally-known actors, and Emmy award-winning graphic technicians, the school has a reputation for alumni success.

Notable Names: Student Academy Award-winning producer Doug Smith, Emmy award-winning graphics specialist Peggy Southerland is the Program Director for Regent's School of Communications, *Arrested Development* actor Tony Hale, Vice President of Zambia Dr. Nevers Mumba

Admission Stats:

Admissions Deadlines: August 14, Oct. 9, Dec. 18, Feb. 26, April 23, June 18

How to Apply: Apply online at http://www.regent.edu/acad/undergrad/admissions/admissions_process.cfm

Application Requirements: Online or paper application, $40 application fee, signed Community of Life form, SAT or ACT scores, high school transcript

Accepts the Common Application: No

Average SAT Score: 1104

Academic Life On-Campus:

Honors program: No

Majors Offered: Communication (Animation, Professional Communication), Global Business (International Management, Management Information Systems), Interdisciplinary Studies, Organizational Leadership and Management, Political Science, Psychology, Religious Studies

Regent University Continued

Pre-professional Programs:

Seminary

Teacher Licensure Program: Yes

Retention Rate: 57%

Student/Faculty Ratio: 7:1

Average Class Size: 12

Cool Programs: Study abroad at Oxford, student-designed majors, Early Start program for high school students, Council for Christian Colleges and Universities member, member of the Virginia Tidewater Consortium along with Christopher Newport University, the College of William and Mary, Norfolk State University, Old Dominion University, and Virginia Wesleyan College

Distance Learning Options: Yes

Financial Stats:

Undergraduate In-State Tuition: $12,115 full time, $420 per credit hour

Yearly Cost of Attendance: $14,115 plus housing (Regent does not offer student housing or meal plans

Receiving Financial Aid: 96%

Life Off-Campus:

Living On-Campus: No housing available for undergrads

ROTC: None

Varsity Sports: None offered

Sports level: N/A

Cool Clubs: Students in Free Enterprise, International Student Organization, Regent Undergrad Council, Student Alumni Ambassadors

Extra Credit: Liberty University, Marymount University, Virginia Intermont College

Roanoke College www.roanoke.edu

221 College Lane, Salem, VA 24153
Admissions Office: (800) 388-2276, admissions@roanoke.edu

The Basics

Type of School: Private
Type of Campus: Suburban
Size: 1,970 undergrads
Male/Female Ratio: 44/56
Diversity: 10% minority
Out of State Students: 43%

FYI: Prepare to work your body and your mind. Recently ranked as the 19th fittest campus in the nation by Men's Fitness magazine, Roanoke College lets you get your kicks in free through on-campus cardio kickboxing classes, hiking to ancient Japanese temples (over 100 study abroad programs available), or competing in any of the school's 19 varsity sports programs. To make it here, you'll have to break a mental sweat too. In addition to their majors, students also complete a four-year interdisciplinary liberal arts curriculum that focuses on developing writing and reasoning skills.

Notable Names: Pulitzer Prize nominee Carol M. Swain, McAfee Anti-Virus creator and entrepreneur John McAfee, 1993 National Coach of the Year Frankie Allen, Lynchburg College President Kenneth Garren, Film Producer David C. Robinson (producer of Man of the Year and Two For the Money), Surh Beung Kiu, the first Korean to graduate from an American college

Admission Stats:

Admissions Deadlines: Early Action – Sept. 30, Early Decision – Dec. 1, Regular Admissions – March 15, Transfer Admissions – Rolling Admissions

How to Apply: Apply online at www.roanoke.edu/apply or request a paper application at http://web.roanoke.edu/x408.xml

Application Requirements: Online or paper application, $30 application fee (waived for online application), high school transcript, SAT or ACT scores

Optional: Essay, three letters of recommendation, at least one from your guidance counselor

Accepts the Common Application: Yes

Average SAT Score: 1105

Roanoke College Continued

Academic Life On-Campus:

Honors program: Yes

Majors Offered: Art, Art History, Athletic Training, Biochemistry, Biology (General Biology, Pre-Medicine track, Pre-Veterinary Medicine track), Business Administration (Accounting, Business Leadership, Finance, Global Business, Health Care Administration, Human Resource Management, Marketing), Chemistry (General Chemistry, Pre-Medicine track), Computer Information Systems, Computer Science, Criminal Justice, Economics, Engineering (Joint degree program with Virginia Tech or the University of Tennessee Knoxville), English (American Literature, British Literature, Communications, Creative Writing), Environmental Policy, Environmental Science, Foreign Languages (French, Spanish), Health and Human Performance (Elementary Education, PK-6, Secondary Education), History (East Asian Studies, European History, Hispanic/Latin American and Caribbean Studies, U.S. History), International Relations (Africa and the African Diaspora, Foreign Politics, Legal Studies) , Mathematics (Statistics), Medical Technology, Music, Philosophy, Physics, Political Science (Africa and the African Diaspora, American Politics, Foreign Politics, Legal Studies), Psychology (Human Development), Religion, Sociology (Health Care Delivery, Information Analysis), Theatre (Dramaturgy, Theatre Performance, Theatrical Design), Theology (Parish Youth Leadership)

Pre-professional Programs:

Dentistry, Law, Medicine, Pharmacy, Veterinary Medicine, Ministry

Teacher Licensure Program: Yes

Retention Rate: 84%

Student/Faculty Ratio: 14:1

Average Class Size: 18

Cool Programs: Study abroad, undergraduate research opportunities, independent studies courses, first year college transition courses, joint degree programs, upperclassmen mentoring program, themed housing

Distance Learning Options: No

Financial Stats:

Undergraduate In-State Tuition: $25,550 full time, $407 per credit hour.

Room and Board Fees: $8,726

Yearly Cost of Attendance: $36,276

Receiving Financial Aid: 85%

Life Off-Campus:

Living On-Campus: 66%

ROTC: None

Varsity Sports: Baseball, basketball (m/w), cross country (m/w), field hockey, golf (m), lacrosse (m/w), soccer (m/w), softball, tennis (m/w), indoor and outdoor track and field (m/w), volleyball (w)

Sports level: NCAA Division III

Cool Clubs: Order of the Phoenix, Roanoke College Films, Billiards Club, Hockey Club, Outdoor Adventures club, Historical Society, College Bowl team

Extra Credit: Sweet Briar College, Emory and Henry College, Bridgewater College

Saint Paul's College

115 College Drive, Lawrenceville, VA 23868
Admissions Office: (434) 848-3111, admissions@saintpauls.edu

The Basics

Type of School: Private
Type of Campus: Rural
Size: 700 total

Male/Female Ratio: 48/52
Diversity: 1%
Out of State Students: 25%

FYI: One of the South's oldest historically black colleges, Saint Paul's has a long history of serving the educational needs of a wide demographic of students. The College is currently the only school in the state to boast an on-campus residential program designed for single parents. Offering single parents specialized housing, mentoring, counseling, and tutoring assistance, the single parents program assists scholarly moms and dads with both academic and career planning help.

Admission Stats:

Admissions Deadlines: Rolling

How to Apply: Download an application at http://www.saint-pauls.edu/admissions/applicationprocess.htm

Application Requirements: Paper application, $20 application fee, two letters of recommendation, SAT or ACT scores, essay, high school transcript

Accepts The Common Application: No

Average GPA: 2.2

Average SAT Score: 731

Academic Life On-Campus:

Majors Offered: Biology, Business Administration (Accounting, General Business Administration, Management, Management Information Systems, Marketing), Computer Science, Criminal Justice, English (Literature, Mass Communications), General Studies, History/Social Science, Mathematics, Political Science, Religious Studies, Sociology (Criminal Justice, General Sociology, Human Services, Social Work)

Pre-professional Programs:

Medicine

Teacher Licensure Program: Yes

Retention Rate: 25%

Student/Faculty Ratio: 18:1

Average Class Size: 25

Cool programs: Study abroad, Single Parent Program, student-designed majors, student leadership program, accelerated degree program,

Distance Learning Options: Yes

Financial Stats:

Undergraduate In-State Tuition: $10,800 full time, $470 per credit hour

Room and Board Fees: $6,190

Yearly Cost of Attendance: $18,210

Receiving Financial Aid: 95%

Life Off-Campus:

Living on campus: 61%

ROTC: Yes

Varsity Sports: baseball, basketball (m/w), bowling (w), cross country (m/w), football, softball, tennis (m), track (m/w), volleyball (w)

Sports level: NCAA Division II

Cool Clubs: Saint Paul's flag football tournaments, Students in Free Enterprise, Poetry Club

Shenandoah University

1460 University Drive, Winchester, VA 22601
Admissions Office: (800) 432-2266, admit@su.edu

The Basics

Type of School: Private
Type of Campus: Small Town
Size: 3,000 total – 1,500 undergrads
Male/Female Ratio: 40/60
Diversity: 9% minority
Out of State Students: 44%

As a private liberal arts institution, Shenandoah University draws creative minds from 46 states and 42 countries to its eye-pleasing campus. In addition to programs you won't find anywhere else in the country (think Theatre for Youth, Contemporary Commercial Music, Nurse Midwifery and Pharmacogenomics), the campus also offers the Citizen Scholars Program designed to promote global citizenship. Citizen Scholars attend seminars covering headliner hot topics such as human rights, terrorism, and the AIDS crisis by day and by night share a residence hall and attend specialized workshops and programs. Whether you're bound for Hollywood or the halls of the U.N., Shenandoah can help you get started.

Notable Names: Broadway star J. Robert Spencer.

Shenandoah University Continued

Admission Stats:

Admissions Deadlines: Rolling Admissions, Priority applications should be in by Nov. 1.

How to Apply: Apply online at https://www.applyweb.com/apply/su/index.html or download an application at http://www.su.edu/undergraduateapplication2006.pdf

Application Requirements: Online or paper application, $30 application fee, high school transcript, SAT or ACT scores, letter of recommendation from your guidance counselor, audition or portfolio if applying to Shenandoah Conservatory.

Accepts The Common Application: No

Average GPA: 3.21

Average SAT Score: 1026

Academic Life On-Campus:

Honors program: Yes

Majors Offered: Acting, Administration of Justice, Arts Management (Acting, Classical Music, Dance, Jazz, Technical, Technical Theatre), Arts Studies, American Studies, Biology (General Biology, Pre-Pharmacy track, Pre-Physical Therapy track, Pre-Physicians Assistant track), Business Administration, Chemistry, Church Music (organ or voice emphasis), Dance (Dance Education, General Dance), Educational Psychology, English, Environmental Studies, History, Individualized Studies, Jazz Studies, Kinesiology (Exercise Science, Pre-Athletic Training), Mass Communications, Mathematics, Music Education (Choral Concentration – Piano, Choral Concentration – Voice, Instrument Concentration – Non-Piano, Instrument Concentration – Piano), Music Performance (Brass and Percussion, Classical Vocal Studies, Opera, Organ, Piano, Woodwinds or String), Music Production and Recording Technology (Classical Emphasis, Jazz Emphasis), Music Therapy (Classical Applied Study, Jazz Applied Study), Musical Theatre, Nursing, Philosophy and Religion, Political Science (General Political Science, Pre-Law track), Psychology (General Psychology, Pre-Occupational Therapy track), Scene and Lighting Design, Sociology, Theatre for Youth

Pre-professional Programs:

Athletic Training, Health Professions, Law, Pharmacy, Physical Therapy, Occupational Therapy

Teacher Licensure Program: Yes

Retention Rate: 75%

Student/Faculty Ratio: 9:1

Average Class Size: 10

Cool programs: Study abroad, undergraduate research opportunities, student-designed majors, independent studies courses, residential learning communities, Student Citizenship Program for rising high school seniors.

Distance Learning Options: Yes

Financial Stats:

Undergraduate In-State Tuition: $21,090 full time, $610 per credit hour

Room and Board Fees: $7,220

Yearly Cost of Attendance: $30,310

Receiving Financial Aid: 87%

Life Off-Campus:

Living on campus: 24%

ROTC: None

Varsity Sports: Baseball, basketball (m/w), cross country (m/w), field hockey, football, golf (m), lacrosse (m/w), soccer (m/w), softball, tennis (m/w), track and field (m/w), volleyball (w). Sports level: NCAA Division III

Cool Clubs: Avalon Literary Magazine, International Association of Jazz Education, Society for Collegiate Journalists, Students in Free Enterprise (SIFE), Colleges Against Cancer.

Sweet Briar College www.sbc.edu

Sweet Briar College, Sweet Briar, VA 24595
Admissions Office: (800) 381-6142, admissions@sbc.edu

The Basics

Type of School: Private
Type of Campus: Rural
Size: 739 total
Male/Female Ratio: 0/100
Diversity: 13% minority
Out of State Students: 62%

FYI: Sweet Briar College is a feast for the eyes as well as the mind. This women's college set on 3,250 acres of rolling Blue Ridge Mountains is consistently named one of the most beautiful campuses in the country. Besides the six nature sanctuaries, 30 academic buildings, and two lakes found on campus, Sweet Briar also uses the land to operate one of the nation's foremost equestrian programs. Giddy up.

Notable Names: Former president of Discovery Communications' Consumer Products Division, Michela English, President and Co-Founder of Crystal-Barkley Corporation,Nella Gray, Actress Diana Muldaur Dozier

Admission Stats:

Admissions Deadlines: Early Decision – Dec, 1, Regular Admissions – Feb. 1, Transfers Admissions - May 1 (fall semester), Nov. 1 (spring semester)

How to Apply: Apply online or download an application at http://sbc.edu/admissions/apply.html

Application Requirements: Online or paper application, $40 application fee, high school transcript, letter of recommendation from a guidance counselor, letter of recommendation from a teacher, SAT or ACT scores, essay, Common Application Supplement (if applicable)

Accepts the Common Application: Yes

Average SAT Score: 1130

Academic Life On-Campus:

Honors program: Yes

Majors Offered: Anthropology, Art History, Art (Studio), Biology, Biochemistry and Molecular Biology, Business Management, Chemistry, Classical Studies, Computer Science, Dance, Economics, Engineering, English (Creative Writing, General English), Environmental Studies and Environmental Science, Foreign Language (French, German, Italian, Spanish) , Government, History, International Relations, Mathematics (General Mathematics, Mathematics – Physics), Music (Applied Music, General Music, History and Theory), Philosophy, Psychology, Physics, Religion, Sociology, Theatre

Pre-professional Programs:

Health Professions, Law, Medicine, Veterinary Medicine

Teacher Licensure Program: Yes

Retention Rate: 79%

Student/Faculty Ratio: 8:1

Average Class Size: 12

Cool Programs: Study abroad, undergraduate research opportunities, student-designed majors, first year leadership program, peer mentoring program, independent studies courses, Seven College Exchange member

Distance Learning Options: No

Financial Stats:

Undergraduate In-State Tuition: $24,740 full time, $820 per credit hour.

Room and Board Fees: $10,040

Yearly Cost of Attendance: $36,780

Receiving Financial Aid: 92%

Life Off-Campus:

Living On-Campus: 97%

ROTC: None

Varsity Sports: Field hockey, lacrosse, soccer, softball, swimming, tennis, volleyball

Sports level: NCAA Division III

Cool Clubs: Amnesty International, Sweet Briar Outdoor Program, Flag Football Intramural team, Sweet Tones, Taps and Toes, SBC Fencing Team

Sweet Briar College Continued

Extra Credit: Hollins University, Roanoke College, University of Mary Washington

University of Mary Washington

www.umw.edu

1301 College Avenue, Fredericksburg, VA 22401
Admissions Office: (540) 654-2000

The Basics

Type of School: Public
Type of Campus: Small Town
Size: 3,900 undergrads, 4,600 total
Male/Female Ratio: 33/67
Diversity: 13% minority
Out of State Students: 26%

FYI: Students who do well academically will thrive at Mary Washington, but it's also for students who know how to have a good time in the process. One of just two public schools in the state without any social fraternities or sororities, Mary Washington encourages students to get involved through the 100+ student organizations available as well as through the concerts, art exhibits, plays, barbeques, book readings, band competitions, volunteer events, food tastings, and film screenings offered on-campus throughout the year. Speakers from the top of their fields also flock to UMW to participate in several of the school's on-campus lecture series. In 2006, UMW brought former Ambassador of Jordan, Edward W. Gnehm Jr., Pulitzer Prize-winning writer, Edward P. Jones, best-selling author Tim Russert, and singer Judy Collins.

Notable Names: Former US Ambassador to El Salvador Rose Likins, Pulitzer Prize-winning poet Claudia Emerson (current professor), Gregory Stanton, Founder of Genocide Watch, Emmy Award-winning correspondent Judy Muller, Civil rights leader James Farmer (former professor)

Admission Stats:

Admissions Deadlines: Non-binding Early Decision/Honors Program Applications – Jan. 15, Regular Admissions – Feb. 1, Transfer Admissions – March 1 (fall semester), Nov. 1 (spring semester)

How to Apply: Apply online or download an application at http://www.umw.edu/admissions/apply/default.php

Application Requirements: Online or paper application, $45 application fee, high school transcript, SAT or ACT scores, honor statement, In-state Tuition Form for VA residents, Common Application Supplement (if applicable)

Accepts the Common Application: Yes

Average SAT Score: 1205

Academic Life On-Campus:

Honors program: Offered in some majors

Majors Offered: American Studies, Anthropology, Art and Art History, Biology, Business Administration, Chemistry, Classics, Computer Science, Economics, Education, English, Environmental Science, Foreign Languages (French, German, Greek, Latin, Spanish), Geography, Geology, Health Education, Historic Preservation, History, Interdisciplinary Studies, International Affairs, Mathematics, Music, Philosophy, Physics, Psychology, Religion , Sociology, Theatre

Pre-professional Programs:

Dentistry, Law, Medicine, Veterinary Medicine

Teacher Licensure Program: Yes

Retention Rate: 86%

Student/Faculty Ratio: 16:1

Average Class Size: 22

Cool Programs: Study abroad, undergraduate research opportunities and grants, first-year leadership program, independent studies courses, first-year seminars, student-designed majors, first-year residential learning communities, upperclassmen mentoring program

Distance Learning Options: Yes

Financial Stats:

Undergraduate In-State Tuition: $6,494 full time, $228 per credit hour

Room and Board Fees: $6,606

Yearly Cost of Attendance: $15,100

Receiving Financial Aid: 54%

University of Mary Washington Continued

Life Off-Campus:

Living On-Campus: 70%

ROTC: None

Varsity Sports: Baseball, basketball (m/w), cross country (m/w), equestrian (m/w), field hockey, lacrosse (m/w), rowing (m/w), soccer (m/w), softball, swimming (m/w), tennis (m/w), track and field (m/w), volleyball (w)

Sports level: Cheap Seats Cinema, Community Outreach and Resources, Giant Productions, Historic Preservation Club, Trek Club, Ultimate Frisbee team

Extra Credit: Sweet Briar College, James Madison University, College of William and Mary

University of Richmond www.richmond.edu

28 Westhampton Way, University of Richmond, VA 23173
Admissions Office: (800) 700-1662, (804) 289-8640, admissions@richmond.edu

The Basics

Type of School: Private
Type of Campus: Suburban
Size: 2,900 undergrads, 3,700 total
Male/Female Ratio: 49/51
Diversity: 18% minority
Out of State Students: 85% (undergrads only)

FYI: It's not quite the Ivies, but it may as well be. With its small classes, distinguished faculty, and impressive selection of academic programs, UR ranks right up there with Harvard, Yale, and the rest of the gang. Besides a strong first-year liberal arts curriculum, 75 study abroad programs, service learning opportunities, and undergraduate research projects, the school is also home to the Jepson School of Leadership Studies, the nation's first undergraduate school dedicated to the study and teaching of leadership. Despite its high price tag, UR also provides generous financial aid to its enrollees. One out of every fifteen incoming students receives a full-tuition merit-based scholarship and meets 100% of demonstrated eligibility for need-based aid.
Notable Names: Pulitzer Prize winning historian Douglas Freeman, musician Bruce Hornsby, former Phillip Morris CEO Frank Resnick, Congressman Virgil Goode, Space Shuttle Astronaut Leland Melvin, Major League baseball players Tim Stauffer, Brian Jordan and Sean Casey.

Admission Stats:

Admissions Deadlines: Early Decision – Nov. 15 and Jan. 15
Richmond Scholars Program Admissions – Dec. 15
Regular Admissions – Jan. 15
Transfer Admissions – Nov. 1 (Fall Semester), Feb. 1 (Spring Semester)

How to Apply: Apply online or download an application at http://admissions.richmond.edu/apply

Application Requirements: Online Common Application or Richmond Web Application, $50 application fee or approved fee waiver, high school transcript, SAT with writing scores or ACT scores, essay, mid-year grade report, Common Application Supplement (if applicable).

Accepts the Common Application: Yes

Average GPA:A-/B+ average unweighted in academic courses

Average SAT Score: 1850 - 2030 (SAT I critical reading, math, writing combined)

Academic Life On-Campus:

Honors program: No, but some majors have honors designations.

Majors Offered: Accounting, American Studies , Art (Studio), Art History, Biochemistry and Molecular Biology, Biology (General Biology, Neuroscience), Business Administration (Accounting, Economics, Finance, General Business, International Business, Management Systems, Marketing), Chemistry, Classical Studies, Computer Science, Criminal Justice, Economics, English, Environmental Studies, Foreign Language (French, German, Greek, Italian, Latin, Russian, Spanish), History, Interdisciplinary Studies, International Studies (Africa, Asia, Individual programs, International Economics, Latin America, Modern Europe, World Politics and Diplomacy), Journalism, Leadership Studies, Mathematics, Mathematical Economics, Music, Philosophy, Physics (General Physics, Interdisciplinary Physics), Religion, Rhetoric and Communication Studies, Sociology, Theatre, Women, Gender, and Sexuality Studies

University of Richmond Continued

Pre-professional Programs:

Engineering, Health Professions, Law, Medicine, Geoscience

Teacher Licensure Program: Yes

Retention Rate: 93%

Student/Faculty Ratio: 10:1

Average Class Size: 16

Cool Programs: Study abroad, undergraduate research opportunities, first-year college transition program, residential learning communities, student-designed majors, independent studies courses, peer mentoring program, engineering joint degree program.

Distance Learning Options: Yes

Financial Stats:

Undergraduate In-State Tuition: $36,550 full time, $1,820.00 per credit hour

Room and Board Fees: $6,060

Yearly Cost of Attendance: $44,610

Receiving Financial Aid: 65%

Life Off-Campus:

Living On-Campus: 92%

ROTC: Army

Varsity Sports: Baseball, basketball (m/w), cross country (m/w), field hockey, football, golf (m/w), lacrosse (w), soccer (m/w), swimming (w), tennis (m/w), track and field (m/w)

Sports level: NCAA Division I

Cool Clubs: Mock Trial Team, Model United Nations Society, Women Involved in Living and Learning (WILL), Richmond Ranger Company, Volunteer Action Council (VAC), The Richmond Steel Project steel drum ensemble, U of R Poetry Symposium

Extra Credit: Washington and Lee University, College of William and Mary, University of Virginia

University of Virginia

www.virginia.edu

P.O. Box 400160, Charlottesville, VA 22904
Admissions Office: (434) 982-3200, undergradadmission@virginia.edu

The Basics

Type of School: Public
Type of Campus: Small City
Size: 13,353 undergrads, 20,397 total

Male/Female Ratio: 45/55
Diversity: 23% minority
Out of State Students: 32%

FYI: No matter where you go, casually drop the fact that you went to UVA and you're bound to turn some heads. Accepting only the best and the brightest (just check out that list of Notable Names), UVA is recognized by nearly every major guidebook as being a powerhouse educational institution. It's not just that the school offers heavily laurelled faculty members and challenging curriculums – it also pushes students to actively use what they learn in class through research, travel, and volunteerism. In addition to offering one of the largest study abroad programs anywhere (more than 200 programs available) and producing more Peace Corps-bound grads than any school in the state, UVA is also the only U.S.-based member of Universitas21, a student exchange partnership of 21 research-intensive schools located in 12 countries worldwide.

Notable Names: Edgar Allan Poe, Saturday Night Live writer Tina Fey, CBS Evening News Anchor Katie Couric, author David Baldacci, Cabinet Secretary Thurgood Marshall, Jr., George Allen, FBI Director Robert S. Mueller III, New York Times puzzle master Will Shortz, NY Giants running back Tiki Barber, Olympic Gold Medalist Dawn Staley, Former MGM President Samuel J. Goldwyn, Jr., President Woodrow Wilson

Admission Stats:

Admissions Deadlines: Regular Admissions – Jan. 2, Transfer Admissions – March 1 (fall semester), Nov. 1 (spring semester)

How to Apply: Apply online or download an application at: http://www.virginia.edu/undergradadmission/apply.html

Application Requirements: Online or paper application, Supplement for First-year Applicants, $60 application fee, high school transcript, First Semester Grade Report, SAT or ACT scores, scores from 2 SAT II tests, guidance counselor recommendation, essay, In-state Tuition Form for VA residents

Accepts the Common Application: No

Average SAT Score: 1325

University of Virginia Continued

Academic Life On-Campus:

Honors program: Yes

Majors Offered: Aerospace Engineering, African American Studies, Anthropology, Architectural History, Architecture, Area Studies, Art, Astronomy, Biology, Biomedical Engineering, Chemical Engineering, Chemistry, Civil Engineering, Classics, Commerce, Comparative Literature, Computer Engineering, Computer Science, Drama, Economics, Electrical Engineering, Engineering Science, English Language and Literatures, Environmental Sciences, Foreign Affairs, Foreign Languages and Literatures (French, German, Italian, Slavic, Spanish), Government, Health and Physical Education, History, Interdisciplinary Studies, Mathematics, Mechanical Engineering, Music, Nursing, Philosophy, Physics, Psychology, Religious Studies, Sociology, Speech Pathology and Audiology, Systems Engineering, Urban and Environmental Planning

Pre-professional Programs:

Medicine

Teacher Licensure Program: Yes

Retention Rate: 97%

Student/Faculty Ratio: 15:1

Average Class Size: 31

Cool Programs: Study abroad, undergraduate research opportunities, upperclassmen mentors, themed housing, independent studies courses, student-designed majors, joint degree programs offered, cooperative education program, Semester at Sea program, January term

Distance Learning Options: Yes

Financial Stats:

Undergraduate In-State Tuition: $8,690 full time, no part-time students admitted.
Room and Board Fees: $7,435

Yearly Cost of Attendance: $18,125

Receiving Financial Aid: 46%

Life Off-Campus:

Living On-Campus: 45%

ROTC: Army, Navy, Air Force

Varsity Sports: Baseball, basketball (m/w), cross country (m/w), field hockey, football, golf (m/w), lacrosse (m/w), rowing (w), soccer (m/w), softball, swimming and diving (m/w), tennis (m/w), track and field (m/w), wrestling, volleyball (w)

Sports level: NCAA Division I

Cool Clubs: Awesome Fishing Club, Boxing Training Club, Ballroom Dancing Club, Human Rights Study Project, UVA Motorsports Engineering Program, UVA Solar Car Program

Extra Credit: Virginia Polytechnic and State University, University of Richmond, College of William and Mary

University of Virginia's College at Wise

www.wise.virginia.edu

One College Avenue, Wise, VA 24293
Admissions Office: (276) 328-0102, info@uvawise.edu

The Basics

Type of School: Public
Type of Campus: Suburban
Size: 1,911 undergrads

Male/Female Ratio: 43/57
Diversity: 9% minority
Out of State Students: 5%

FYI: Think of it as UVA Lite. The smaller, cozier version of U.Va.'s main campus, UVa-Wise is significantly less selective than its Charlottesville-based counterpart. While you won't get weed-out classes and a grueling admissions process, you will get an academically supportive environment built around student success. From the First-Year Experience program (designed to help freshmen adjust to collegiate work and life) to post-graduation career counseling, UVa-Wise students never find themselves without administrative support. Studies show that the helping hand pays off. After graduation, 97% of UVa-Wise students have a job or are accepted into graduate school.

University of Virginia's College at Wise Continued

Admission Stats:

Admissions Deadlines: Early Action – Dec. 1, Feb. 1, Regular Admissions – Rolling

How to Apply: Apply online or download an application at: http://www.wise.virginia.edu/admissions/download_forms.html Application Requirements: Online or paper application, $25 application fee, high school transcript, SAT or ACT scores, 2 letters of recommendation, In-state Tuition Form for VA residents

Accepts the Common Application: No

Average SAT Score: 1006

Academic Life On-Campus:

Honors program: Yes

Majors Offered: Accounting, Administration of Justice, Art (Studio), Biology, Business Administration, Chemistry, Communication, Computer Science, Economics, English Literature, Environmental Science , Foreign Languages (French, German, Spanish), Government (Political Science, Public Administration), History, Interdisciplinary Studies, Management Information Systems, Mathematics, Medical Technology, Nursing, Pre-Denistry, Pre-Forestry, Pre-Law Studies, Pre-Medicine, Pre-Pharmacy, Pre-Physical Therapy, Pre-Veterinary, Psychology, Sociology, Software Engineering, Theatre

Pre-professional Programs:

Dentistry, Forestry, Law, Medicine, Pharmacy, Physical Therapy, Veterinary Medicine

Teacher Licensure Program: Yes

Retention Rate: 73%

Student/Faculty Ratio: 17:1

Average Class Size: 15

Cool Programs: The only undergraduate degree program in software engineering in Virginia. Study abroad, undergraduate research opportunities, upperclassmen mentors, cooperative education program in some majors, independent studies courses, introductory courses for first-year students only

Distance Learning Options: Yes

Financial Stats:

Undergraduate In-State Tuition: $6,151 full time, $141 per credit hour

Room and Board Fees: $6,742

Yearly Cost of Attendance: $14,893

Receiving Financial Aid: 80%

Life Off-Campus:

Living On-Campus: 33%

ROTC: None (currently under consideration)

Varsity Sports: Baseball, basketball (m/w), cross country (m/w), football, golf (m), softball (w), tennis (m/w), volleyball (w)

Sports level: National Association of Intercollegiate Athletics, Division II

Cool Clubs: Bass Fishing Club, Medieval Appreciation Society, Undergraduate Research Association, Wallyball Tournament, Step Team, Tandem Skydiving

Extra Credit: Christopher Newport University, Roanoke College, Randolph-Macon College

Virginia Commonwealth University www.vcu.edu

910 West Franklin Street, Richmond, VA 23284
Admissions Office: (804) 828-1222, ugrad@vcu.edu

The Basics

Type of School: Public
Type of Campus: Urban
Size: 21,260 undergrads, 30,381 total
Male/Female Ratio: 38/62
Diversity: 40% minority
Out of State Students: 12%

FYI: Boasting one of the best fine arts programs in the state, the nation's top advertising program, one of the nation's leading health care centers, and the first undergrad Homeland Security and Emergency Preparedness program to be offered by a U.S. research university, VCU is a cornucopia of learning opportunities. Nestled in the heart of the state's capital, VCU offers students first-class research facilities (like a full-scale medical center, a bioinformatics computing lab, and a nucleic acid research center), opportunities to intern with major companies and state government offices, and the chance to have their work displayed at a wide array of city venues. Diversity, both in terms of the student body as well as the academic programs offered, is the buzzword here. Notable Names: Gesundheit! Institute Founder and subject of the film Patch Adams, Dr. Hunter "Patch" Adams, Nobel Laureates John Fenn and Baruj Benacerraf, Authors David Baldacci and Tom Robbins, Hepatitis B Vaccine Discoverer Saul Krugman

Admission Stats:

Admissions Deadlines: Admissions with Scholarship Consideration – Jan. 5, Regular Admissions – Feb. 1 (fall semester), Dec. 1 (spring semester), Transfer Admissions – June 1 (fall semester), Dec. 1 (spring semester)

How to Apply: Apply online or download an application at: http://www.vcu.edu/ugrad/apply/index.html

Application Requirements: Online or paper application, $30 application fee ($55 if applying to the School of the Arts), high school transcript and profile, SAT or ACT scores, essay (for scholarship consideration), letters of recommendation, In-state Tuition Form for VA residents, portfolio for School of the Arts applicants

Accepts the Common Application: No

Average SAT Score: 1065

Academic Life On-Campus:

Honors program: Yes

Majors Offered: Accounting, African American Studies, Anthropology, Art Education, Art History (Architectural History, General Art History), Bioinformatics (Biology/Genomics, Computational Science Bioinformatics, Quantitative/Statistical Bioinformatics), Biology, Business Administration (Entrepreneurship and Small Business Management, Finance, General Business Administration, Human Resource Management, International Management, Operations Management, Real Estate and Urban Land Development), Chemistry (Biochemistry, General Chemistry, Chemical Modeling), Clinical Laboratory Sciences , Clinical Radiation Sciences (Nuclear Medicine Technology, Radiation Therapy, Radiography), Communication Arts (General Communication Arts, Medical Illustration), Computer Science, Craft and Material Studies (Ceramics, Fiberwork/Fabric Design, Glassworking, Metalsmithing/Jewelry, Woodworking/Furniture Design), Criminal Justice (Forensic Crime Scene Investigation, Justice), Dance and Choreography, Dental Hygiene, Economics, Engineering (Biomedical, Chemical and Life Science, Computer, Computer Science, Electrical, Mechanical), English, Environmental Studies, Fashion (Design, Merchandising), Financial Technology, Foreign Language (French, German, Spanish), Forensic Science (Biology, Chemistry), Graphic Design, Health, Physical education, and Exercise Science (Applied Health Science, Athletic Training, Clinical Exercise Science, Community Health Education, Physical Education), History, Homeland Security and Emergency Preparedness, Information Systems (Application Development, Business Analysis, Network Management), Interdisciplinary Studies (General Liberal Studies, Individualized Studies, Women's Studies), Interior Design, International Studies (Africa, Asia, Global Studies, Latin America, Mediterranean, Middle East, Russia and Eastern Europe, Western Europe), Kinetic Imaging, Marketing, Mass Communications (Advertising, Journalism, Public Relations), Mathematical Sciences (Applied Mathematics, Mathematics, Operations Research, Statistics), Military Science and Leadership, Music (Composition, Education, Performance), Nursing, Painting and Printmaking, Philosophy (Ethics and Public Policy) , Photography and Film, Physics, Political Science, Psychology (Applied Psychology, Life Science, Urban Psychology), Religious Studies, Sculpture, Social work, Sociology, Theatre (Costume Design, Lighting Design, Performance, Scene Design, Stage Management, Theatre Education), Urban Studies and Geography (Generalized, Geography, Urban Studies)

Virginia Commonwealth University Continued

Pre-professional Programs:

Clinical Laboratory Sciences, Clinical Radiation Sciences, Dental Hygiene, Dentistry, Law, Medicine, Nursing, Occupational Therapy, Optometry, Pharmacy, Physical Therapy, Veterinary Medicine

Teacher Licensure Program: Yes

Retention Rate: 81.3%

Student/Faculty Ratio: 14:1

Average Class Size: 28

Cool Programs: Study abroad, undergraduate research opportunities, first-year summer research opportunities, cooperative education program in some majors, independent studies courses, college introduction course for first-year students only, first-year residential learning communities, themed housing, student leadership program

Distance Learning Options: Yes

Financial Stats:

Undergraduate In-State Tuition and Fees: $6,196 full time, $244.35 per credit hour

Room and Board Fees: $7,567 (depending on dorm and meal plan)

Yearly Cost of Attendance: $13,763

Receiving Financial Aid: 67%

Life Off-Campus:

Living On-Campus: 16.1%

ROTC: Army

Varsity Sports: Baseball, basketball (m/w), cross country (m/w), field hockey, golf (m), soccer (m/w), tennis (m/w), track and field (m/w), volleyball (w)

Sports level: NCAA Division I

Cool Clubs: Cancer Awareness Team, Independent Film Club, Sierra Student Coalition, Skydiving Club, Whitewater at VCU (Team WAV), Contemporary Craft Society

Extra Credit: Virginia Polytechnic and State University, George Mason University, Christopher Newport University

Virginia Intermont College www.vic.edu

1013 Moore Street, Bristol, VA. 24201
Admissions Office: (800) 451-1-VIC, viadmit@vic.edu

The Basics

Type of School: Private
Type of Campus: Small Town
Size: 916 undergrads

Male/Female Ratio: 30/70
Diversity: 6% minority
Out of State Students: 68%

FYI: Saddle up partner, Virginia Intermont College is one of the few schools in the country to offer an accredited four-year degree in Equine Studies. Split between the traditional classroom and the school's 125-acre riding facility (which boards 60 horses year-round), the program trains students for a wide array of careers in the horse industry. If you prefer two to four-legged animals, no sweat. VIC also offers a strong selection of liberal arts majors including notable programs in Photography, Youth Ministry, and Legal Studies.

Admission Stats:

Admissions Deadlines: Rolling Admissions

How to Apply: Apply online at www.vic.edu or call (800) 451-1842 for a paper application

Application Requirements: Online or paper application, $25 application fee, high school transcript, SAT or ACT scores

Optional: SAT II tests, letters of recommendation, personal statement

Accepts the Common Application: No

Average SAT Score: 970

Virginia Intermot College Continued

Academic Life On-Campus:

Honors program: Yes
Majors Offered: Art (General art, Pre-Art Therapy track), Biology (Evironmental Science, General Biology, Nutrition, Pre-Medicine track, Pre-Veterinary Medicine track), Business Administration (Business Education, General Business, Management, Marketing), Computer Information Management, Criminal Justice, Dance, English (Language and Literature, Written Communication), Equine Studies , History, Interdisciplinary Studies, Legal Studies (Business Paralegal, Litigation Paralegal, Pre Law track), Liberal Arts, Photography and Digital Imaging, Physical Education (General Physical Education, Pre-Physical Therapy track), Political Science , Psychology, Religion (General Religion, Youth Ministry), Social Work, Sport Management, Theatre (Acting, Musical Theatre)

Pre-professional Programs:

Law, Medicine, Veterinary Medicine

Teacher Licensure Program: Yes

Retention Rate: 74%

Student/Faculty Ratio: 12:1

Average Class Size: 10

Cool Programs: Study abroad, student-designed majors, independent studies courses

Distance Learning Options: No

Financial Stats:

Undergraduate In-State Tuition: $16,895 full time, $220 per credit hour up to 6 hours, $420 per credit hour over 6 hours

Room and Board Fees: $6,095

Yearly Cost of Attendance: $24,990

Receiving Financial Aid: 85%

Life Off-Campus:

Living On-Campus: 60%

ROTC: None

Varsity Sports: Baseball, basketball (m/w), cross country (m/w), equestrian (m/w), golf (m), soccer (m/w), softball, tennis (m/w), track and field (m/w), volleyball
Sports level: National Association of Intercollegiate Athletics

Cool Clubs: Venturing Club, Equestrian Club, Photography Club, Aikido Club, Cardinal Key leadership organization

Extra Credit: Mary Baldwin College, Virginia Wesleyan College, Lynchburg College

Virginia Military Institute

www.vmi.edu

319 Letcher Avenue, Lexington, VA 24450
Admissions Office: (800) 767-4207, admissions@vmi.edu

The Basics

Type of School: Public
Type of Campus: Small City
Size: 1,300 undergrads
Male/Female Ratio: 93/7
Diversity: 15% minority
Out of State Students: 45%

FYI: Throw out everything you know about college. The nation's first state-supported military college, VMI requires its new recruits to stay physically, academically, and mentally fit. On top of completing a rigorous set of classes, all new cadets are required to shave their heads (or cut their hair short for women) during their first months at the Institute, complete four years of ROTC training, endure intense military training, and live without luxuries such as televisions, telephones, and civilian clothing. If you can survive, you'll be rewarded. VMI grads are EXTREMELY well-prepared for life after college, whether they choose to enroll in the armed forces or not.
Notable Names: Nobel Prize Winner and former U.S. Army Chief of Staff George Marshall, comedian Fred Willard, Long and Foster Real Estate CEO P. Wesley Foster, Jr., Arctic Explorer Admiral Richard E. Byrd, WWII General George Patton, Pulitzer Prize winner John H. Crider

Virginia Military Institute Continued

Admission Stats:

Admissions Deadlines: Honors Institute Applicants – Jan. 15, Early Decision – Nov. 15, Regular Admissions – Feb. 15, Rolling Admissions after Feb. 15

How to Apply: Apply online or download an application at: http://www.vmi.edu/show.asp?durki=3902

Application Requirements: Online or paper application, $35 application fee, high school transcript and profile, SAT or ACT scores, letter of recommendation, medical approval

Optional: Essay or Personal Statement, extra letter of recommendation

Accepts the Common Application: No

Average SAT Score: 1148

Academic Life On-Campus:

Honors program: Yes

Majors Offered: Biology (General Biology, Molecular Cellular and Biological Chemistry), Chemistry (General Chemistry, Molecular Cellular and Biological Chemistry) , Computer Science , Civil Engineering (Construction Management, Environmental Engineering, Fluid Mechanics & Hydraulic Engineering, Geotechnical Engineering, Hydrology & Water Resources Engineering, Structural Engineering, Transportation and Planning Engineering), Economics & Business (Financial Management, General Business, General Economics), Electrical & Computer Engineering (Computer Science Engineering, General Electrical Engineering, Microelectronics Engineering), English (Fine Arts, General English, Writing), Foreign Languages and Cultures (Arabic, French, German, Japanese, Spanish), History, International Studies and Political Science, Mathematics, Mechanical Engineering (Aerospace Engineering, General Mechanical Engineering), Physics (Astronomy, General Physics) , Psychology (General Psychology, Leadership, Philosophy)

Pre-professional Programs:

None

Teacher Licensure Program: Yes

Retention Rate: 84%

Student/Faculty Ratio: 11:1

Average Class Size: 14.8

Cool Programs: Study abroad, undergraduate research opportunities, Teacher Certification consortium in partnership with Mary Baldwin College and Washington and Lee University, cooperative education program in some majors, optional first-year summer transition program, independent studies courses, upperclassmen mentoring program

Distance Learning Options: No

Financial Stats:

Undergraduate In-State Tuition: $5,062 full time (part-time isn't offered)

Room and Board Fees: $6,108

Yearly Cost of Attendance: $24,990

Receiving Financial Aid: 75%

Life Off-Campus:

Living On-Campus: 100%

ROTC: Army, Navy, Marines, Air Force

Varsity Sports: Baseball, basketball (m), cross country (m/w), football, lacrosse (m), soccer (m/w), rifle (m/w), swimming (m/w), tennis , track and field (m/w), wrestling

Sports level: NCAA Division I

Cool Clubs: Clay Target Shooting club, Glee Club, Firefighters, Rat Disciplinary Committee, Combat Support Group, Boxing Team, Alpine Ski Team, Fencing Team, Cadet Investment Group

Extra Credit: Washington and Lee University, Virginia Polytechnic Institute and State University, Christopher Newport University

Virginia Polytechnic Institute and State University (Virginia Tech) www.vt.edu

201 Burruss Hall, Blacksburg, VA 24061
Admissions Office: (540) 231-6267, vtadmiss@vt.edu

The Basics

Type of School: Public
Type of Campus: Small City
Size: 22,000 undergrads, 26,000 total
Male/Female Ratio: 58/42
Diversity: 8% minority
Out of State Students: 28%

FYI: As Virginia's leading research university offering the widest variety of studies, Virginia Tech spends more than $290 million on research and development programs every year and is one of the best places in the country to get your study on. Undergrads who want to be a part of ground-breaking studies can find opportunities (some of them paid) in the 3,500 active projects the school now hosts. From an interactive virtual reality theater to a full-scale veterinary hospital, VT facilities are second to none as are the faculty. When taking a break from the lab, VT students have plenty of opportunities to gain practical training. Besides offering internships, externships, job shadowing programs, and cooperative education programs, the school's long list of more than 600 student organizations includes clubs such as the Aerial Unmanned Vehicle Team, Walking Robot Team, and the Solar De-Cathalon Team.

Notable Names: Atlanta Falcons quarterback Michael Vick, Former Exxon CEO Clifton C. Garvin, Federal Reserve Bank president Jack Guynn, Butyl Rubber co-inventor Robert M. Thomas, Dateline NBC Correspondent Hoda Kotb, Astronaut John B. McKay, Nobel Prize winner Robert C. Richardson

Admission Stats:

Admissions Deadlines: Early Decision – Nov. 1, Regular Admissions – Jan. 15, Transfer Admissions – Feb. 15 (fall semester), Oct. 1 (spring semester)

How to Apply: Apply online at http://www.admiss.vt.edu/apply/apply_online.php or download an application at http://www.admiss.vt.edu/forms
Application Requirements: Online or paper application, $50 application fee, high school transcript and profile, SAT or ACT plus writing scores, midyear high school report, Supplement High School Information form (completed by guidance counselor or principal), In-State Tuition Form for VA residents

Optional: Essay or Personal Statement

Accepts the Common Application: No

Average SAT Score: 1231

Academic Life On-Campus:

Honors program: Yes
Majors Offered: Accounting and Information Systems, Aerospace Engineering, Agricultural and Applied Economics, Agricultural Sciences, Agricultural Technology, Agriculture, General, Animal and Poultry Sciences, Apparel, Housing, and Resource Management, Architecture, Art , Art History , Biochemistry (Agricultural Biochemistry, General Biochemistry), Biological Sciences, Biological Systems Engineering, Biology, Building Construction, Business, Business Information Technology, Chemical Engineering, Chemistry, Civil and Environmental Engineering, Classical Studies, Communication, Computer Engineering, Computer Science, Construction Engineering and Management, Crop and Soil Environmental Sciences, Dairy Science, Economics (Business Economics, General Economics), Electrical Engineering, Engineering, General, Engineering Science and Mechanics, English, Environmental Policy and Planning, Environmental Science, Finance, Fisheries Science, Food Science and Technology, Foreign Languages and Literatures (French, German, Russian, Spanish), Forestry, Geography, Geology, Geosciences, Graphic Design, History, Horticulture, Hospitality and Tourism Management, Human Development, Human Nutrition, Foods and Exercise, Industrial and Systems Engineering, Industrial Design, Interdisciplinary Studies, Interior Design, International Studies, Landscape Architecture, Management, Marketing, Materials Science and Engineering, Mathematics, Mechanical Engineering, Mining and Minerals Engineering, Music, Natural Resources Conservation, Ocean Engineering, Philosophy, Physics, Political Science, Psychology, Public and Urban Affairs, Sociology, Statistics , Theatre Arts, Wildlife Science, Wood Science and Forest Products

Virginia Tech Continued

Pre-professional Programs:

Clinical Science, Dentistry, Law, Medicine, Optometry, Pharmacy, Physical Therapy, Veterinary Medicine

Teacher Licensure Program: Yes

Retention Rate: 89%

Student/Faculty Ratio: 16:1

Average Class Size: 41

Cool Programs: Study abroad, undergraduate research opportunities, independent studies courses, cooperative education program, upperclassmen mentoring program, themed housing, first-year seminars, first-year residential learning communities, student-designed majors, joint degree programs

Distance Learning Options: Yes

Financial Stats:

Undergraduate In-State Tuition: $5,772 full time, $240 per credit hour

Room and Board Fees: $5,088

Yearly Cost of Attendance: $12,860

Receiving Financial Aid: 67%

Life Off-Campus:

Living On-Campus: 41%

ROTC: Army, Navy, Air Force

Varsity Sports: Baseball, basketball (m/w), cross country (m/w), football, golf (m), lacrosse (w), soccer (m/w), softball, swimming and diving (m/w), tennis (m/w), track and field (m/w), volleyball (w), wrestling

Sports level: NCAA Division I

Cool Clubs: Hoorah Cloggers, Musicals for a Cause, Aerial Unmanned Vehicle Team, Billiards Club, Wildland Fire Crew, Walking Robot Team, VTunes Internet Radio, Through Being Cool club, Solar DeCathalon Team, Paintballers club

Extra Credit: University of Virginia, Virginia Commonwealth University, George Mason University

Virginia State University

www.vsu.edu

1 Hayden Drive, Petersburg, VA 23806
Admissions Office: (800) 871-7611, admiss@vsu.edu

The Basics

Type of School: Public
Type of Campus: Suburban
Size: 4,300 undergrads, 5,000 total

Male/Female Ratio: 38/62
Diversity: 96% minority
Out of State Students: 29%

FYI: If you're looking for a nurturing academic environment, this is the place to find it. Unlike large, impersonal universities, VSU's small student body and big academic advising and support systems ensure that all students will have the tools they need to make it through the college years. More than 9 out of every 10 students receives financial aid, the school's Bridges to Baccalaureate program helps students with an interest in the sciences transition from two-year schools to VSU, and the Ronald E. McNair program provides financial support for students driven to earn their Ph.D.

Notable Names: VSU's first president, John Mercer Langston, became the first African-American elected to Congress from Virginia

Admission Stats:

Admissions Deadlines: Regular Admissions - May 1 (Fall semester), Oct. 15 (Spring semester), Transfer Admissions - Dec. 15

How to Apply: Apply online or download an application at: http://www.vsu.edu/pages/1873.asp

Application Requirements: Online or paper application, $25 application fee, high school transcript and profile, SAT or ACT scores, two letters of recommendation, personal statement

Accepts the Common Application: No

Average SAT Score: 794

Virginia State University Continued

Academic Life On-Campus:

Honors program: Yes

Majors Offered: Accounting and Finance, Agriculture, Art and Design (Studio), Biology, Chemistry, Computer Engineering, Computer Information Systems, Computer Science, Criminal Justice, Economics, Engineering Technology, English, Family and Consumer Sciences, Foreign Language (French, German, Spanish), Health and Physical Education (General Health, Recreation, Sport Management), History, Hospitality Management , Industrial Education and Technology, Individualized Studies, Management and Marketing, Manufacturing Engineering, Mass Communications, Mathematics, Music (Choral, Instrumental, Performance), Political Science, Physics, Psychology, Public Administration, Sociology, Social Work

Pre-professional Programs:

Dentistry, Law, Medicine, Veterinary

Teacher Licensure Program: Yes

Retention Rate: 72%

Student/Faculty Ratio: 17:1

Average Class Size: Information Not Available

Cool Programs: Study abroad, undergraduate research opportunities, independent studies courses, cooperative education program, student-designed majors

Distance Learning Options: Yes

Financial Stats:

Undergraduate In-State Tuition: $5,396 full time, $181 per credit hour

Room and Board Fees: $7,340

Yearly Cost of Attendance: $14,736

Receiving Financial Aid: 67%

Life Off-Campus:

Living On-Campus: 53%

ROTC: Army

Varsity Sports: Baseball, basketball (m/w), bowling (w), cross country (m/w), football, golf (m/w), softball, tennis (m/w), track and field (m/w), volleyball (w)

Sports level: NCAA Division II

Cool Clubs: Betterment of Brothers and Sister, National Society of Pershing Rifles, Kerojo Modeling Agency, Student Ambassadors, VSU National Assoc. of Parliamentarians

Extra Credit: Virginia Union University, Norfolk State University, Ferrum College

Virginia Union University

www.vuu.edu

1500 North Lombardy Street, Richmond, VA 23220
Admissions Office: (804) 342-3570, admissions@vuu.edu

The Basics

Type of School: Private
Type of Campus: Urban
Size: 1,250 undergrads, 1,580 total
Male/Female Ratio: 1.2:1
Diversity: 97% minority
Out of State Students: 52%

FYI: As one of the nation's oldest and most well-respected Historically Black Colleges or Universities, Virginia Union has a long-standing reputation for producing successful graduates. Alumni include the first elected African American governor in the United States, the first African American admiral in the U.S. Navy, several of the first African American mayors of cities, 22 college presidents, numerous ministers, senators, teachers, doctors, lawyers, businesspersons, and professional athletes. Alumni success can, in part, be chalked up to the school's first-year mentoring and undergraduate research programs.

Notable Names: Former governor, L. Douglas Wilder; NBA players Charles Oakley and Ben Wallace; First African American Admiral in the United States Navy, Samuel Lee Gravely, Jr.; Stu Gardner, former musical director, The Cosby Show; Henry L. Marsh III, first African American mayor of Richmond, VA

Virginia Union University Continued

Admission Stats:

Admissions Deadlines: Rolling Admissions, Cut off date is June 30 for fall semester, Nov. 30 for spring semester

How to Apply: Apply online or download an application at: http://www.vuu.edu/admissions/apply.htm

Application Requirements: Online or paper application, $25 application fee, high school transcript, SAT or ACT scores, essay

Optional: SAT II tests, letters of recommendation

Accepts the Common Application: Yes

Average SAT Score: 749

Academic Life On-Campus:

Honors program: Yes

Majors Offered: Accounting, Biology, Chemistry, Computer Information Systems, Criminology/Criminal Justice, English, Entrepreneurial Management, Finance and Banking, Interdisciplinary Studies, Marketing, Mathematics, Media Arts Political Science and Public Administration, Psychology, Religious Studies, Social Work

Pre-professional Programs:

None

Teacher Licensure Program: Yes

Retention Rate: 59%

Student/Faculty Ratio: 18:1

Average Class Size: 18

Cool Programs: Student leadership program, first year mentoring program, dual-degree programs with other universities, undergraduate research opportunities, summer science enrichment program

Distance Learning Options: No

Financial Stats:

Undergraduate In-State Tuition: $12,188 full time, $507 per credit hour

Room and Board Fees: $6,054

Yearly Cost of Attendance: $24,479

Receiving Financial Aid: 67%

Life Off-Campus:

Living On-Campus: 54%

ROTC: Army through Virginia State University

Varsity Sports: Basketball (m/w), bowling (w), cross country (m/w), football, golf (m/w), softball, tennis (m/w), track and field (m/w), volleyball (w)

Sports level: NCAA Division II

Cool Clubs: ME Step Team, University Players Drama Club, College Students Against Cancer, Panther's Claw pep squad, Rotaract Club

Extra Credit: Virginia State University, Norfolk State University, Ferrum College

Virginia Wesleyan College www.vwc.edu

1584 Wesleyan Drive, Norfolk, VA 23502
Admissions Office: (800) 737.8684, admissions@vwc.edu

The Basics

Type of School: Private
Type of Campus: Small Town
Size: 1,400 undergrads
Male/Female Ratio: 36/64
Diversity: 21% minority
Out of State Students: 21%

FYI: Sandwiched between Norfolk and Virginia Beach, Virginia Wesleyan gives students all of the internship, research, and career opportunities that come with a city as well as the recreational activities of a beach town. The school's PORTfolio Program allows students to supersize their education by adding a four-year, hands-on, interdisciplinary curriculum to their major. Adding team-taught seminars, off-campus activities, service learning projects, externships, shadowing experiences, and internships to what's taught in class, PORTfolio acts the ultimate career counselor, perfecting your resume every year you're in school. Whether you enroll in the PORTfolio program or not, all VWC students have the chance to beef up their resume during the school's three-week Winter Session. Offering courses ranging from Kitchen Science to Extreme Religion, Winter Session gives students the chance to explore topics they'd never touch otherwise.

Admission Stats:

Admissions Deadlines: Rolling Admissions, Wesleyan Scholarship Applications – Jan. 1, Priority Spring Semester Applications – Jan. 1, Priority Fall Semester Applications – March 1, Academic and Leadership Scholarships – March 15

How to Apply: Apply online or download an application at: http://www.vwc.edu/admissions/apply.php

Application Requirements: Online or paper application, $40 application fee, high school transcript, SAT or ACT scores, essays, letter of recommendation from a dean, counselor, or advisor

Optional: SAT II tests

Accepts the Common Application: No

Average SAT Score: 1010

Academic Life On-Campus:

Honors program: Yes
Majors Offered: American Studies, Art (Art Education, Studio Art), Biology, Chemistry, Classical Studies, Communication (Journalism, Media Studies), Computer Science, Criminal Justice, Earth and Environmental Sciences, English, Environmental Studies, Foreign Language (French, German, Spanish), Health and Human Services, History, Humanities, International Studies, Liberal Arts Management Program (Management/Business/Economics), Liberal Studies, Latin, Mathematics, Music, Natural Sciences and Mathematics, Philosophy, Political Science, Psychology, Recreation and Leisure Studies, Religious Studies, Social Sciences, Social Studies, Sociology, Theatre, Women's and Gender Studies

Pre-professional Programs:

Dentistry, Environmental Studies, Health Professions, Law, Medicine, Seminary, Veterinary Medicine

Teacher Licensure Program: Yes

Retention Rate: 66%

Student/Faculty Ratio: 13:1

Average Class Size: 14

Cool Programs: Student-designed majors, first year college transitional seminars, joint degree program with Eastern Virginia Medical School, PORTfolio program, winter term, study abroad, independent studies courses, undergraduate research opportunities, member of the Virginia Tidewater Consortium along with Christopher Newport University, the College of William and Mary, Norfolk State University and Old Dominion University

Distance Learning Options: Yes

Financial Stats:

Undergraduate In-State Tuition: $24,355 full time, $1,015 per credit hour

Room and Board Fees: $6,900

Yearly Cost of Attendance: $33,255

Receiving Institutional Financial Aid: 96%

Virginia Wesleyan College Continued

Life Off-Campus:

Living On-Campus: 48%

ROTC: Army through Old Dominion University

Varsity Sports: Baseball, basketball (m/w), cross country (m/w), field hockey, golf (m), lacrosse (m/w), soccer (m/w), softball, tennis (m/w), track (m/w), volleyball (w)

Sports level: NCAA Division III

Cool Clubs: Campus Kaleidoscope, Cultural Arts Society, Model United Nations, Fencing Club, Wesleyan Beekeepers Association, Student Environmental Awareness League

Extra Credit: Longwood University, Lynchburg College, Bridgewater College

Washington and Lee University

www.wlu.edu

Lexington, VA 24450
Admissions Office: (540) 458.8710, admissions@wlu.edu

The Basics

Type of School: Private
Type of Campus: Small City
Size: 1,749 undergrads, 3,004 total

Male/Female Ratio: 51/49
Diversity: 15%
Out of State Students: 85%

FYI: Slackers beware – students at Washington and Lee are expected to be self-motivated from the day they step foot on campus. While the school supplies an army of top-notch faculty members (97% of whom hold the highest degree in their field) as well as an array of innovative academic and travel-study programs (imagine yourself interning in Bolivia, presenting research in California, or fighting poverty at home in Lexington), it's up to the students to take advantage of all their school has to offer. Fortunately, that's not hard to do. Washington and Lee's month-long Winter Term gives students the opportunity to explore trips and classes they simply can't fit into their semester schedules.

Notable Names: Authors Tom Wolfe, Tom Robbins, and Terry Brooks, U.S. Senator John Warner, former Secretary of Labor William Brock, Pulitzer Prize-winning reporter Alex S. Jones, former congressmen Jim Davis and David Gardiner Tyler

Admission Stats:

Admissions Deadlines: Early Decision – Nov. 15, Feb. 1, Honors Scholarship Applications – Dec. 15, Regular Admissions – Jan. 15, Transfer Admissions – April 1 (fall semester), Nov. 1 (spring semester)

How to Apply: Apply online or download an application at: http://admissions.wlu.edu/web/page/normal/101.html

Application Requirements: Online or paper application, $50 application fee, high school transcript, SAT or ACT scores, scores from two SAT II tests, two letters of recommendation from teachers, letter of recommendation from a dean, counselor, or advisor, mid-year report, essay, Common Application Supplement (if applicable)

Optional: Admissions interview

Accepts the Common Application: Yes

Average SAT Score: 1386

Academic Life On-Campus:

Honors program: Yes

Majors Offered: Accounting and Business Administration, Archaeology and Anthropology, Art (Art History, Studio Art), Biology, Business Administration, Chemistry (Biochemistry, Chemistry/Engineering, General Chemistry), Classical Studies, Combination Work in Law (3-3), Computer Science, East Asian Languages and Literatures, Economics, English, Environmental Studies in Geology, French, Geology, German Language and German Literature, History, Independent Studies, Journalism and Mass Communications (Business, Electronic, and Print Journalism), Mathematics, Medieval and Renaissance Studies, Music, Neuroscience, Philosophy, Physics (General Physics, Physics/Engineering), Politics, Psychology, Public Accounting, Religion, Romance Languages (French, Italian, Portuguese, Spanish), Russian Area Studies, Sociology and Anthropology, Spanish, Theater

Waskington and Lee university Continued

Pre-professional Programs:

Engineering, Health Professions, Law, Medicine, Seminary, Social Work

Teacher Licensure Program: Yes

Retention Rate: 87%

Student/Faculty Ratio: 10:1

Average Class Size: 16

Cool Programs: Study abroad, independent studies courses, student-designed majors, themed housing, joint degree programs with Columbia University, Rensselaer Polytechnic Institute, and Duke University, undergraduate research opportunities, consortium agreement with Duke University Marine Labs, Shepherd poverty studies program, Executive-In-Residence Program, first year leadership program, first year residential learning communities, first year transition to college curriculum

Distance Learning Options: No

Financial Stats:

Undergraduate In-State Tuition: $34,650 full time, $1,155 per credit hour

Room and Board Fees: $7,525

Yearly Cost of Attendance: $42,175

Receiving Institutional Financial Aid: 33%

Life Off-Campus:

Living On-Campus: 40%

ROTC: Army through Virginia Military Institute

Varsity Sports: Basketball (m/w), cross country (m/w), equestrian (w), field hockey, football, golf (m), lacrosse (m/w), soccer (m/w), swimming (m/w), tennis (m/w), track (m/w), volleyball (w), wrestling

Sports level: NCAA Division III

Cool Clubs: Club Ice Hockey, Club Squash, Film Society, Fencing Club, Foxhunting Club, March of Dimes committee, Mindbending Productions, Martial Arts club, Mock Trial club

Extra Credit: University of Virginia, University of Richmond, College of William and Mary

Summer Enrichment Index

52 Ways to Use Your Brain This Summer:

A Guide to Pre-College and Summer Enrichment Programs

1. All Arts and Science Camp

Where: College of William and Mary (Charlottesville, VA), Virginia Polytechnic Institute and State University (Blacksburg, VA)

About: Students ages 7 to 15 get creative during this week-long day or residential summer camp. Upper-level classes include auto design, animal science, digital photography, fashion design, food chemistry, medical mysteries, podcasting, myth-busting, sports medicine, and stage make-up to name a few.

Dates: Virginia Tech – June 24 – 29, William and Mary – July 8 – 13
Costs: $599 for day campers, $699 for residential campers.

Application Deadline: Registration ends one month before camp begins.
For More Information: Go to http://web.uncg.edu/dcl/web/allarts/default.asp or contact All Arts and Science Camp at (866) 334-CALL.

2. Appalachian Institute Summer Enrichment Camp

Where: Emory and Henry College (Emory, VA)

About: Students in grades 3 through 12 dive into a diverse array of classes during this one to two-week residential summer camp. Classes aim to get students to look at the world in new scientific or artistic ways. Classes will cover topics such as medical ethics, enigmas, baseball statistics, puppetry, internal combustion, knitting, photography, and monsters.

Dates: July 16 – 22 and July 23 - 29
Costs: $600 for one week, $1,150 for two (early bird special); $650 for one week,, $1,250 for two weeks if applying after June 15

Application Deadline: February 1st for reduced rate, June 15 for regular rate
For More Information: Go to www.appalachianinstitute.org or contact the Appalachian Institute at (800) 951-7442.

3. Camp Curtain Call

Where: Camp Curtain Call (Dugspur, VA)

About: Students ages 7 to 18 come to Carroll County, VA for one to seven weeks of theatre, music, visual arts, dance, and variety act-intensive study. When not performing, campers have a huge selection of evening activities ranging from model rocketry to fire eating to enjoy during this residential camp.

Dates: June 10 – August 5
Costs: $965 - $6,895 depending on length of stay
Application Deadline: Rolling admissions

For More Information: Go to www.campcurtaincall.com or call Camp Curtain Call at (865) 573-7002 during the year or (276) 730-0233 during June and July.

Christendom College High School Summer Program

Where: Christendom College (Front Royal, VA)

About: Rising seniors get their first taste of college by taking Catholic-based courses that focus theology, philosophy, history, and literature. Students will search for answers to heavy-hitting questions such as "what is the relationship between faith and reason?" and "can one man make a difference?" during this one to two week-long residential program.

Dates: Session I occurs June 24 – July 1, Session II occurs in July 8 - 22.
Costs: $850 for two weeks, $425 for one, limited scholarships available
Application Deadline: Rolling admissions, first come, first serve
For More Information: Go to www.christendom.edu/admissions/hssummer.shtml or contact Christendom admissions at (800) 877-5456, extension 292.

5. Commonwealth Youth Conference for Leadership Effectiveness

Where: Virginia Polytechnic Institute and State University (Blacksburg, VA)

About: Rising 10th graders with a passion for leadership are invited by the Virginia Police Chiefs Foundation to attend a series of summer leadership conferences. Topics covered will include understanding yourself, positive interactions, teamwork, decision-making, effective communication, and relating to others.

Dates: June 17 – 22, June 24 – 29, July 8 – 13, July 22 – 27, July 29 – August 3
Costs: Free
Application Deadline: February 21, Students must be recommended through their school resource officer. If interested in this program, talk to your guidance counselor about the recommendation process in early January.
For More Information: Go to www.vachiefs.org/vpcf/vpcf_cycle.html or contact the Virginia Police Chiefs Foundation at (804) 285-8227.

Computers and Technology at Virginia Tech

Where: Virginia Polytechnic Institute and State University (Blacksburg, VA)

About: Rising junior and senior ladies with an interest in computers, listen up. VA Tech's C-Tech2 summer camp program will give you the opportunity to explore math, science, and engineering topics at one of the best places in the state to do it.

Dates: July 1 – July 14
Costs: $500 plus personal expenses. Full and partial scholarships are available based on financial need.
Application Deadline: March 9
For More Information: Go to www.eng.vt.edu/academics/what.php or contact CTech2 Program Director, Whitney Edmister, at (540) 231-3973 or ctech2@vt.edu.

7. CyberCamp

Where: George Mason University (Fairfax, VA), Northern Virginia Community College (Alexandria, VA), Oak Marr RECenter (Fairfax, VA)

About: Turn your love for video games into a career...or at least something to help get your foot in the door of a good college. Students ages 7 to 18 learn about game modding, robotics, programming, animation, and graphic design during this day or residential camp.

Dates: Held throughout July and August, dates vary from campus to campus.
Costs: $699 per week for day campers, $1,098 per week for residential campers.
Application Deadline: Rolling admissions
For More Information: Go to www.cybercamps.com or call (888) 904-CAMP.

8. Eastern Mennonite University Intensive English Program

Where: Eastern Mennonite University (Harrisonburg, VA)

About: EMU's IEP program is designed to help middle and high school students for whom English is a second language get prepared for college-level language. Students may enroll in beginning, intermediate, or advanced-level courses. Those who complete both intermediate and advanced levels and enroll at EMU for undergraduate study may receive up to 15 college credits before regular classes begin.

Dates: July 16 – August 3 or July 23 – August 17
Costs: $1,625 for the three-week program, $2,145 for the four-week program.

Application Deadline: June 1
For More Information: Go to www.emu.edu/iep/ or contact IEP at EMU by calling (540) 432-4053.

9. George Mason University Institute in Forensics

Where: George Mason University (Fairfax, VA)

About: Top forensics coaches in the nation come together with eager competitors from both dramatic and oratorical events. In this residential camp, students prepare and perfect the forensic pieces they'll be performing during the upcoming year. An optional four-day extended program allows students to take their pieces one step further and work one-on-one with award-winning coaches.

Dates: July 19 – August 2 (Extended Program: August 2 – 5th)
Costs: $1,199 ($949 for commuter students), additional $399 ($299 for commuters) to attend the extended session.

Application Deadline: April 1, rolling admissions after.
For More Information: Go to www.gmuforensics.org/gmif/ or contact Program Director Dr. Peter Pober at (703) 993-4119.

10. George Mason University Mathematics and Technology for Talented Youth

Where: George Mason University (Fairfax, VA)

About: Designed to help refresh and enrich students in the areas of mathematics and computers, this day camp provides both refresher courses for rising 6th through 12th graders. Math courses from pre-algebra through calculus level are offered as well as computer courses including C++ programming, visual BASIC, and Intro to JavaScript.

Dates: Sessions run from June 25 – August 3
Costs: $400 - $500 depending on course taken
Application Deadline: End of May, rolling admissions after that.

For More Information: Go to http://talentedyouth.org/ or contact Program Director, Dr. J.E. Lin at (703) 973-6889.

11. George Mason University Summer Study for High School Students

Where: George Mason University (Fairfax, Arlington, and Princeton campuses)

About: Rising juniors and seniors can earn college credit by taking freshmen-level courses on GMU's campus. In 2006, courses were available in anthropology, art and visual technology, communications, economics, English, government, history, information technology, math, philosophy, and sociology.

Dates: July 2 – August 3
Costs: $245 per credit hour plus a $40 application fee ($60 if submitting a paper application)

Application Deadline: April 30
For More Information: Contact GMU Summer Term at (703) 993-2300 or via e-mail at summer@gmu.edu.

12. Global Youth Village

Where: Global Youth Village (Bedford, VA)

About: Bedford, VA may not look like a center for international culture, but it becomes one each summer. Students ages 13 to 18 from around the world come to the Blue Ridge Mountains to live in the woods for seven weeks and learn about culture in a global context. By day, students take morning workshops that focus on developing intercultural dialogue and cultivating global awareness and by night, learn sports from around the world and attend performances by international artists.

Dates: July 15 – August 4
Costs: $1,900 plus money for personal expenses.
Application Deadline: Rolling admissions, preference given to applications submitted by April 15.

For More Information: Check out http://globalyouthvillage.org or contact Global Youth Village at (540) 297-9081.

13. Hampton University A-Plus

Where: Hampton University (Hampton, VA)

About: 50 lucky students between the ages of 12 and 16 congregate on Hampton U's campus for a week of hands-on study. This year's theme is history. Students will delve into general history as well as develop life and study skills.

Dates: June 24 – 30
Costs: $500
Application Deadline: Rolling admissions, students should get their application in by February.

For More Information: Go to www.hamptonu.edu/academics/summer/aplus.htm or contact Dr. Freddye Davy at (757) 727-5076.

14. Hampton University Pre-College Program

Where: Hampton University (Hampton, VA)

About: Rising seniors and college freshmen are invited to Hampton U's campus to get a jump on college. Students live and take introductory college courses at Hampton while earning college credit. Weekends are reserved for field trips and outings.

Dates: June 22 – July 27
Costs: $1,300 (includes tuition, room, and board) plus approximately $300 for books.
Application Deadline: May 25

For More Information: Go to www.hamptonu.edu/academics/summer/precollege/index.htm or contact the Pre-College Program office at (757) 727-5511.

15. Hampton University Summer High School Band Camp

Where: Hampton University (Hampton, VA)

About: If you play an instrument, twirl a baton, or simply move to the music, this is the place for you. Student musicians, majorettes, dancers, and flag corps members get ready for the upcoming school year in this day or residential camp.

Dates: July 8 – 14
Costs: $350 (residential), $250 (commuters)
Application Deadline: June 30

For More Information: Go to www.hamptonu.edu/academics/summer/band_camp.htm or call (757) 728-6876.

16. High School Senior Enrichment Program

Where: Virginia State University (Petersburg, VA)

About: Rising high school seniors are invited to VSU campus to learn the basics of engineering and get in some great SAT preparation. This is a residential program.

Dates: June 2007
Costs: Free, stipend of $400 given to participants
Application Deadline: End of January

For More Information: Contact Dr. Ali Ansari at (804) 524-5566.

17. Hollinsummer

Where: Hollins University (Roanoke, VA)

About: Pottery, forensic chemistry, psychology, navigation, and politics in literature are just a few of the courses offered to 9th, 10th, and 11th grade girls at Hollinsummer. Students spend their days getting a taste of the wide variety of courses college offers then spend their nights hanging out with friends, exploring the Roanoke area, and enjoying Hollins' recreational facilities including the college's indoor swimming pool.

Dates: July 8 – 20
Costs: $1,150
Application Deadline: June 1

For More Information: Go to www.hollins.edu/specprog/hollinsummer/holsum.htm or contact Hollins at (800) 456-9595.

18. Inside Architecture Workshop

Where: Virginia Polytechnic Institute and State University (Blacksburg, VA)

About: Future builders of America gather here each summer to get a glimpse of the real world of architecture. In this 5-day, hands-on day or residential camp, students learn about what it takes to major in architecture and what it means to become a professional architect.

Dates: June 25 – 29
Costs: Estimated costs are $440 for day students
Application Deadline: Rolling admissions

For More Information: Go to www.archdesign.vt.edu/students/inside-architecture or contact the Virginia Tech School of Architecture at (540) 231-5383.

19. Internal Drive Tech Camp

Where: College of William and Mary (Williamsburg, VA), the University of Virginia (Charlottesville, VA), Virginia Polytechnic Institute and State University (Blacksburg, VA).

About: This is how you get in the game...literally. Offered throughout the state, iD Tech Camps allow students (ages seven through seventeen) to go behind the scenes of their favorite video games and create games of their own. Students may opt to attend the day camp or a residential summer camp and can choose classes such as 3D Game Design, Game Modding, and Digital Video and Editing.

Dates: Sessions run throughout June and July and vary from campus to campus.
Costs: $729 - $1,129 depending on course residency status.
Application Deadline: Rolling admissions, registration is encouraged no later than a week before camp starts.

For More Information: Check out www.internaldrive.com/virginia/ or contact Internal Drive at (888) 709-TECH.

20. Liberty Institute for Young Champions

Where: Liberty University (Lynchburg, VA)

About: 10th, 11th, and 12th grade students eager to explore collegiate life as well as their relationship with Jesus Christ head to Liberty U every year for a week of worship and study. Students spend their mornings diving into college coursework and their evenings taking advantage of the resources both Liberty and Lynchburg have to offer. Whether you're buried in poli-sci books, ice skating with friends, or studying the Bible alongside likeminded students, the Liberty Institute for Young Champions is a great way to make Christian college connections.

Dates: June 24 – 29
Costs: $375 if paid before March 15, $425 after March 15
Application Deadline: May 31

For More Information: Go to www.liberty.edu/index.cfm?PID=10137 or contact the program director at (434) 582-2087.

21. Marine Science Consortium Pre-College Summer Program

Where: Marine Science Consortium, Wallops Island, Virginia

About: Students ages 13 – 18 get their feet wet by living and working on Wallops Island. Students may register for one or several week-long marine science workshops held throughout the summer. Courses range from Fintastic Fishes to Adventures in Sea Kayaking to Dolphin and Marine Mammal Behavior.

Dates: Sessions run June 24 – July 28
Costs: $480 per week
Application Deadline: Rolling admissions

For More Information: Head to www.msconsortium.org/Precollegesummer.htm or contact the Marine Science Consortium at 757-824-5636.

22. National Aeronautics and Space Administration Mentorship Program

Where: Christopher Newport University (Newport News, VA)

About: Rising 11th and 12th graders hone their engineering skills in this four-week residential program.

Dates: June 24 – July 21
Costs: Free
Application Deadline: Students apply through their school in October/November. To be considered as the nominee from your school, contact your principal or guidance counselor.

For More Information: Contact the Virginia Institute of Marine Science at 804.684.7698 or go to www.pen.k12.va.us/VDOE/Instruction/Govschools/SRGS/ to download an application.

23. New Horizons Leadership Camp

Where: George Mason University (Fairfax, VA)

About: Rising 7th through 10th grade students hone their leadership and problem-solving skills during this day camp. Topics explored include alternatives to consumerism, conflict resolution, and gender stereotyping. Students also spend one day working in the surrounding community and one day doing team-building exercises in a nearby park.

Dates: July 9 – July 13
Costs: $400
Application Deadline: Rolling admissions

For More Information: Go to www.ncc.gmu.edu/enrichmentcamps/horizons/index.html or contact Program Director Suzanne Scott at (703) 993-1819.

24. Northern Virginia Writing Project Summer Student Institute

Where: George Mason University (Fairfax, VA)

About: Select rising 5th through 12th graders work collaboratively to publish an anthology of written work. During this two-week day camp, students will gain an intro to mystery, novel, short story, and poetry writing as well as perfect their own work. The Advanced Institute for 11th and 12th graders also includes one night of camping.

Dates: July, 2007
Costs: Estimated costs are $375 for grades 5 – 10, $415 for grades 11 and 12

For More Information: Go to www.nvwp.org/ or contact Program Director Mark Farrington at (703) 993-1168.

25. Radford University College of Information Science and Technology Summer Bridge Program

Where: Radford University (Radford, VA)

About: Rising junior and senior ladies with a knack for all things electronic are invited to strut their stuff on Radford's campus. Students choose a database, networks, or web site design track and will spend all three days developing their technical skills and gaining and introduction to the world of IT.

Dates: June 25 - 29
Costs: $100 - $200
Application Deadline: Early June

For More Information: Go to www.radford.edu/~bridge/ or contact Radford Summer Bridge at (540) 831-6054 or (540) 831-6277.

26. RAPME Summer Engineering Institute

Where: Virginia State University (Petersburg, VA), Virginia Commonwealth Univesrity (Richmond, VA), J. Sargeant Reynolds Community College (Richmond, VA)

About: Designed to encourage minority students interested in engineering fields, the Richmond Area Program for Minorities in Engineering summer program blends traditional engineering coursework with computer and robotics workshops. The 7th and 8th grade program focuses on introducing students to engineering professions and projects while the high school program goes more in-depth, allowing students to conduct their own research and earn five hours of college credit.

Dates: Late June – July, dates vary from campus to campus
Costs: $50
Application Deadline: April, 2007

Scholarship Deadline: May 15
For more information: Check out RAPME online at www.rapme.org or call (804) 524-5591.

27. Sea Camp

Where: Old Dominion University (Norfolk, VA)

About: Students ages 13 through 17 dissect fish, kayak the open waters, conduct oceanographic experiments, and take ODU's 55-foot research vessel out to sea during this week-long day camp.

Dates: June 18 – 22, July 9 – 13, July 23 – 27, August 6 – 10
Costs: $195 per week
Application Deadline: Rolling admissions, students are advised to get their applications in as close to January as possible.

For More Information: Go to http://sci.odu.edu/oceanography/seacamp/ or contact Sea Camp at (757) 683-4943.

28. Space Flight Adventure Camp

Where: Wallops Flight Facility (Wallops Island, VA)

About: Get ready to blast off. Students ages 11 to 15 build and launch model rockets, create their own robots, master flight simulators, and tour NASA launch facilities during this week-long residential camp.

Dates: Offered throughout June, July, and August
Costs: $645, limited scholarships available
Application Deadline: Two weeks before camp date

For More Information: Go to www.vaspaceflightacademy.org or contact the Virginia Space Flight Academy at (866) 757-7223.

29. Summer Residential Governor's School for Agriculture

Where: Virginia Polytechnic and State Institute (Blacksburg, VA)

About: Animals, plants, and agricultural economy, oh my! Rising 11th and 12th grade students in this four-week intensive program cover the ins and outs of agriculture, environmental planning, and the economy of land.

Dates: July 1 - 28
Costs: Free
Application Deadline: Students apply through their school in October/November. To be considered as the nominee from your school, contact your principal or guidance counselor.

For More Information: Check out www.gsa.vt.edu/index.htm or contact Virginia Polytechnic and State Institute at (540) 231-6836. To download an application, head to www.pen.k12.va.us/VDOE/Instruction/Govschools/SRGS.

30. Summer Residential Governor's School for Humanities

Where: University of Richmond (Richmond, VA)

About: Rising 11th and 12th graders nominated from their school convene for four-weeks of archaeological digs, film screenings, mock trials, and everything in between. Students live and study on-campus and when they're not in the classroom, enjoy special performances and group outings.

Dates: July 1 - 28
Costs: Free
Application Deadline: Students apply through their school in October/November. To be considered as the nominee from your school, contact your principal or guidance counselor.

For More Information: Check out www.richmond.edu/govschool/ or call (804) 289-8945. To download an application, head to www.pen.k12.va.us/VDOE/Instruction/Govschools/SRGS/.

31. Summer Residential Governor's School for the Performing Arts

Where: University of Richmond (Richmond, VA)

About: Rising 11th and 12th grade dancers, singers, actors, musicians, and artists nominated from their school convene for four weeks of creative exploration. Students live and study on-campus and when they're not in the classroom, enjoy special performances and group outings.

Dates: July 1 - 28
Costs: Free
Application Deadline: Students apply through their school in October/November. To be considered as the nominee from your school, contact your principal or guidance counselor. Students must also audition at the University of Richmond, Shenandoah University, or Emory and Henry College no later than January 20.

For More Information: Go to www.richmond.edu/govschool/ or call (804) 289-8945. To download an application, head to www.pen.k12.va.us/VDOE/Instruction/Govschools/SRGS/.

32. Summer Residential Governor's School for Mathematics, Science, and Technology

Where: Lynchburg College (Lynchburg, VA)

About: Rising 11th and 12th graders nominated from their school convene for four-weeks of exploring anatomy, astronomy, and anything else related to math or science. Students live and study on-campus and when they're not in the classroom, enjoy special performances and group outings.

Dates: July 1 - 28
Costs: Free
Application Deadline: Students apply through their school in October/November. To be considered as the nominee from your school, contact your principal or guidance counselor.
For More Information: Contact Lynchburg College at (434) 544-8609. To download an application, head to www.pen.k12.va.us/VDOE/Instruction/Govschools/SRGS/

33. Summer Residential Governor's School for Life Sciences and Medicines

Where: Virginia Commonwealth University (Richmond, VA)

About: Rising 11th and 12th graders nominated from their school spend four weeks living on campus, conducting clinical research under the advisement of mentors in the medical and life science professions.

Dates: June 24 – July 20
Costs: Free
Application Deadline: Students apply through their school in October/November. To be considered as the nominee from your school, contact your principal or guidance counselor.
For More Information: Call VCU Life Sciences at (804) 827-5600 or go to www.vcu.edu/lifesci/centers/cen_lse_governors.html. To download an application, head to www.pen.k12.va.us/VDOE/Instruction/Govschools/SRGS/.

34. Summer Transportation Institute

Where: Virginia State University (Petersburg, VA), Hampton University (Hampton, VA)

About: One in seven jobs is in the transportation industry. Here's your chance to find out more first-hand. Rising 9th, 10th, and 11th grade students learn about the transportation industry from the ground up. Covering highway design, transportation of people and cargo, laws and regulations, safety, and career opportunities, this camp will focus on honing engineering and science skills and preparing students for the SATs.

Dates: June 25 – July 1 (Hampton campus), June 2007 (VSU campus)
Costs: Free
Application Deadline: April 10 (Hampton site), End of March (VSU campus)
For more information: For information on the Hampton University site, go to www.hamptonu.edu/academics/summer/trans_institute.htm or contact Dr. Sonja Pollard-Mitchell at (757) 727-5867. For more information on the Virginia State University location, go to www.vsu.edu/pages/3009.asp or contact Dr. Ali Ansari at 804-524-5566.

35. University of Richmond Summer Scholars Program

Where: University of Richmond (Richmond, VA)

About: Rising juniors and seniors earn four credits at the University of Richmond during this three week-long residential program. Courses for 2007 include Biogenetics, Disaster Science and Homeland Security, and Into the Green: Explorations of Text and Trail.

Dates: July 8 – July 28
Costs: $3,950
Application Deadline: April 15

For More Information: Go to http://summer.richmond.edu/scholars/ or contact the Summer Scholars program at (804) 289-8382.

36. University of Virginia Introduction to Engineering Pre-College Program

Where: University of Virginia (Charlottesville, VA)

About: Rising juniors, seniors, and recent high school grads gain a hands-on intro to the wide world of engineering in this program. Students live on-campus and explore introductory engineering concepts through both seminars and experimentation with the assistance of UVA faculty.

Dates: July 8 - 14
Costs: $275 - $300, limited scholarships available
Application Deadline: April 13

For More Information: Head to www.seas.virginia.edu/diversity/pre_college/ite.html or contact UVA's Center for Diversity in Engineering office at (434)-924-0618.

37. University of Virginia Summer Enrichment Program

Where: University of Virginia (Charlottesville, VA)

About: Rising 9th through 11th grade students live and work on UVA campus, taking courses such as Visual Journaling, Cryptography, Post WW-II American Art, and the 5-Minute Play. In their off time, students take advantage of the recreation amenities on UVA's campus.

Dates: June 17 – 28, July 1 – 12, July 15 - 26
Costs: $1,000, limited financial aid is available
Application Deadline: February 15

For More Information: Head to http://curry.edschool.virginia.edu/index.php?option=com_content&task=view&id=715&Itemid=64 or contact the Summer Enrichment Program at (434) 924-3182.

38. University of Virginia Young Writer's Workshop

Where: University of Virginia (Charlottesville, VA)

About: High school fiction, nonfiction, poets, and songwriters hone their craft under the tutelage of bigwig writers (including Pulitzer Prize and T.S. Eliot Prize winners as well as Poet Laureates). Students will receive critiques on their work and an introduction to the world of publication. Students live and work on-campus.

Dates: Session I (beginners through experts): June 24 – July 6, Session II (advanced writers only) July 8 – July 27
Costs: $1,200 for Session I, $1,850 for Session II, limited scholarships available.
Application Deadline: Postmarked by March 5

For More Information: Go to http://web.virginia.edu/yww/ or contact the Young Writer's Workshop at (434) 924-0836 or writers@virginia.edu.

39. Vernon L. Smith High School Workshops in Experimental Economics

Where: George Mason University (Fairfax, VA)

About: Rising juniors, seniors, and college freshmen get the chance to explore the foundations of economics during this hands-on day camp. Students will brush up on (or learn for the first time) the basics of supply and demand, game theory, asset markets, and personal and impersonal exchange.

Dates: June 25 – 29 (Session I), July 9 – 13 (Session II)
Costs: $50 up front. Students can also earn cash based on how well they perform in economics-based games.

Application Deadline: April 1
For More Information: Go to http://ices.gmu.edu/subcategory.php/107.html or contact GMU at (703) 993-4850.

40. Virginia Commonwealth University Summer String Camp

Where: Virginia Commonwealth University (Richmond, VA)

About: Rising 6th through 12th grade musicians become better players with the help of the pros. Students will participate in chamber as well as orchestral ensembles, learn about improvisation, and hear VCU faculty performances. Students may choose to live on campus or attend the program as a day student.

Dates: July 8 – 14
Costs: $65 for students from Chesterfield, Henrico, Hanover, Goochland counties, and the city of Richmond; $265 for all other students; $515 for residential students. Limited scholarships available.

Application Deadline: April 30
For More Information: Go to www.pubinfo.vcu.edu/artweb/music/orch/camp/index.htm or contact VCU Orchestral Studies at (804) 828-4040.

41. Virginia Institute of Marine Science Summer Governor's School Mentorship Program

Where: Christopher Newport University (Newport News, VA)

About: Six lucky rising 11th and 12th graders live, breathe, eat, and sleep marine science in this four-week residential program. VIMS apprentices get hands-on experience, conducting their own marine research and working with faculty sponsors.

Dates: June 24 – July 1
Costs: Free
Application Deadline: Students apply through their school in October/November. To be considered as the nominee from your school, contact your principal or guidance counselor.
For More Information: Contact the Virginia Institute of Marine Science at 804.684.7698 or via e-mail at seitz@vims.edu. To download an application, head to www.pen.k12.va.us/VDOE/Instruction/Govschools/SRGS/.

42. Virginia's Governor's Foreign Language Academies

Where: Virginia Commonwealth University (Richmond, VA)

About: Parlez-vous francais? You will once you're through. Rising 11th and 12th grade students studying French, German, or Spanish are welcomed to VCU's campus for a four-week, total immersion program. That means check your English at the door. Students studying Latin, Japanese, or Russian are also welcome for a partial immersion program.

Dates: June 23 – July 15 (French, German, Spanish), June 24 – July 15 (Latin, Japanese, Russian)
Costs: Free
Application Deadline: January 11

For More Information: Go to www.doe.virginia.gov/VDOE/Instruction/Language/GAindex.html or call (804) 225-3666. To download an application, head to www.pen.k12.va.us/VDOE/Instruction/Govschools/SRGS/.

43. Virginia State University DuPont Pre-College Readiness Program

Where: Virginia State University (Petersburg, VA)

About: Ladies and racial minorities who reside in the Tri-Cities or Southside Virginia areas and who are in grades ten through twelve can prepare for college math, science, and engineering before they graduate high school in this summer intensive program. Lasting three summers, students tackle introductory material the first summer then move on to upper level chemistry, engineering, and SAT preparation work during the latter portion of the program.

Dates: June 26 – July 25
Costs: Free, Students who complete the program will receive a $300 stipend and a free TI-84 graphing calculator.
Application Deadline: June 12

For more information: Contact the program director, Dr. George Wimbush at (804) 524-5920 or gwimbush@vsu.edu. To get an application, contact your guidance counselor.

44. Virginia State University Minority Science and Engineering Improvement Program

Where: Virginia State University (Petersburg, VA)

About: This science, engineering, and technology-intensive program is designed for ladies and racial minorities who reside in the Tri-Cities or Southside Virginia areas and who are in grades seven through ten. Combining traditional classroom learning with hands-on labs and field trips, students prepare for college-level math and science courses by doing rather than seeing.

Dates: June 21 – July 6 (7th and 8th grade), July 10 – 20 (9th and 10th grade)
Costs: None
Application Deadline: June 7 (7th and 8th grade), June 28 (9th and 10th grade)

For more information: Contact the program director, Dr. George Wimbush at (804) 524-5920 or gwimbush@vsu.edu. To get an application, contact your guidance counselor.

45. Virginia Tech Summer Music Camp

Where: Virginia Polytechnic Institute and State University (Blacksburg, VA)

About: Rising 7th – 10th grade students spend their summer making music and living the college life on Virginia Tech's campus. Courses are offered in such areas as conducting, jazz, improvisation, composition, and computer applications in music and optional private lessons are available. By the end of the week-long residential camp, students perform a final concert.

Dates: June 24 – 30
Costs: $350 for residential campers, $250 for commuters, $15 per half-hour private lesson.
Application Deadline: June 1

For More Information: Go to www.music.vt.edu/outreach/camp/ or contact the Summer Music Camp at (540) 231-5685.

46. WGMU Summer Radio Camp

Where: George Mason University (Fairfax, VA)

About: Learn how to write and produce a radio show from inside the studio. 9th – 12th graders work with WGMU staff to create their own live broadcasts. At the conclusion of this four-day day camp, student deejays broadcast their own shows from GMU's web site.

Dates: July 17 - 24
Costs: $275
Application Deadline: Rolling admissions

For More Information: Contact Program Director Rodger Smith at (703) 993-2940 or via e-mail at rsmith6@gmu.edu

47. Washington and Lee Summer Scholars Program

Where: Washington and Lee University (Lexington, VA)

About: Ready to live the college life? Now you can do it without graduating from high school. Rising high school seniors invade Washington and Lee's scenic campus every summer to get a taste of college life both in and outside of the classroom. Students enroll in one of six curriculums (Humanities and Culture, Journalism, Law & Society, Policy-Making in a Global Context, Research, or Science and Medicine), live in dorms, and enjoy the benefits of Washington and Lee's award-winning faculty.

Dates: July 1 - 27
Costs: $2,800 plus money for books and personal expenses, limited scholarships are available.
Application Deadline: May 30

For More Information: Go to http://summerscholars.wlu.edu/ or contact the Summer Scholars office at (540) 458-8727 or summerscholars@wlu.edu.

48. William and Mary Pre-College Program in Early American History

Where: College of William and Mary (Williamsburg, VA)

About: Juniors and Seniors who aren't afraid to get down and dirty with American history get the chance to live on-campus and earn four academic credits that count as a freshman seminar, History 150. A background in U.S. History isn't required, but a passion for learning is.

Dates: June 24 – July 14 (Session I) and July 15 – August 4 (Session II)
Costs: $3,250 for in-state students, financial aid available

Application Deadline: April 23
For More Information: Go to www.wm.edu/niahd/precollegiate.php or contact the program at (757) 221-7652.

49. William and Mary Science Training and Research Program (S.T.A.R.)

Where: College of William and Mary (Williamsburg, VA)

About: 11th graders from disadvantaged background congregate on William and Mary grounds for a month to get a hands-on introduction to the real world of science, technology, and research.

Dates: June 24 – July 21
Costs: Free
Application Deadline: May 9

For More Information: www.wm.edu/multiculturalaffairs/starprogram.php or call (757) 221-2300.

50. William and Mary Summer Enrichment Program

Where: College of William and Mary (Williamsburg, VA)

About: Gifted students in grades Pre-K through 10 flock to William and Mary's campus to take a wide array of summer enrichment courses. Offering elective courses such as Introductory Chinese, Rocketry, and Jazz Poetry, students come here to explore topics traditional high schools never touch.

Dates: July 9 – 13 (Session I), July 16 – 27 (Session II)
Costs: Approximately $165 for the one-week session, approximately $210 for the two-week session.

Application Deadline: June 1
For More Information: Contact William and Mary's Center for Gifted Education at (757) 221-2458.

51. Youth Conservation Camp

Where: Virginia Polytechnic Institute and State University (Blacksburg, VA)

About: Students in grades 9 – 12 gather on VA Tech's scenic campus to explore Virginia's natural resources and how best to protect them during this week-long residential camp. In addition to learning about fisheries management, water quality, agriculture, and forestry, students will also kick back by playing volleyball, canoeing the New River, visiting Mountain Lake, and hiking the Cascades.

Dates: July, 2007
Costs: Free

For More Information: Go to www.vaswcd.org/youth-camp.htm or contact the Virginia Association of Soil and Water Conservation at (804) 559-0324.

52. Youth Leadership Forum

Where: Christopher Newport University (Newport News, VA)

About: 25 Virginia high school students with disabilities are selected each year to attend this five-day leadership development program

Dates: July 9 - 14
Costs: Free
Application Deadline: February 25

For More Information: Go to www.vaboard.org/ylfprarchives.htm#09 or contact the Virginia Board for People with Disabilities' Youth Leadership Forum at (800) 846-4464.

OTHER RESOURCES:

Idealist.org – Find volunteer or internship opportunities with nonprofit organizations at home and abroad.

Americorps – Here students 17 and older can gain real-world experience, see the country, and earn cash for college. For more information, call (202) 606-5000 or go to Americorps.org.

Getthatgig.com – In addition to finding insanely awesome internship opportunities, you'll also find information on paid positions with big-name companies and non-profit organizations.

MonsterPartTime.com – Find jobs and scholarships all in one place. This search engine will help you find funds as well as paid positions near you.

Virginia Scholarships and Grants Index

Your search for college cash starts here. These scholarship and grant programs are only available to Virginia students.

American Fire Sprinkler Association, Virginia Chapter

Eligibility: High school seniors across the state compete to construct the best essay on a given fire safety-related topic.
Where Funds Can Be Used: Any college or university in the U.S.
Type of Award: Merit-based
Amount: Up to $1,500 statewide and the opportunity to compete for an additional $2,000 nationally.
Deadline: March 1
Renewable: No
For More Information: Go to www.afsavirginia.com/ or contact the Virginia Chapter of the American Fire Sprinkler Association at (804) 371-7156

American Legion's National High School Oratorical Contest

Eligibility: High school students ages 16 to 18 with a knack for public speaking and a love of the constitution are invited to enter this oratorical contest. Speech topics vary from year to year, but all students will be required to prepare a short three to five minute speech as well as a five to eight minute speech.
Where Funds Can Be Used: Any accredited college or university in the U.S.
Type of Award: Merit-based award
Amount: Up to $5,000 on the state level, up to $10,000 on the national level
Deadline: Deadlines vary from locale to locale, contact your local American Legion post for information on how to apply. State competition is held in March.
Renewable: No
For More Information: Contact your principal, college counselor, or guidance counselor for more information.

Armed Forces Communication and Electronics Association, Virginia Chapters

Eligibility: Graduating high school seniors in Fort Belvoir, VA as well as undergrad and graduate students from the Northern Virginia area. Students must be pursuing degrees in the areas of computer science, information technology, engineering, physical or natural sciences, mathematics, or other national security-related fields.
Where Funds Can Be Used: Any accredited college or university in the U.S.
Type of Award: Merit-based
Amount: Up to $4,000
Deadline: April 1
Renewable: No
For More Information: Go to www.afcea.org/education/scholarships/undergraduate/northeast.asp or contact the AFCEA Fort Belvoir chapter at vpscholarships@belvoir.afceachapter.org or the AFCEA Northern Virginia chapter at (703) 281-0022.

Associated General Contractors of Virginia Scholarship Program

Eligibility: Rising college juniors seeking careers in construction. Students must be enrolled in a construction-related program of study.
Where Funds Can Be Used: Any accredited college or university in Virginia
Type of Award: Need and merit-based
Amount: $2,000 on the state level, students may also compete nationally for up to $10,000. The AGC also offers district scholarships, contact your local AGC chapter for details.
Deadline: Early Spring, deadline varies from year to year
Renewable: No
For More Information: Go to www.agcva.org/Brochure/scholarships.htm or contact AGC of VA at (804) 364-5504.

Bank of America Lori Ann Robinson Memorial Scholarship

Eligibility: High school seniors in Richmond City, Henrico, Chesterfield, Hanover, or King and Queen counties who are planning to major in accounting, finance, economics, or business administration.
Where Funds Can Be Used: Any accredited two or four-year college or university in the continental U.S.
Type of Award: Need-based
Amount: Up to $1,500
Deadline: March 10
Renewable: Yes
For More Information: Go to www.tcfrichmond.org/ for more information or contact The Community Foundation Serving Richmond and Central Virginia at (804) 330-7400.

Brighter Futures Scholarship Program

Eligibility: Students attending any of the 15 colleges in the Virginia Foundation of Independent Colleges consortium are eligible to compete for regular scholarships as well as undergraduate research stipends. The Brighter Future Scholarship program is extensive and includes a wide range of financial aid opportunities for students attending VFIC schools. See your financial aid officer for information on specific opportunities available at your institution.
Where Funds Can Be Used: Any Virginia Foundation of Independent Colleges member school.
Type of Award: Need-based
Amount: $1,000 and up
Deadline: November 1
Renewable: Yes, students may need to re-apply each year.
For More Information: Contact your school's financial aid office. Information on Virginia Foundation of Independent College scholarships is available at www.vfic.org/scholarship/scholarship_index.html. A list of member colleges in the VFIC can be found here: www.vfic.org/member/member_index.htm.

Brown vs. the Board of Education Scholarship

Eligibility: Applicants must be domiciled VA residents who were students of Charlottesville, Norfolk, Prince Edward County, or Warren County where public schools were closed to avoid desegregation between 1954 and 1964.
Type of Award: Non-need based
Where Funds Can Be Used: Two-year, four-year, GED, and transitional degree programs.
Amount: Up to full tuition price
Deadline: March 1
Renewable: Yes, but students must re-apply each year.
For More Information: Go to http://dls.state.va.us/brown.htm or contact Mrs. Brenda H. Edwards, Scholarship Coordinator, at (804) 786-3591.

Central Virginia Scholarship

Eligibility: Outstanding high school seniors in Richmond City, Henrico, Chesterfield or Hanover counties.
Where Funds Can Be Used: Any accredited college or university in the U.S. Preference given to students attending private colleges in Virginia.
Type of Award: Need-based
Amount: Up to $5,000
Deadline: March 10
Renewable: Yes
For More Information: Go to www.tcfrichmond.org/ for more information or contact The Community Foundation Serving Richmond and Central Virginia at (804) 330-7400.

College Scholarship Assistance Program

Eligibility: Designed for students with extreme financial need, the College Scholarship Assistance Program provides monetary support for students attending both public and private VA schools. To be eligible, students need to file a FAFSA and if attending a private institution, a Virginia Tuition Assistance Grant application as well.
Where Funds Can Be Used: Two and four-year VA schools.
Type of Award: Need-based
Amount: Up to $5,000
Deadline: Corresponds to your school's financial aid deadline
Renewable: Yes, but students must re-apply each year.
For More Information: Contact your school's financial aid office.

Commonwealth Award

Eligibility: Undergrads and graduate students admitted to a two or four-year public school in Virginia may be eligible to receive a significant chunk off of their tuition bill. Students must be enrolled at least half-time.
Where Funds Can Be Used: Public two and four-year Virginia colleges and universities.
Type of Award: Need-based
Amount: Up to full tuition and fees
Deadline: Corresponds to your school's financial aid deadline.
Renewable: Yes
For More Information: Contact your school's financial aid office.

Farm Bureau Insurance Virginia High School League Achievement Award

Eligibility: High school students who participate in VHSL sports or activities (including debate, drama, forensics, school publications, and scholastic bowl competitions) may compete for cash prizes. Students must maintain a 3.0 GPA and be nominated by their high school. VHSL also offers one scholarship for a student who does not participate in VHSL activities, but has overcome substantial adversities.
Where Funds Can Be Used: Any accredited college or university in the U.S.
Type of Award: Merit-based
Amount: $1,000
Deadline: March 15
Renewable: No
For More Information: Ask your principal or guidance counselor about how to obtain a nomination from your school. For information on the scholarship itself, contact the Virginia High School League Scholarship Program at (434) 977-8475.

Granville P. Meade Scholarship

Eligibility: Virginia high school seniors with outstanding academic records and financial need may be eligible to receive up to $8,000 in free college cash. Students must be recommended by their high school principal and will compete for 5 state-wide awards.
Where Funds Can Be Used: Virginia colleges and universities
Type of Award: Need-based
Amount: $2,000 per year
Deadline: March 14
Renewable: Yes, up to four years.
For More Information: Contact your high school principal or guidance counselor for more information.

Hellenic Society of Paideia of Virginia Scholarship Program

Eligibility: Students of Greek-American heritage with a 3.0 GPA
Where Funds Can Be Used: Any accredited four-year college or university in Virginia
Type of Award: Merit-based
Amount: $1,000
Deadline: February 15
Renewable: No
For More Information: Go to http://hellenicpaideiaofvirginia.org/scholarship.html or contact the Hellenic Society of Paideia of Virginia at (540) 552-6504 or mhatzios@radford.edu.

Higher Education Teacher Assistance Program

Eligibility: Undergraduate students studying to become elementary, middle, or high school teachers. Students must be enrolled full-time, demonstrate financial need, maintain at least a 2.5 GPA, and be nominated by a faculty member from their undergraduate institution. Preference will be given to students enrolled in a teacher shortage area.
Where Funds Can Be Used: Virginia two and four-year institutions
Type of Award: Need-based
Amount: $2,000 per year at four-year institutions, $1,000 per year at two-year institutions.
Deadline: Corresponds with your school's financial aid deadline.
Renewable: Yes
For More Information: Contact your school's financial aid office as well as your school's Education department.

Julian S. Wise Scholarship/Fred E. (Freddy) Weymouth II Scholarship

Eligibility: Members of the Virginia Association of Volunteer Rescue Squads, auxiliary units, junior squads, and their dependents are eligible to receive up to $500 to further their education. Applicants must be under the age of 30.
Where Funds Can Be Used: Any accredited college or university in the U.S.
Type of Award: Need-based
Amount: Up to $500
Deadline: July 1
Renewable: No
For More Information: Go to www.vavrs.com or contact the Virginia Association of Volunteer Rescue Squads at (800) 833-0602.

Kimball L. Glass Memorial Scholarship

Eligibility: Members of the Virginia Association of Volunteer Rescue Squads, auxiliary units, junior squads, and their dependents are eligible to receive up to $500 to further their education. Students must be entering and Emergency Medical Services-related career.
Where Funds Can Be Used: Any accredited college or university in the U.S.
Type of Award: Need-based
Amount: Up to $500
Deadline: May 15
Renewable: No
For More Information: Go to www.vavrs.com or contact the Virginia Association of Volunteer Rescue Squads at (800) 833-0602.

Lee-Jackson Scholarship

Eligibility: Virginia high school juniors, seniors, and homeschoolers with a knack for the written word can try their hand at this essay contest. Topics will focus on history as well as social context.
Where Funds Can Be Used: Accredited in-state four-year colleges and universities or transfer programs at VA-based community colleges.
Type of Award: Merit-based
Amount: Up to $10,000
Deadline: Students must file their essay along with an application form to their high school principal no later than January 5
Renewable: No
For More Information: Go to www.lee-jackson.org/ or contact the Lee-Jackson Foundation at (434) 977-1861.

Micron Science and Technology Scholars Program

Eligibility: Virginia, Colorado, Idaho, Utah, or Texas-based high school seniors who have a combined Critical Reading or Writing and Math SAT score of at least 1350 or a composite ACT score of at least 30. Students must also have an unweighted grade point average of at least 3.5, demonstrate leadership skills in school as well as extracurricular activities, and plan to major in computer science, physics, chemistry, material sciences, or engineering.
Where Funds Can Be Used: Any four-year accredited college or university in the U.S.
Type of Award: Merit-based
Amount: Up to $55,000
Deadline: January 19
Renewable: Yes
For More Information: Go to www.sms.scholarshipamerica.org/micron/program.html or contact the Micron Science and Technology Scholars Program at (800) 537-4180.

Miss Virginia Scholarship

Eligibility: High school senior ladies between the ages of 17 and 24 are eligible to compete for scholarships and all the fame you could ever need. Contestants must be unmarried, of high moral character, and drug and alcohol free.
Where Funds Can Be Used: Any accredited college or university in the U.S.
Type of Award: Merit-based
Amount: Up to $8,000
Deadline: Deadlines vary between qualifying pageants
Renewable: No
For More Information: Go to http://www.missva.com or contact Miss Virginia at lithses@aol.com.

Roger L. Foster Scholarship Program

Eligibility: Dependent children of active police officers in the Commonwealth of Virginia. Students must be pursuing their first undergraduate degree.
Where Funds Can Be Used: Any accredited college or university in the U.S.
Type of Award: Need-based
Amount: Varies from year to year
Deadline: April 6
Renewable: Yes, but students must reapply.
For More Information: Go to www.vachiefs.org/vpcf/vpcf_scholar.html or contact the Virginia Police Chiefs Foundation at (804) 285-8227.

Senior Citizens Tuition Waiver

Eligibility: Seniors ages 60 and over may be eligible to receive up to a full tuition waiver at Virginia public colleges and universities. Certain income limitations apply.
Where Funds Can Be Used: Virginia public colleges and universities
Type of Award: Non-need based
Amount: Full tuition waiver
Deadline: Corresponds to your school's financial aid deadline
Renewable: Yes
For More Information: Contact your school's financial aid office.

United Daughters of the Confederacy, Virginia Division

Eligibility: Lineal descendents of Confederate Veterans who have the documentation to prove it. Recipients must maintain a 3.0 GPA.
Where Funds Can Be Used: Virginia colleges and universities
Type of Award: Need-based
Amount: Varies from year to year
Deadline: April 30
Renewable: Yes, but students must apply for renewal and must maintain a 3.0 GPA
For More Information: Go to http://vaudc.org/ or contact the United Daughters of the Confederacy, Virginia Division at (804) 355-1636. Information on general UDC scholarships is also available here: http://hqudc.org/.

Virginia Army National Guard Tuition Assistance Program

Eligibility: Give one weekend a month, two weeks a year and you could attend college for free. Students must be 17 or older to apply.
Where Funds Can Be Used: Any accredited college, university, technical school, or professional development school in Virginia
Type of Award: Merit-based
Amount: Up to full tuition and up to a $20,000 cash bonus and up to $20,000 in student loan repayment, additional federal programs are available as well.
Deadline: Rolling
Renewable: Yes
For More Information: Go to www.geocities.com/virginianationalguard/ or contact the VA Army National Guard at 800.572.3019.

Virginia Child Care Provider Scholarship

Eligibility: Child care employees and those looking to be are eligible to receive up to two courses per semester (8 total classes) or up to $1,707.60 courtesy of the Virginia Department of Social Services. Students must already be accepted to an approved child care program at either a two or four-year Virginia school.
Type of Award: Merit-based based
Where Funds Can Be Used: Approved two and four-year Virginia schools.
Amount: 8 free classes or up to $1,707.60
Deadline: Oct. 15 - Dec.15 (spring semester), March 15 - May 1 (summer semester), June 1 - August 10 (fall semester)
Renewable: Up to 8 classes. Students must re-apply each semester.
For More Information: Contact the Virginia Child Care Provider Scholarship Program at (866) 636-1608.

Virginia Community College System Tuition Grant

Eligibility: Students who were in foster care, custody of a social service agent, or were a special needs adoption at the time they received their high school diploma or GED. Applicants are required to enroll in the community college of their choice full-time and must file a FAFSA and submit appropriate documentation to the VA Department of Social Services.
Where Funds Can Be Used: Any Virginia community college
Type of Award: Need-based
Amount: Up to full tuition and fees
Deadline: Corresponds to your school's financial aid deadline
Renewable: Yes
For More Information: Go to www.dss.virginia.gov/family/tuitiongrant.html or contact the financial aid officer at your community college.

Virginia Congress of Parents and Teachers Scholarship Program

Eligibility: VA high school grads who plan on going into the teaching profession. Students must have at least a 2.5 GPA
Where Funds Can Be Used: Any accredited college or university in the U.S.
Type of Award: Merit-based
Amount: Up to $1,200
Deadline: March 1
Renewable: No
For More Information: Go to http://www.vapta.org/Programs/student_programs.htm or contact VAPTA at info@vapta.org or (866) 4-vakids.

Virginia Congress of Parents and Teachers Citizenship Essay Project

Eligibility: Students in grades 6 – 12 are encouraged to express their views on character and citizenship in this essay contest.
Where Funds Can Be Used: Any accredited college or university in the U.S.
Type of Award: Merit-based
Amount: Up to $1,000
Deadline: February 1
Renewable: No
For More Information: Go to http://www.vapta.org/Programs/student_programs.htm or contact VAPTA at info@vapta.org or (866) 4-vakids.

Virginia Department of Transportation Engineering Scholarship Program

Eligibility: College sophomore, junior, and senior civil engineering majors at four-year institutions with at least a 2.5 GPA may be eligible to receive college cash in addition to work experience and professional mentorship. Applicants must be Virginia residents or attend a Virginia college or university.
Where Funds Can Be Used: Any accredited college or university
Type of Award: Merit-based
Amount: $7,000 per year and a summer job
Deadline: January 15
Renewable: Yes
For More Information: Go to http://virginiadot.org/jobs/engscholarprog.asp or contact the VDOT Scholarship Program at scholarship@vdot.virginia.gov.

Virginia Fire Chief's Association Scholarship Program

Eligibility: Anyone. Priority given to active fire service personnel as well as their spouses and dependents.
Where Funds Can Be Used: Any college, university, National Fire Academy classes, or approved courses or seminars.
Type of Award: Awarded based on need and merit
Amount: Up to $1,000
Deadline: December 1
Renewable: No
For More Information: Go to www.vfca.us/vfca_scholarships.htm or contact the Virginia Fire Chief's Association at (757) 810-1690.

Virginia Golf Foundation Scholarship

Eligibility: Virginia high school students with an interest in golf who also demonstrate academic achievement, citizenship, and character.
Where Funds Can Be Used: Accredited colleges and universities in Virginia
Type of Award: Need and merit-based awards offered
Amount: Up to $6,000
Deadline: February 28
Renewable: Some scholarships are renewable, some are not.
For More Information: Contact the Virginia State Golf Association at www.vsga.org or (804) 378-2300.

Virginia Guaranteed Assistance Program

Eligibility: VA high school grads with demonstrated financial need and at least a 2.5 high school GPA can get a helping hand from the state. Students must be enrolled in an approved degree, certificate, or diploma program and be classified as a dependent student.
Where Funds Can Be Used: Public two and four-year schools in VA.
Type of Award: Need-based
Amount: Up to tuition, books, and fees.
Deadline: Corresponds with your school's financial aid deadline
Renewable: Yes for up to three years
For More Information: Contact your school's financial aid office.

Virginia High School League Charles E. Savedge Journalism Scholarship

Eligibility: High school seniors who have made significant contributions to school publications (as editors, writers, photographers, ad salesmen, designers, etc.).
Where Funds Can Be Used: Any accredited college or university in the U.S.
Type of Award: Merit-based
Amount: $500
Deadline: March 1
Renewable: No
For More Information: Ask your principal or guidance counselor about how to obtain a nomination from your school. For information on the scholarship itself, contact the Virginia High School League Scholarship Program at (434) 977-8475.

Virginia Smiles College Scholarship Program

Eligibility: Virginia high school seniors and college students who were born with a cleft lip or palate.
Where Funds Can Be Used: Any accredited college or university in the U.S.
Type of Award: Merit-based
Amount: $1,000
Deadline: May 31
Renewable: No
For More Information: Go to www.virginia-smiles.org or contact Virginia Smiles at info@virginia-smiles.org.

The Virginia Space Grant Consortium Aerospace Research Awards

Eligibility: Undergraduate and graduate students enrolled at the College of William and Mary, Hampton University, Old Dominion University, University of Virginia, or Virginia Tech could get paid just to go to school. Students must be in an aerospace-related field of study.
Where Funds Can Be Used: The College of William and Mary, Hampton University, Old Dominion University, University of Virginia, or Virginia Tech
Type of Award: Merit-based
Amount: Up to $5,000 for graduate students, up to $8,500 for undergraduate students
Deadline: February 5
Renewable: Yes for graduate students, no for undergraduate students
For More Information: Go to www.vsgc.odu.edu/Menu3_1_1.htm or contact the Virginia Space Grant Consortium at (757) 766-5210.

The Virginia Space Grant Consortium Teacher Education Scholarship

Eligibility: College students, high school seniors, and Masters degree students interested in becoming certified teachers are eligible to receive monetary support. Priority is given to those majoring in technology education, mathematics, or earth/space/ environmental science.
Where Funds Can Be Used: The College of William and Mary, Hampton University, Old Dominion University, University of Virginia, or Virginia Tech
Type of Award: Merit-based
Amount: Up to $1,000
Deadline: February 26
Renewable: No
For More Information: Go to www.vsgc.odu.edu/Menu3_1_1.htm or contact the Virginia Space Grant Consortium at (757) 766-5210.

The Virginia Space Grant Consortium Community College Scholarship

Eligibility: Students enrolled in a Virginia community college who are majoring in a technological field that supports the aerospace industries.
Where Funds Can Be Used: Virginia community colleges
Type of Award: Merit-based
Amount: Up to $1,500
Deadline: February 26
Renewable: No
For More Information: Go to www.vsgc.odu.edu/Menu3_1_1.htm or contact the Virginia Space Grant Consortium at (757) 766-5210.

Virginia Teaching Scholarship Loan Program

Eligibility: College students on track to obtain their teaching licensure are eligible to receive financial help. Students must be nominated by their college or university, have at least a 2.7 GPA, be at or beyond the sophomore year in college, and majoring in a critical teaching shortage area. Students may receive a scholarship-loan for up to $3,720 and can pay the loan back by teaching four semesters in a Virginia public school in their critical shortage field upon graduation.
Where Funds Can Be Used: The 37 colleges or universities in Virginia with approved teaching programs.
Type of Award: Merit-based
Amount: Up to $3,720
Deadline: Check with your school's financial aid office
Renewable: Yes
For More Information: Go to www.doe.virginia.gov/VDOE/newvdoe/vtslp.pdf or contact the Virginia Department of Education at (800) 292-3820.

Virginia Tuition Assistance Grant

Eligibility: VA students pursuing degrees in anything but religion, religious studies, or theology are eligible for a sizeable grant that can be used at accredited private in-state schools.
Where Funds Can Be Used: Accredited four-year private VA schools
Type of Award: Non-need based.
Amount: Up to $2,700 for undergraduates, Up to $1,900 for graduate students
Deadline: July 31st prior to the year of enrollment
Renewable: Yes
For More Information: Contact your school's financial aid office for an application or if you have questions.

Virginia Military Survivors and Dependents Education Program

Eligibility: One of the applicant's parents must have been killed, permanently disabled, or gone MIA in the line of duty. Students must be between the ages of 16 and 25.
Where Funds Can Be Used: Public colleges and universities in VA.
Type of Award: Non-need based
Amount: Full tuition and fee waiver
Deadline: Rolling
Renewable: Yes
For More Information: Go to www.dvs.virginia.gov/education_benefits.htm or contact the Virginia Department of Veteran's Affairs at (540) 857-7104.

Wachovia Citizenship Award

Eligibility: VHSL participants that demonstrate exemplary citizenship, sportsmanship, and leadership skills. Students must be nominated by their high school in order to be eligible.
Where Funds Can Be Used: Any accredited college or university in the U.S.
Type of Award: Merit-based
Amount: $1,000
Deadline: March 15
Renewable: No
For More Information: Ask your principal or guidance counselor about how to obtain a nomination from your school. For information on the scholarship itself, contact the Virginia High School League Scholarship Program at (434) 977-8475.

The Wildlife Society, Virginia Chapter

Eligibility: Juniors and seniors enrolled at an accredited Virginia college or university. Students must be majoring in a natural resources program and have at least a 3.0 GPA.
Where Funds Can Be Used: Any accredited college or university in Virginia
Type of Award: Merit-based
Amount: $500
Deadline: January 31
Renewable: No
For More Information: Go to http://fwie.fw.vt.edu/vatws/ScholarshipAnnounce.pdf or contact The Wildlife Society, Virginia Chapter scholarship program at (703) 432-6774.

About the Author

Photo by Ed Blackshaw

Christina Couch is a freelance writer based in Richmond, Virginia and a graduate of James Madison University. Her work has appeared in Aol.com, Msn.com, *WORKMAGAZINE, Wired Magazine, Entrepreneur Magazine,* the *Christian Science Monitor,* Yahoo! Finance, *Virginia Business Magazine,* Go!, and Time Out Chicago. Her work can also be found in 18 college guidebooks produced by Hobsons Publications and Sparknotes Publications.

Index

ORDER FORM

Please send in this form with a check or money order payable to Palari Publishing.
Or visit www.palaribooks.com to order online.

Name____

Street____

City, State, ZIP____________________________________

Phone____

FREE SHIPPING! FREE SHIPPING! FREE SHIPPING!

Quantity	Book	Price
________	Virgina Colleges 101	$14.95
	TOTAL:__________	

Mail to:

Palari Publishing
PO Box 9288
Richmond, VA 23227-0288

www.palaribooks.com

orders@palaribooks.com